St Lucia, Dominica and Martinique are a series of volcanic peaks jutting out of the sea. They form a barrier between the Atlantic Ocean and the Caribbean Sea and have a wild, blustery east coast and a calm, sheltered west coast with lovely natural harbours and picturesque fishing villages. Sulphur fumaroles and hot springs are evidence of the dormant, but not dead, volcanoes, while the volcanic soil provides immense fertility. There are large areas of lush rainforest with national parks protecting places of biodiversity or natural beauty on land and underwater. The islands are a haven for birds with lots of endemic species, while the sea is teeming with fish and other marine life, including whales and dolphins. Hikers and birdwatchers are spoilt for choice, with many rewarding trails through forested mountains, following rivers and along beaches. There is always something to do and an action-packed holiday can include any number of watersports, such as sailing, kayaking, diving and snorkelling. And then you can kick back on a beach under the Caribbean sun with a rum punch, or enjoy Creole cuisine and live music at local 'jump-ups' around the islands.

These islands were all at one time colonized by the French and share a cultural heritage, even though St Lucia and Dominica eventually became British before getting their independence. Martinique has remained French and is a part of France: a Département. Imported African slaves brought to work on plantations have added to the rich ethnic mix. This Caribbean melting pot of people and cultures has produced a language known as Kwéyòl, which is widely spoken, with regional differences. St Lucia and Dominica have retained French names for many of their towns and villages, where the older colonial buildings are decorated with gingerbread fretwork and jalousie shutters. However, the official language is English, cars drive on the left and cricket is the most popular sport.

Lizzie Williams

Best of
St Lucia &
Dominica

top things to do and see

❶ Castries Central Market

Castries market is a hive of activity, especially when a cruise ship is in town. It's a wonderful place to shop for tropical fruits and vegetables, as well as a staggering array of spices, including enormous chunks of cinnamon bark and shiny brown nutmegs, traditional coal pots and other souvenirs. Page 34.

❷ Rodney Bay

Rodney Bay is St Lucia's tourist and beach holiday hub and is a hive of activity with many hotels, restaurants and shops. Its picturesque crescent-shaped Reduit Beach of glittering white sand is one of the island's most popular stretches, and it is enclosed to the north by Pigeon Island National Landmark for walks and views. Page 39.

❸ Marigot Bay

Lush hillsides plunge to the pretty palm-fringed beach, and yachts bob on the blue waters of this beautiful bay. The harbour is so deep and sheltered that the British fleet supposedly hid here from the French by covering their masts with palm fronds. Water taxis ferry people across to restaurants and hotels on the opposite side. Page 50.

Footprint Handbook
St Lucia &
D

LIZZ

0142010429

This is
St Lucia &
Dominica

❻ Soufrière and Scotts Head

This marine reserve off the south coast of Dominica is the most picturesque bay on the island both above and below the water. Characterized by warm underwater sulphur vents and abrupt coral reef drop-offs, it's a site for pelagic fish and cetaceans, including spinner dolphins and sperm whales. Page 94.

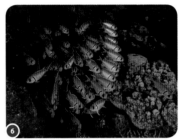

❹ Diamond Falls Botanical Gardens and Mineral Baths

Part of St Lucia's Soufrière Estate, the attractions here are beautiful tropical gardens planted among coconut, cocoa and red cedar trees, a dramatic waterfall coloured by mineral deposits, healing mineral hot spring baths, originally built for the troops of King Louis XVI of France, and a restaurant in an 18th-century sugar mill. Page 54.

❺ The Pitons

When you hear the words 'St Lucia', an image of the Pitons will most likely spring to mind; the twin volcanic peaks are the most photographed landmark on the island. Rising like skyscrapers out of the sea, the ancient forest-clad plugs are a majestic backdrop for the charming town of Soufrière. Page 59.

❼ Trafalgar Falls

On the west side of Morne Trois Pitons National Park, and known as Mother and Father, these twin waterfalls lie at the end of an easy 10- to 15-minute hike through a forest of ginger plants and vanilla orchids; you can take a dip in the hot and cold pools at their base. Page 95.

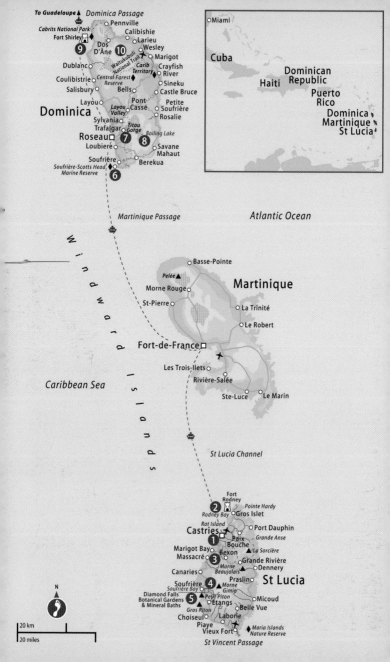

Dominica Passage
To Guadeloupe
Dominica Passage
Cabrits National Park
Fort Shirley
Pennville
Calibishie
Larieu
Wesley
Dos D'Âne
Marigot
Crayfish River
Carib Territory
Dublanc
Coulibistrie
Central Forest Reserve
Sineku
Salisbury
Bells
Castle Bruce
Dominica
Layou
Layou Valley
Pont Cassé
Petite Soufrière
Rosalie
Sylvania
Titou Gorge
Trafalgar
Roseau
Boiling Lake
Loubiere
Savane Mahaut
Soufrière
Berekua
Soufrière-Scotts Head
Marine Reserve

Martinique Passage

Atlantic Ocean

Windward Islands

Basse-Pointe
Pelée ▲
Morne Rouge
Martinique
St-Pierre
La Trinité
Le Robert
Fort-de-France
Caribbean Sea
Les Trois-Ilets
Rivière-Salée
Ste-Luce
Le Marin

St Lucia Channel

Fort Rodney
Pointe Hardy
Rodney Bay
Gros Islet
Rat Island
Port Dauphin
Castries
Paix Bouche
Grande Anse
Marigot Bay
Bexon
La Sorcière
Massacré
Grande Rivière
Dennery
Canaries
Morne Beaujolais
Praslin
Soufrière
Morne Gimie
St Lucia
Soufrière Bay
Diamond Falls
Botanical Gardens
& Mineral Baths
Etangs
Micoud
Petit Piton
Gros Piton
Belle Vue
Choiseul
Laborie
Piaye
Maria Islands
Vieux Fort
Nature Reserve
St Vincent Passage

N

20 km
20 miles

Miami
Cuba
Dominican Republic
Haiti
Puerto Rico
Dominica
Martinique
St Lucia

❽ Boiling Lake

Part of the Morne Trois Pitons National Park in Dominica's mountainous volcanic interior, a rigorous hike through the Valley of Desolation brings you to the second largest boiling lake in the world. Like a cauldron of bubbling milky-blue water, it's often enveloped in a cloud of vapour giving it an other-worldly feel. Page 96.

❾ Fort Shirley, Cabrits Peninsula

A former military outpost on a scenic peninsula in the north of the island, Fort Shirley is Dominica's most important historic site. The 18th-century British garrison once housed more than 600 soldiers. Some of the ruins have been rebuilt, while others lie half-buried in the jungle and are fun to explore. Page 100.

❿ Waitukubuli Trail

This coast-to-coast hiking trail winds its way for 115 miles (185 km) through lush virgin rainforest, over steep mountainous ridges, past waterfalls, coastal villages and down to the sea again. It's a showcase of Dominica's rich cultural and natural heritage and can be completed as a series of day hikes. Page 118.

Marigot Bay palm tree

Route planner

St Lucia is a Caribbean island in two parts. To the north of the capital, Castries, is the resort area around Rodney Bay, a self-contained region for typical sun, sea and sand holidays where you'll find everything you need for some fun and relaxation. But much of St Lucia is mountainous and covered in a blanket of thick emerald-green rainforest, and the southwest corner has arguably the most arresting sight in the whole Caribbean: the breathtaking views of the green and precipitous volcanic cones of the Pitons rising out of the brilliantly blue sea. Nearby are a number of other natural attractions such as waterfalls and sulphur hot springs, good snorkelling and diving and hiking trails. Few visitors miss this contrasting second part of the island, and most itineraries combine beach time with the island's spectacular scenery in the south.

Thanks to its lush vegetation and varied flora and fauna, **Dominica** – the 'Nature Island' of the Caribbean and the most mountainous island of the Lesser Antilles – is the place to hike in the rainforest and admire its volcanic peaks. You arrive either at the Douglas-Charles Airport in the northeast of the island or by ferry with L'Express des Iles (perhaps via Martinique) in the capital, Roseau, on the west coast. Both are on the one road that encircles the island, so any itinerary will depend on where you start, but will undoubtedly include exploring the trails, rivers, waterfalls and geothermal pools of the interior, and maybe snorkelling or diving off the southwest coast of the island.

One week

If you have only a week to spend on St Lucia you will probably want to spend most of your time relaxing on the beach with a sun lounger, umbrella and rum punch. Rodney Bay is probably the best area to base yourself; it has good-value mid-range accommodation and plenty to keep holidaymakers occupied, like beach bars, watersports, shopping malls, casual restaurants and lively nightlife. It is worth spending a few hours stretching your legs and enjoying the views at Pigeon Island National Landmark, across the bay, a pleasant day can be spent watching cricket (if a match is on) at the stadium near Gros Islet, and you should definitely try and take in the Friday evening activities: the fish fry at **Anse La Raye**

Best activities

- **Birdwatching** in the Edmund Forest, deep in the tropical nature reserve, page 56.
- **Canyoning** in Titou Gorge where a narrow channel ends in a torrential waterfall, pages 97 and 117.
- **Diving** in the marine park at Soufrière; a pristine underworld adventure, pages 52 and 77.
- **Diving** or **snorkelling** off Soufrière and Scotts Head, swimming through the bubbles of underwater hot springs at a site known as Champagne, pages 95 and 117.
- **Hiking** some or all of the Waitukubuli National Trail, taking in Dominica's dense forests, volcanic hills, rivers and waterfalls, page 118.
- **Kiteboarding** or **windsurfing** at Anse de Sables, where wind conditions are exciting but you won't get carried out to the ocean, pages 48 and 79.
- **Mountain biking** on the jungly hillsides above Anse Mamin, looking out for birds, orchids and 18th-century French colonial ruins, page 77.
- **Sailing** from Rodney Bay down the west coast for a view of the cliffs, forests and majestic Pitons, page 78.
- **Watching a Test Match** at St Lucia's Darren Sammy National Cricket Stadium, one of the best pitches in the West Indies, page 77.
- **Whale watching** in Soufrière Bay with playful dolphins leaping in and out of your wake, pages 52 and 79.

or the jump-up at **Gros Islet**, both street parties where the food and booze are in abundance and you are guaranteed a good time. And you mustn't miss a day trip to Soufrière and the Pitons – either by boat from Rodney Bay Marina, or by road (tour operators pick up at hotels in the area).

On **Dominica**, you will probably want to do something active, such as a day's diving or snorkelling, a couple of days' hiking the mountain trails, and perhaps canyoning or whale watching. There are no white sandy beaches (or typical holiday resorts), but there are some out-of-the-way stretches of black volcanic sand and, while the sea may not always be safe for swimming, they are great for beach-combing, walking and splashing around in the shallows. Accommodation on Dominica is mostly in small and relatively remote lodges and guesthouses dotted around hillsides overlooking both the Caribbean and Atlantic coasts and this undeveloped and low-key tourism is part of the attraction of Dominica; your days might just swerve between adventurous pursuits in the mountains and forests and utter relaxation.

Two weeks or more

If you have more than a week, you could consider a two-centre holiday, split between the two parts of **St Lucia**. You could divide your time between the good beach, restaurants and bars, and activities at more developed **Rodney Bay** in the northwest, and the rural peace and beauty around **Soufrière** in the southwest. The area around the Pitons has most of the island's special and most luxurious places to stay – many popular with honeymooners – with drop-dead views, as well as some fine restaurants and extra attractions such as the Diamond Falls Botanical Gardens and Mineral Baths, the Sulphur Springs Park and a few hiking trails – including the ultimate challenge of climbing Gros Piton itself. The beaches are mostly dark volcanic sand, but it doesn't mean they are not attractive; in particular Anse Chastanet and Anse Mamin to the north of Soufrière, and Anse des Pitons right in the 'cleavage' of the Pitons, are tremendous. You can hire a car for a day or two for a leisurely around-island tour, which could also include stops in Castries (to visit the markets or the military ruins on Morne Fortuné), Marigot Bay (to admire the yachts in the pretty, forested steep-sided bay), or Mamiku Botanical Gardens (to see rare plants and orchids).

On **Dominica**, it would again be worth dividing your time between the north and the south to enjoy all the attractions without backtracking on the awfully twisty roads. You could stay either in Roseau or at one of the dive lodges on the west coast at Castle Comfort. From here you can explore the markets, head up into the Roseau Valley to Trafalgar Falls, and enjoy the southern stretch of coast down towards Scotts Head. Head up the west coast to the second city of Portsmouth to visit Fort Shirley and the Cabrits National Park; definitely make time for a boat trip on the Indian River. From here you can cross over to the east coast for a spectacular view of the Atlantic side of the island; from Calibishie head north to Guadeloupe, and then turn inland on one of the transinsular roads back to Roseau, perhaps via the Emerald Pool or stopping to hike one of the interior trails. Really keen hikers can attempt the arduous day trip to the Boiling Lake, or even spend an entire two weeks hiking all 14 segments of the Waitukubuli National Trail covering the length of the island on foot.

It is well worth making the ferry journey between the two islands, dividing your holiday between St Lucia and Dominica. International flight connections are better to St Lucia, so the option is to start and finish there, or you can opt for an open-jaw international flight from one of the other islands such as Antigua or Barbados and take a local connecting flight from Dominica to there. Martinique lies between the two, and a stopover in Fort-de-France is recommended, even if it's just for one night to do a bit of sightseeing and while away the evening over Creole food washed down with a bottle of good French wine. For details of L'Express des Iles services, see page 132, and for a taster of what to expect in Fort-de-France, see page 82.

When to go

Climate

The climate is tropical. The volcanic mountains and forests of St Lucia, Dominica and Martinique attract more rain than some other, more low-lying islands in the Caribbean such as Barbados or Antigua. The driest and coolest time of year is usually December to April, coinciding with the winter peak in tourism as people from Europe and the US escape to the sun. However, there can be showers, which keep things green. Temperatures can fall to 20°C during the day, depending on altitude, but are normally in the high 20s, tempered by cooling trade winds. The mean annual temperature is about 26°C. At other times of the year the temperature rises only slightly, but greater humidity can make it feel hotter if you are away from the coast, where the northeast trade winds are a cooling influence. The main climate hazard is hurricane season, which runs from June to November, with September and October the likeliest months for major tropical storms that can cause flooding and mudslides; the latest, Tropical Storm Erica, battered Dominica in 2015. In terms of price, accommodation rates are much higher from mid-December to April than at other times of year (especially over Christmas/New Year and Easter, when additional premiums are often charged), while in the quietest and wettest months of September and October, some hotels, restaurants and bars close altogether.

Weather St Lucia and Dominica

January	February	March	April	May	June
29°C	29°C	30°C	30°C	31°C	31°C
22°C	22°C	22°C	23°C	24°C	25°C
95mm	69mm	60mm	74mm	88mm	131mm

July	August	September	October	November	December
31°C	31°C	32°C	31°C	30°C	30°C
24°C	24°C	24°C	23°C	23°C	22°C
171mm	219mm	200mm	250mm	222mm	138mm

Festivals

You can time your visit to coincide with one of the islands' festivals. On St Lucia, **Carnival** is celebrated in July with colourful parades and pageants, music and competitions; visitors are welcome to join in. Dominica's carnival, which takes place in February/March, is one of the friendliest in the Caribbean and is a celebration of calypso, building up to two days of street jump-up. The greatest influx of visitors is usually for St Lucia's annual **Jazz Festival** in May, when open-air concerts by internationally renowned artists are held around the island. In October, Dominica hosts the **World Creole Music Festival** attracting artists from across the globe. Other events to consider are **Test Matches**, when cricket fans travel to support their team, or the arrival of the **Atlantic Rally for Cruisers** in the first week of December, when Rodney Bay on St Lucia fills with yachts and their crew, hell-bent on enjoying themselves on terra firma. For further details, see page 74 for St Lucia's festivals and page 116 for those in Dominica.

Improve your travel photography

Taking pictures is a highlight for many travellers, yet too often the results turn out to be disappointing. Steve Davey, author of Footprint's *Travel Photography*, sets out his top rules for coming home with pictures you can be proud of.

Before you go

Don't waste precious travelling time and do your research before you leave. Find out what festivals or events might be happening or which day the weekly market takes place, and search online image sites such as Flickr to see whether places are best shot at the beginning or end of the day, and what vantage points you should consider.

Get up early

The quality of the light will be better in the few hours after sunrise and again before sunset – especially in the tropics when the sun will be harsh and unforgiving in the middle of the day. Sometimes seeing the sunrise is a part of the whole travel experience: sleep in and you will miss more than just photographs.

Stop and think

Don't just click away without any thought. Pause for a few seconds before raising the camera and ask yourself what you are trying to show with your photograph. Think about what things you need to include in the frame to convey this meaning. Be prepared to move around your subject to get the best angle. Knowing the point of your picture is the first step to making sure that the person looking at the picture will know it too.

Compose your picture

Avoid simply dumping your subject in the centre of the frame every time you take a picture. If you compose with it to one side, then your picture can look more balanced. This will also allow you to show a significant background and make the picture more meaningful. A good rule of thumb is to place your subject or any significant detail a third of the way into the frame; facing into the frame not out of it.

This rule also works for landscapes. Compose with the horizon two-thirds of the way up the frame if the foreground is the most interesting part of the picture; one-third of the way up if the sky is more striking.

Don't get hung up with this so-called Rule of Thirds, though. Exaggerate it by pushing your subject out to the edge of the frame if it makes a more interesting picture; or if the sky is dull in a landscape, try cropping with the horizon near the very top of the frame.

Fill the frame

If you are going to focus on a detail or even a person's face in a close-up portrait, then be bold and make sure that you fill the frame. This is often a case of physically getting in close. You can use a telephoto setting on a zoom lens but this can lead to pictures looking quite flat; moving in close is a lot more fun!

Interact with people

If you want to shoot evocative portraits then it is vital to approach people and seek permission in some way, even if it is just by smiling at someone. Spend a little time with them and they are likely to relax and look less stiff and formal. Action portraits where people are doing something, or environmental portraits, where they are set against a significant background, are a good way to achieve relaxed portraits. Interacting is a good way to find out more about people and their lives, creating memories as well as photographs.

Focus carefully

Your camera can focus quicker than you, but it doesn't know which part of the picture you want to be in focus. If your camera is using the centre focus sensor then move the camera so it is over the subject and half press the button, then, holding it down, recompose the picture. This will lock the focus. Take the now correctly focused picture when you are ready.

Another technique for accurate focusing is to move the active sensor over your subject. Some cameras with touch-sensitive screens allow you to do this by simply clicking on the subject.

Leave light in the sky

Most good night photography is actually taken at dusk when there is some light and colour left in the sky; any lit portions of the picture will balance with the sky and any ambient lighting. There is only a very small window when this will happen, so get into position early, be prepared and keep shooting and reviewing the results. You can take pictures after this time, but avoid shots of tall towers in an inky black sky; crop in close on lit areas to fill the frame.

Bring it home safely

Digital images are inherently ephemeral: they can be deleted or corrupted in a heartbeat. The good news though is they can be copied just as easily. Wherever you travel, you should have a backup strategy. Cloud backups are popular, but make sure that you will have access to fast enough Wi-Fi. If you use RAW format, then you will need some sort of physical back-up. If you don't travel with a laptop or tablet, then you can buy a backup drive that will copy directly from memory cards.

Available in both digital and print formats, Footprint's Travel Photography by Steve Davey covers everything you need to know about travelling with a camera, including simple post-processing. More information is available at www.footprinttravelguides.com

What to do

Cricket

Since the **Beausejour Cricket Ground** was built in 2002, St Lucia has hosted a number of Test and international matches, including the World Cup in 2007. The 15,000-seater stadium was renamed the **Darren Sammy National Cricket Stadium** in 2016, after St Lucian Darren Sammy who captained the West Indies side when they won the 2016 ICC World Twenty20 in India. See page 77 for details.

In Dominica, **Windsor Park** in Roseau is the national stadium and cricket ground. It was built in 2007 and has a capacity of 12,000. However, Dominica does not currently have a major presence in cricket, and Dominican players generally play for the West Indies ('Windies'). Nevertheless, the stadium occasionally hosts local friendly games.

Cycling

There are dedicated mountain biking trails through the forest above **Anse Mamin Beach**, part of the Anse Chastanet Estate (see page 53) in the southwest, and on the **Errard Estate** on the east coast of St Lucia (see page 47). **St Lucia Cycling Association** (T758-721 7756, see Facebook), organizes road races, time trials and public fun rides with BMX, mountain bikes and road bikes and competitors of all ages. Visitors will have to negotiate to borrow a bike.

Dominica has lots of trails that would be excellent for off-road cycling but, as yet, mountain biking is very small scale. Nevertheless, there are occasional events; contact the **Dominica Cycling Association** (T758-245 0811, see Facebook) for more information.

Diving and snorkelling

St Lucia

There is some very good diving off the west coast off St Lucia, although this is somewhat dependent on the weather, as heavy rain tends to create high sediment loads in the rivers and sea. Diving off the east coast is not so good and can be risky unless you are a competent diver. One of the best snorkelling and beach entry dive locations in the Caribbean is directly off **Anse Chastanet**, where an underwater shelf drops off from about 3 m down to 20 m and there is a good dive over **Turtle Reef** in the bay, where there are over 25 different types of coral. The area in front of the Anse Chastanet Resort is buoyed-off, and a roped-off area by the jetty is used by snorkellers and beginner divers. Just south and below the **Petit Piton** are impressive sponge and coral communities on a drop to 70 m of spectacular wall and, at the northern entrance to Sourfrière Bay, the Keyhole Pinnacles is an impressive site where four pinnacles are grouped within a radius of 150 m and rise to within 3 m of the surface; there are gorgonians, black coral trees, huge barrel sponges and plenty of other beautiful reef life. This whole area is part of a marine reserve administered by the **Sourfrière Marine Management Area** (SMMA; www.smma.org.lc), and it stretches between Anse Jambon, north of Anse Chastanet, and Anse L'Ivrogne to the south. There are other popular dive sites off **Anse L'Ivrogne**, **Anse La Raye** and **Anse Cochon**, not forgetting the **wrecks**, such as the *Volga* (in 6 m of water north of Castries harbour, well broken up, subject to swell, requires caution), and the 55-m *Lesleen M* (deliberately sunk in 1986 off Anse Cochon Bay in 20 m of water). For dive operators, see page 77. See also the Coral reef box, page 57.

Dominica

Dominica is highly regarded as a diving destination and, due to deep waters close to shore and heavy sediments from volcanic sands, visibility averages 24 m year-round; even after heavy rains the sediments subside within hours and good visibility returns. Features include wall dives, drop-offs, reefs, hot, freshwater springs under the sea, sponges, black coral, pinnacles and wrecks, all in unpolluted water. The most popular sites are south of Roseau in the **Soufrière-Scotts Head Marine Reserve** (SSMR;

www.ssmrdominica.org). Here, an unusual site is **Champagne Reef**, with underwater hot springs where you swim through bubbles (hence the name); it is also excellent for snorkelling. There are also good diving and snorkelling in the north off the Cabrits Peninsula and in Toucari Bay, where there are reefs dropping off sharply over barrel sponges and corals that attract schools of fish, and along the south and southeast coast there are more dive sites; however, because of the Atlantic currents, these are for experienced, adventurous divers only. For dive operators, see page 117.

Fishing

On **St Lucia**, fishing trips for barracuda, blue marlin, yellowfin, white marlin, sailfish, wahoo and dolphin fish (mahi mahi) can be arranged, and fishing is particularly good February-May when most of these game fish are in season (Augusut-December for blue marlin). One of the most popular places to head out from is Rodney Bay Marina, where there are a number of fishing charter boats, and where the annual five-day St Lucia **International Billfish Tournament** is held at the end of October (for more information, check the St Lucia Game Fishing Association's Facebook page). For fishing operators, see page 77.

On **Dominica**, most deep-sea fishing is done on the leeward side of the island and in the Guadeloupe Channel off the north coast, and popular catches include barracuda, bonito, dorado, mackerel, blue marlin, sailfish, tarpon, wahoo and yellowfin. Fishing is particularly good

December-June when most of these game fish are in season (August-December for blue marlin). There's a very good chance of seeing whales when out on a fishing excursion from Dominica (see below). For fishing operators, see page 118.

Golf

Unlike some of the other flatter Caribbean islands where golf is very popular, St Lucia's rugged and hilly terrain means there are only two golf courses on the island: a nine-hole course at the **Sandals Regency La Toc** resort near Castries (Sandals guests only), and the 18-hole course at the **St Lucia Golf Club** (see page 78), located at Cap Estate on the northern end of the island, which may not be as glamourous as other golf clubs in the Caribbean, but has fantastic views of both the Atlantic Ocean and Caribbean Sea from its greens. There are no golf courses on Dominica.

Hiking and birdwatching

St Lucia

St Lucia has an extensive network of hiking trails in the interior of the island managed and maintained by the **Forestry Department**. Permits are usually available at the rangers' stations at the start of the trails, where you can also pick up a guide – particularly useful if you are birdwatching. On a couple of trails guides are mandatory and you will have to pre-organize one with the Forestry Department or go with a tour operator. Trails that are particularly good for birdwatching, with the chance of seeing the St Lucian parrot and other endemic birds such as

the St Lucia oreole and St Lucia warbler, include the **Forestiere Trail** in the north of the island (see page 45); the **Barre le l'Isle Rainforest Trail** at the high point of the transinsular road (see page 46); the **Des Cartiers Rainforest Trail** on the east coast (see page 48); and the **Millet Bird Sanctuary Trail** on the west coast (see page 51). There are numerous other opportunities for hiking: for example, along the coast around **Cas-en-Bas Beach**; the **Tet Paul Nature Trail** in the southwest, which offers extraordinary views of the Pitons; and the **Gros Piton Nature Trail** itself for the tremendous 360-degree view of the southern part of the island.

Dominica

Hiking on Dominica can take anything from a couple of hours to a couple of weeks. Many of the trails are self-guided and there are also plenty of guides and tour companies to show you the way to some outstanding sights and beauty spots. To visit any of the places maintained by the **Division of Forestry, Wildlife and National Parks** you will need a site pass (see page 119), usually payable at the trailheads. The **Morne Trois Pitons National Park** has a number of trails to some natural wonders; the most fascinating and challenging is to the **Boiling Lake**, a strenuous hike of three hours uphill to the boiling fumarole, often taking in a stop at the **Valley of Desolation** along the way, followed by a plunge into the waters of **Titou Gorge** to cool off. Anyone wanting some serious hiking should consider all or parts of the

Waitukubuli National Trail, which is the Caribbean's first long-distance walking trail; it is divided into 14 manageable sections and covers the whole island, from Scotts Head in the south to the Cabrits Peninsula in the north, see box, page 118.

Remember that on either island, hiking in the forests can be wet and muddy, so bring appropriate clothing and footwear as well as hat, sun protection and insect repellent.

Sailing

As some of the best views are from the sea, it is recommended to take at least one boat trip. One of the most popular day excursions on **St Lucia** is to sail down the west coast to Soufrière, where you can admire the Pitons from the sea and alight at the town's jetty to visit some local sights such as the Sulphur Springs, Diamond Falls Botanical Gardens and Mineral Baths or Anse Chastanet Beach for swimming and snorkelling. Other possibilities include two- to three-hour sunset cruises and day trips to Martinique. See page 78. On **Dominica**, excursions by boat include whale watching (below), diving and snorkelling trips and fishing (above). See also page 119.

Whale watching

St Lucia

Whales generally visit the waters around St Lucia between December and April. Sperm and short-finned pilot whales are the most commonly seen, but humpbacks, Bryde's whales and orcas are also occasionally sighted. Dolphins include spinner, spotted, Fraser and bottlenose, usually in pods of 30-60 family members, but sometimes they can be seen in their hundreds. In season, boat trips for whale and dolphin watching are operated by the same charter companies that operate fishing trips. A good vantage point for land-based whale watching on the west coast is from the top of the hills at the Pigeon Island National Landmark overlooking Rodney Bay. See page 79.

Dominica

Whale watching off Dominica is particularly good; the best chance of seeing them in the eastern Caribbean. The deep, sheltered bays make ideal calving and breeding grounds and it's one of the few places in the world where there are resident sperm whales and family groups tend to remain off the island's west coast year-round – although the best season for spotting them in great numbers is November to March. On a good day, you could be treated to the sight of mothers and their young swimming close to the boat, or young males making enormous jumps before diving below the waves. Other species include short-fin pilot whales, false killer whales, melon-headed whales and humpback whales. Even if you are unlucky enough to miss the whales, your boat is likely to be accompanied by large pods of Fraser's, bottlenose, spinner and spotted dolphins. Boat trips are arranged by all the dive operators year-round. See page 119.

Windsurfing and kiteboarding

The winds off **Anse de Sables** in the extreme south of St Lucia are very good for both windsurfing and kiteboarding, with the latter taking place off a cove slightly to the north. January, February, May and June are the best months, with winds blowing unobstructed cross-onshore from the left. The sickle-shaped beach is bordered on the leeward side by the **Moule à Chique Peninsula**, so you won't drift off into the Atlantic. Windsurfing and kiteboarding are also good at **Cas-en-Bas** in the northeast, where the winds come in off the Atlantic. On the Caribbean side of the island several resorts offer equipment for lazy windsurfing and **Reduit Beach** in Rodney Bay is good for beginners. See page 42.

Where to stay

from all-inclusives to basic guesthouses

St Lucia

St Lucia has a wide and varied selection of resorts, hotels, guesthouses, apartments and villas. The majority of hotels are small, friendly and offer flexible service. They cater for all budgets, from the height of luxury in hotels with three-walled rooms featuring their own infinity pools to simple guesthouses in Gros Islet where you fall into bed after the Friday night jump-up. Rodney Bay is the place to stay if you want the beach, restaurants and nightlife on your doorstep, while the marina makes excursions convenient by boat, whether for day sails, diving or whale watching. Several hotels around Soufrière enjoy fabulous views of the Pitons and the coast, perched on hillsides in beautiful tropical gardens and forests; truly peaceful and romantic, but you will have to arrange car hire or taxis to get around or go to restaurants. Elsewhere, there are several remote all-inclusive resorts, providing everything their guests need for a relaxing holiday or honeymoon. Castries is obviously good for business travellers, but is also convenient for people who want to explore the island by bus. There are lots of villas to rent on St Lucia, particularly near the northern tip of the island in and around the upmarket Cap Estate, from where it's a short drive to Rodney Bay; there are also a number of very lavish villas to rent around Soufrière in the southwest, some of which have astonishing views of the Pitons. In fancier villas, the services of a chef and cleaner maybe included in the rates.

Price codes

Where to stay

$$$$ over US$300
$$$ US$150-300
$$ US$75-150
$ under US$75

Price codes refer to a standard double/twin room in high season.

Restaurants

$$$ over US$30
$$ US$15-30
$ under US$15

Price codes refer to the cost of a two-course meal, excluding drinks or service charge.

The top hotels in sublime locations and offering every conceivable service and luxury can cost over US$800 per room per night, while mid-range places, say around Rodney Bay Village, are in the US$150-300 per room range, and are generally good value for families or friends, with perhaps a pull-out sofa bed for children, a kitchenette and a wide selection of hotel amenities, such as a pool, bar and restaurant. Cheap and cheerful lodging can be found on St Lucia for US$50-100 a night, but it will be inland, not on the beach. High season – mid-December to mid-April – is when rates are at their most expensive. There are often discounts of around 30% in low season – September and October – but this is also the worst time for rainy weather and many hotels close altogether. Hotel VAT (10%) and service charge (10%) is charged across the board, usually as a single charge of 20%; check if this has been included in quotes. Rates are room-only, B&B or all-inclusive, meaning you get three meals a day and sometimes local drinks. Opting for an all-inclusive rate, or staying at a specifically all-inclusive resort where everything such as watersports is also included, can be appealing as you know exactly what you are getting for your money. But you will miss out on the fun of selecting from the huge choice of restaurants on the island, and you may only mix with guests of one nationality (depending on where the resort is marketed).

Almost all places have websites, which gives the opportunity to ask questions, get further information from the proprietors/reservations teams and to book direct. Good listings can be found on the website of the **St Lucia Tourist Board**, ⓘ *www.stlucia.org*, and St Lucia is well represented on accommodation websites such as www.expedia.com, www.booking.com, www.ownersdirect. co.uk and www.airbnb.com.

Dominica

With no long-distance flights bringing mass tourism to the island, and no large beaches to accommodate the crowds, Dominica has no large, all-inclusive resorts. Instead there are small and intimate places to stay, whether higher end or low budget or somewhere in between. There are hotels, guesthouses, B&Bs, rental cottages, specialist dive lodges and rustic eco-resorts, inland or on the coast. There are hardly any places that would fall into the super-luxury category – only Secret Bay on the northwest coast would pass the US$500 per night price range – but there are a few good mid- to upper-range hotels, from Roseau's Fort Young Hotel to a couple of resorts on the east coast in the US$200-400 range. More prolific and scattered all around the island, are small inns, guesthouses and self-catering cottages in the US$75-150 range. You are unlikely to get amenities like TV or air conditioning but you may well be surrounded by bountiful gardens and the sounds of the forest, and you might be able to swim in a river on the property. These are peaceful places to base yourself while you explore, although a bit of pre-planning is required to buy food and other provisions (most owners will assist with this). Some places may be a little rough around the edges, but if the paint is peeling it is more likely to be because of the ravages of the tropical climate and frequent rain rather than any lack of care by the owners. Generally the cheaper low season is June to November, but this is also the most likely time for rain. Hotel VAT (10%) and service charge (10%) is charged across the board, usually as a single charge of 20%. Check if this has been included in quoted rates. There are accommodation listings on the website of the **Discover Dominica Authority** ⓘ *www.dominica.dm*, as well as www.avirtualdominica.com, www. expedia.com, www.booking.com and www.airbnb.com.

Food
& drink

The historical movement of people along the chain of Caribbean islands means that the food is a blend of cultural influences from the islands' immigrants over the centuries. Known as Creole cuisine, it's a blend of starchy, high-carbohydrate vegetables ('provisions') that were introduced to sustain African slaves, gourmet sauces and garnishes dating from the days when the French governed the islands, and other flavours such as spices from when Indians were bought over as indentured labourers to work on the plantations. Difficulties in storing meat and fish in the tropical heat led to the common use of salt-curing, pickling and other preservatives, and sugar, the main crop of the islands for generations, features heavily in both food and drink, reaching perfection in the production of rum.

Food

As you might expect of islands, there is a wide variety of seafood on offer which is fresh and tasty and served in a multitude of ways. Fish and seafood of all sorts are commonly available and are usually better quality than local meat. Flying fish, dorado, kingfish and tuna are likely to be among the catches of the day, as well as spiny lobsters and octopus. Beef and lamb are often imported from the USA or Argentina, but goat, pork and chicken are produced locally. There is no dairy industry to speak of, so cheeses are also usually imported. There is, however, a riot of tropical fruit and vegetables and a visit to a local market will give you the opportunity to see unusual and often unidentifiable objects as well as more familiar items found in supermarkets in Europe and North America but with 10 times the flavour.

The best bananas in the world are grown on small farms in the Windward Islands; they are cheap, incredibly sweet and unlike anything you can buy at home. You will come across many of the wonderful tropical fruits in the form of juices or ice cream. Don't miss the rich flavours of the soursop (*chirimoya*, *guanábana*), the guava, tamarind or the sapodilla (*zapote*). Breakfast buffets are usually groaning under the weight of tropical fruits, from banana, pineapple, melon, orange and grapefruit, to mango, of which there are nearly 100 varieties, papaya/pawpaw (*papay* in Kwéyòl), carambola (star fruit) and sugar apple (custard apple or sweetsop). Mangoes in season drip off the trees and those that don't end up on your breakfast plate can be found squashed in abundance all over the roads. Caribbean oranges are often green when ripe, as there is no cold season to bring out the orange colour; they are better for juicing than peeling. Portugals are like tangerines and easy to peel.

Avocados are nearly always sold unripe, so wait several days before attempting to eat them. Avocados have been around since the days of the Arawaks, who also cultivated cassava and cocoa, but many vegetables have their origins in the slave trade, brought over to provide a starchy diet for the slaves. The breadfruit, a common staple, rich in carbohydrates and vitamins A, B and C, was brought from the South Seas in 1793 by Captain Bligh, perhaps more famous for the mutiny on the *Bounty*. A large, round, starchy fruit, usually eaten fried or boiled, it grows on huge trees with enormous leaves and is known as *bwapen* in Kwéyòl. Christophene is another local vegetable which can be prepared in many ways, but is delicious baked in a cheese sauce. Dasheen is a root vegetable with green leaves, rather like spinach, which are used to make the tasty and nutritious callaloo soup. Plantains are eaten boiled or fried as a savoury vegetable, while green bananas, known as figs, can be cooked before they are ripe enough to eat raw as a fruit.

Drink

For non-alcoholic drinks, there is a range of refreshing fruit juices, including orange, mango, pineapple, grapefruit, lime, guava and passionfruit. Local soft drinks include sorrel, a bright red drink made with hibiscus sepals and spices, and tamarind, a bitter sweet drink made from the pods of the tamarind tree. Both are watered down like a fruit squash and they can be refreshing with lots of ice. Teas are made from a variety of herbs, often for medicinal purposes. Cocoa tea, however, is drunk at breakfast as is hot chocolate, usually flavoured with spices. Try the sea-moss drink in Dominica, rather like a vanilla milk shake (with a reputation as an aphrodisiac).

Like most islands, St Lucia has its own rum, produced by **St Lucia Distillers**, used in cocktails and liqueurs or drunk on the rocks. There are over 20 different products, of which the amber **Bounty** is the most popular. Others include the white **Crystal**, used in cocktails, or the aged rums, **Chairman's Reserve** and **Admiral's**. Denros is a 150° proof rum to be treated with extreme caution. Rum shops stock five-gallon plastic containers of the stuff, combining it with fruits and spices and calling it 'spice'. Flavoured rums are popular with those who like an alcoholic, liquid sweet, including the award-winning

Tip...
Try coconut water – the clear liquid inside young green coconuts which is very refreshing and often served by using a machete to cut open the nut. Look for barrows and stalls piled high with coconuts and a knife-wielding vendor in markets, on the side of village streets and in car parks at the beaches.

Nutz&Rum. On Dominica you can find the local **Macoucherie**, **Soca** or **Red Cap** rums. If you drink in a rum shop, rum and other drinks are bought by the bottle. The smallest size is a mini, then a flask, then a full bottle. The shop will supply ice and glasses, you buy a mixer, and serve yourself.

The local St Lucian beer is **Piton**, brewed in Vieux Fort. A shandy on St Lucia is a mixture of beer and ginger ale; if it's a **Piton** shandy it can be with lemon or sorrel. **Kubuli** is the local beer on Dominica. Both are drunk very cold for maximum refreshment. Water is of good quality on St Lucia and most hotels treat it, but there is bottled water if you prefer. Dominicia however does generally not have good tap water as much of it comes directly from rivers and maybe untreated; best to stick to bottled water.

Eating out

St Lucia

The standard of cooking in St Lucian restaurants is high, but for really authentic local food you should try cafeterias and street vendors. A typical lunch, such as at any of the stalls at Castries Central Market, will feature the likes of meat or fish with rice and peas, plantains, macaroni and salad, washed down with a passionfruit juice, and will cost around US$6-10. The best places for freshly caught seafood on St Lucia, cooked to your specification, are at 'fish frys'; the weekly street parties at Anse La Raye, Dennery and Gros Islet, where local fishermen sell their catch to be cooked on huge oil drum barbecues. Beach bars are good places for seafood at lunchtime, especially grilled fish, and you can make a day of it with cocktails and sun loungers on the sand. Formal restaurants will charge around US$12-30 for a main course, and quality is good and the settings often special; you may get an open-air table on a garden terrace or with a gorgeous view. The majority of places to eat international food are at Rodney Bay Village, where there is a wide variety allowing you to indulge in Italian, Mexican, Indian, French, Japanese or whatever takes your fancy. Elsewhere, like in the smart hotel restaurants around Soufrière, the menus tend to lean towards refined and well-presented Creole cooking using local ingredients.

Dominica

Eating out on Dominica is nearly always in small family-run local eateries or at the few hotel restaurants, and you can expect an abundance of fish and seafood, vegetables and root crops ('provisions'), and fruit on menus around the island – good for nourishing tired bodies after hiking. There is a concentration of restaurants in Roseau and Portsmouth; particularly popular are the cafeteria-type places, that are busy from midday as Dominicans eat their main meal at lunchtime, where you will get a filling plate of food for around US$6-10. There are also lots of 'snackettes' in these towns serving (you guessed it, snacks), a small spattering of restaurants around the island including at Castle Comfort, Calibishie and Marigot, and rum shops in villages may cook a lunchtime meal of the day or serve the likes of grilled chicken or fish. Hours can vary, and many restaurants will be closed on Sundays and, except for the few top-end ones and those in hotels, restaurants on Dominica will not generally accept credit cards. Restaurants are supposed to quote prices on menus that include the 15% VAT; the more formal ones do, but the small, casual, family-run places don't usually bother with it.

St Lucia

Whether you're after adventure, relaxation, or a bit of both – St Lucia (pronounced 'Loosha') ticks all the boxes. Its crescent-shaped beaches are golden or black sand and many are favoured by nesting sea turtles, while offshore is good diving and snorkelling in the marine reserve along part of the west coast. Castries, the island's capital and cruise ship port, offers a colourful slice of St Lucian life at its lively market, as well as some historic landmarks. In the northwest, the resort zone around Rodney Bay provides fun in the sun, watersports, good restaurants and nightlife and has one of the best yacht marinas in the Caribbean. The mountainous interior is outstandingly beautiful and there are several reserves to protect the St Lucia parrot and other wildlife, as well as a number of hiking trails through the rich rainforests. In the southwest, sightseeing opportunities include small fishing villages, geothermal sulphur springs, cascading waterfalls, and the towering Pitons, St Lucia's famous twin volcanic peaks clad in emerald-green forest. St Lucia has a rich cultural heritage too, having alternated between the French and English colonial powers, which is reflected in colonial fortifications and plantations.

Essential St Lucia

Finding your feet

Hewanorra International Airport (UVF; T758-454 6355, www.hewanorrainternational airport.com) on the outskirts of Vieux Fort in the very south of the island, handles the majority of long-haul flights. The journey to Castries is about 1½ hours by road and most traffic goes via the east coast road as it's quicker than going around the west coast. The travel time from the airport to Soufrière on the west coast is about one hour. Sample taxi fares from the airport are: to George F L Charles Airport/Castries, US$75; to Soufrière, US$75; and to Rodney Bay US$85. You can sometimes negotiate a ride with one of the transfer buses from hotels for less; enquire at **St Lucia Reps** (T758-456 9100, www. stluciareps.com) who also offer other transfer services, including limousines, private minibuses, shared minibuses and private cars, with advance booking.

The smaller short-haul/inter-island **George F L Charles Airport** (SLU) (T758-452 1156, www.georgeflcharlesairport. com), is on the Vigie Peninsula just outside Castries. If you are travelling light you can walk to the main road and catch a minibus or route taxi the short distance into town.

Otherwise sample taxi fares are: to Rodney Bay US$25; to Soufrière, US$90; and to Marigot Bay, US$30. There is an air shuttle between the two airports by helicopter with **St Lucia Helicopters** (T758-453 6950, www.stluciahelicopters.com) which takes about 10 minutes, US$165 per person, or 15 minutes, US$180 for a more scenic route around the Pitons and Soufrière. See also page 80 for details and additional helicopter tours. If you are arriving on L'Express des Iles ferry from Guadeloupe, Dominica and Martinique, the terminal is on La Toc Road on the south side of Castries' harbour, a short taxi ride from any of the hotels in and around the capital.

Getting around

Hiring a car is the best way of exploring the island and a normal car is sufficient if you stick to the main roads, but remember that the mountain roads into the forests are very poor when a 4WD or at the very least a high-clearance vehicle is recommended. If you don't want to drive yourself, there are tours to anywhere you might want to go and guides can always be arranged. Minivans provide a reasonable public transport system but will not get you far off the beaten track.

Weather Castries

	January	February	March	April	May	June
High	29°C	29°C	30°C	30°C	31°C	31°C
Low	22°C	22°C	22°C	23°C	24°C	25°C
Rainfall	95mm	69mm	60mm	74mm	88mm	131mm

	July	August	September	October	November	December
High	31°C	31°C	32°C	31°C	30°C	30°C
Low	24°C	24°C	24°C	23°C	23°C	22°C
Rainfall	171mm	219mm	200mm	250mm	222mm	138mm

St Lucia

Pointe du Cap
Smuggler's Cove
Cap Estate
St Lucia Golf Club
13
Pointe Hardy
Donkey Beach
Pigeon Island National Landmark
Fort Rodney
20
14
Cas-en-Bas
Gros Islet
10
32
Massade
Anse Levoutte
Comerette Point
Anse Comerette
Rodney Bay
26
Darren Sammy National Cricket Stadium
Anse Lapins
Espérance Harbour
Rodney Bay Village
Labrellotte Beach
21
Monchy
Cap Marquis
Labrellotte Bay
8
St Lucia Megaplex 8
1
Port Dauphin
Marisule Estate
Rat Island
Choc Bay
Grande Rivière
Cassimi Point
Vide Bouteille Point
5
Gablewoods Shopping Mall
Marquis River
Morne Monier
Tanti Point
Sandals Halcyon Beach Resort & Spa
George F L Charles Airport
Vigie Beach
11
Lushan Country Life
Paix Bouche
Grande Anse
D'Estrées Point
Vigie
Morne Chaubourg
Castries
Babonneau
Des Barra
Tortue Point
La Toc Bay
La Toc Point
La Toc Beach
Coubaril Point
Sandals Regency La Toc
Morne Fortuné
Fort Charlotte
Fond Cacao
SDA
Chassin
Good Lands
Cul de Sac Bay
Eudovic's Art Studio
Fond Assor
Rainforest Adventures
Castries Waterworks Forest Reserve
Louvet Point
Anse Massacré
9
34
23
Hess Oil Terminal
24
Marigot Bay
La Sorcière
Anse Louvet
Povert Pt
Roseau Bay
6
Roseau
Forestiere
Piton Flore
Forestiere Trail
St Lucia Distillery
La Croix Maingot
Bexon
Au Leon
La Caye
Mamelles Pt
Massacré
Jacmel
Vanard
Ravine Poisson
Grande Rivière
L'Anse la Raye
Pointe La Ville
Sarot
Fond River
Fond D'Or Bay
Anse Cochon
33
Plas Kassav
Roseau River
Morne La Combe (231m)
Barre de l'Isle Rainforest Trail
Morne Beaujolais
Dennery
Dennery Bay
Anse Jambette
Canaries
Millet
Millet Bird Sanctuary Trail
Errard
Treetop Adventure Park
Linnis Point
Anse La Liberté
Grand Bois Forest
Errard Falls
Praslin
Praslin Island
Praslin Bay
Blanche Point
Mamiku Botanical Gardens
3
Anse Mamin Beach
17
Morne Tabac (678m)
Mon Repos
Trou Gras Point
Anse Chastanet
30
2
Morne Gimie (950m)
Diamond Falls Botanical Gardens & Mineral Baths
Quillesse Forest Reserve
Mahaut
Patience
Anse Chapeau
Soufrière
18
Toraille Waterfall & Gardens
Fond Bay
Soufrière Bay
Morne Coubaril Estate
22
Sulphur Springs Park
Edmond Forest Reserve
La Tille Waterfalls
Port Volet
Micoud
29
19
Petit Piton
27
4
Fond St Jacques
New Jerusalem Mineral Baths
Rabot Estate
7
Ti Rocher
Jalousie Bay
Anse des Pitons
Fond Doux Plantation & Resort
Morne Grand Magazin (616m)
Blanchard
Troumassé Bay
Tet Paul Nature Trail
16
Desruisseaux
Gros Piton Nature Trail
Fond Gens Libre
Etangs
Anse Ger
Gros Piton (771m)
Anse L'Ivrogne
Victoria Junct
Monzie
Dacretin
Belle Vue
Point Lamarre
La Pointe
31
Saltibus
Caraïbe Point
Banse
Pierrot
Anse L'Islet
Gertrine
Augier
Sauzay
Sab Wee-Sha Beach
Choiseul
15
Laborie
1
Piaye
Laborie Bay
Hewanorra International Airport
2
25
Maria Islands Nature Reserve
Black Bay
4
Vieux Fort
28
Anse de Sables Beach
Caesar Point
Moule à Chique Lighthouse
Cap Moule à Chique

32•St Lucia

N

| 2 km |
| 2 miles |

Where to stay

Best views on St Lucia

Best beaches

Best places to eat

Fact file

Location One of the Windward Islands chain lying between the Atlantic Ocean and the Caribbean Sea, with Martinique to the north and St Vincent to the south
Capital Castries, 14° 1′ 0″ N, 60° 59′ 0″ W
Time zone Atlantic standard time GMT -4 hrs, EST +1 hr
Telephone country code +758
Currency East Caribbean dollar, EC$

The picturesque capital, Castries, is set on a natural harbour against a mountainous background. Ships and boats of all sizes come in here: mammoth cruise ships, cargo and container ships, the ferry to Dominica and the French Antilles, yachts and brightly painted fishing boats, all jostling for space at their respective berths. The centre of Castries is small enough to walk around, but to get to outlying districts you can catch a bus (minivan) or taxi or hire a car.

★ Market area and around

Largely rebuilt after being destroyed by major fires, the last in 1948, the city's commercial centre and government offices are today built of concrete. Only the buildings to the south of Derek Walcott Square and behind Brazil Street survived that fire, when over three-quarters of the city was engulfed in flames. Here you will see late 19th- and

> **Tip...**
> To benefit from lower, duty-free prices, you'll need to show your passport and airline ticket (or travel documents for cruise ship passengers) when making a purchase.

early 20th-century French-style three-storeyed wooden buildings, their gingerbread fretwork balconies overhanging the pavement. The other area which survived was the **Castries Central Market** ⓘ *Mon-Sat 0700-1800*, on the north side of Jeremie Street. The simple building with its metal roof and clock above the entrance was constructed in 1891 by Bruce and Still, Civil Engineers of Liverpool, England. There are dozens of stalls inside and out for the fruit, vegetable and flower sellers, piled high with bananas, plantains, coconuts, limes, breadfruit, soursop, dasheen and much else besides. On the first floor and in the Vendor's Arcade across John Compton Highway, are people selling T-shirts, crafts, spices, basketwork and St Lucia's famous hot pepper sauce. The Vendor's Arcade also has booths offering good Creole meals and local juices. There are some 300 vendors but this swells to more than 400 on Saturday, which is the traditional market day across the island, when more stalls are set up beneath a multitude of shady umbrellas.

About 300 m to the west of the market and by the main berth at Queen Elizabeth II Dock is **La Place Carenage** ⓘ *Jeremie St, T758-453 2451 www.carenagemall.com, daily 0900-2000*, a modern, three-storey duty-free shopping centre for cruise ship passengers selling jewellery, clothes, souvenirs, locally made arts and crafts, crystal, perfume, liquor and tobacco; there are also two restaurants. At the St Lucia Cruise Ship Terminal across the harbour to the north, and reached by water taxi or by road around the bay, **Pointe Seraphine Shopping Centre** ⓘ *T758-457 3425, www.pointeseraphine.lc, Mon-Fri 0900-1630, Sat 0900-1400, Sun 0900-1400 if there's a cruise ship in port*, is another waterfront complex selling similar items. Some 400 cruise ships on average call in to Castries every year from October to April (between 500,000 and 700,000 passengers), and on the days that ships are in port Castries is heaving. Prices in both the market areas and the shops take a distinct hike when cruise ship passengers are around; on 'dry days' (as the shop owners like to call them), haggling over prices is acceptable whether it's for bananas or a diamond ring.

Derek Walcott Square

Bounded by Bourbon, Brazil, Laborie and Micoud streets, Derek Walcott Square is a 2-acre (0.8-ha) park established in the 1760s by the French as the Place d'Armes. The British renamed it Promenade Square, then it became Columbus Square in 1893 and was the original site of the courthouse and the market. In 1993, exactly 100 years after the last name change, it was renamed in honour of Derek Walcott, the St Lucian author who in 1992 won the Nobel Prize for Literature (see box, page 36). There is a bust of him, and one

Castries

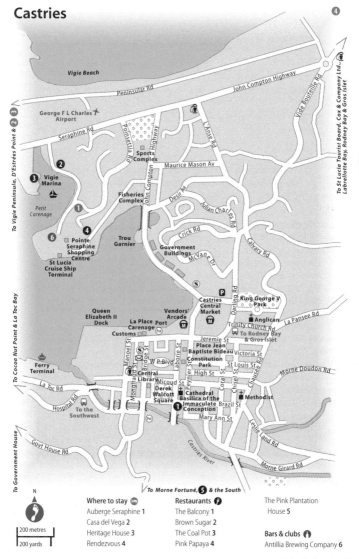

Where to stay 🛏
Auberge Seraphine 1
Casa del Vega 2
Heritage House 3
Rendezvous 4

Restaurants 🍴
The Balcony 1
Brown Sugar 2
The Coal Pot 3
Pink Papaya 4

The Pink Plantation House 5

Bars & clubs 🍸
Antillia Brewing Company 6

BACKGROUND

Derek Walcott

One of the Caribbean's most renowned poets and playwrights, Derek Walcott, was born in Castries in 1930. Both his grandmothers were said to have been descended from slaves, and his father was a painter and his mother headmistress of a Methodist school. He published his first collection of poems at the age of 19 and a year later, in 1950, he staged his first play and went to study English literature, French and Latin at the newly established University College of the West Indies in Jamaica. He lived and worked for many years in Trinidad and the US, and in later life was Professor of Poetry at the University of Essex in the UK. Walcott wrote many acclaimed collections of poetry including what is considered his masterpiece: the 1990 *Omeros*, a Caribbean reimagining of *The Odyssey*. This epic poem's parallels with *The Odyssey* include replacing the story of the Trojan War with that of a fishermen's fight. Walcott was awarded the Nobel Prize for Literature in 1992, and received many other literary awards over the course of his career. An OBE since 1972, he was also awarded Knight of the Order of Saint Lucia for exceptional and outstanding service of national importance in 2016. Walcott died at his home in Cap Estate in the north of St Lucia in March 2017. He is buried at Morne Fortuné.

of St Lucia's other Nobel Laureate, Sir Arthur Lewis, plus a bandstand and a monument to St Lucia's war dead. The giant saman tree in the middle is about 425 years old. The park is now used for ceremonial occasions and entertainment, including 'Jazz on the Square' concerts during the annual **Jazz Festival**.

On the west side of the square, Bourbon Street, the **Central Library** was completed in 1924 thanks to a £2500 grant from US millionaire Andrew Carnegie of the Carnegie Foundation. The first building miraculously escaped the 1927 Castries fire, but the 1948 fire gutted the building and over 20,000 books were destroyed. After the fire, the library was rebuilt using the old walls; it now features gracious columns and balustrades.

Running along the south side of Derek Walcott Square, Brazil Street has several buildings which survived the 1948 fire and are therefore some of the oldest in the capital. Here you can see latticed overhanging balconies and gingerbread fretwork. There are even some remaining chattel houses, made of wood on a stone base. They were built in such a way as to be easily dismantled; families often had to move with 'all their goods and chattels'.

Basilica of the Immaculate Conception
Laborie St, T758-452 2271, daily 0800-1700, Mass Sat 0800, Sun 0600, 0800, 1030.

On the east side of Derek Walcott Square, on Laborie Street, is the Roman Catholic Cathedral, which was built in 1897 and looks fairly plain and sombre from the outside, but the splendid and colourfully painted interior is a different story. The ceiling, supported by iron arches and braces, is decorated with panelled portraits of the apostles. Above the central altar with its four carved screens, the apse ceiling has paintings of five female saints with St Lucy in the centre. The walls have murals of the Stations of the Cross and are unusual in that the people in the paintings are black. They are by Dunstan St Omer, one of St Lucia's better known artists. The 12 stained-glass windows were created by his son,

Giovanni. Suffused with yellow light, the side altars are often covered with flowers, while votive candles placed in red, green and yellow jars giving a fairytale effect. The cathedral is open to visitors all day, although funerals sometimes take place in the late afternoon, which often means a large crowd dressed in black, white and purple, the local colours of mourning. As part of its centenary celebrations, the cathedral was given the honorary status of a Minor Basilica in 1999.

La Toc

To get to La Toc, follow Millennium Highway west from town past the ferry terminal and turn on to La Toc Road at the roundabout.

On the southern tip of the bay is **La Toc Point** from where you can see Martinique to the north on a clear day. Here is **La Toc Battery** ① *T758-452 7921, daily 0900-1500*, which was built in 1888 as part of the fortifications to protect the harbour, although it was abandoned in 1905. It's the best restored of the military buildings around Castries and has a mostly intact gun emplacement with cannons, a fire signal tower, and underground rooms and corridors that housed the shell store and soldiers' dormitory. These now exhibit artefacts found in and around the area, including a collection of over 900 bottles found by divers in Castries harbour, some dating from 1720.

Below the point, the crescent-shaped **La Toc Beach** is dominated by the all-inclusive, adults-only, **Sandals Regency La Toc** ① *La Toc Rd, T758-452 3081, www.sandals.com*. At the resort's lower gate, the staff will show you the path that leads down to the beach – many of St Lucia's beaches are dominated by resorts, but they are all public. The water here is beautifully clear and there's good swimming once you get past the drop-off and a little rocky patch, although at times the waves can get rough. The sand is pale yellow and is littered with seashells and is kept clean by the resort. There is the option of getting a day pass for Sandals (over 18s only, 1000-1800 US$100, 1000-0200 US$200), which includes unlimited food and drink in the nine restaurants/bars, use of the three swimming pools, non-motorized watersports such as snorkelling, kayaking, hobies, stand-up paddle boarding and windsurfing, and use of sun loungers and umbrellas on the beach.

Morne Fortuné

The ridge of Morne Fortuné ('hill of good luck') just south of the city centre enjoys wonderful views over Castries and the harbour and receives pleasant breezes to temper the tropical sunshine. For this reason the British built their grand houses up here as well as their military buildings. From the town centre, head south down Micoud Street then turn right into Government House Road, up the hill and onto Morne Road. It is very twisty and steep and dangerous to walk because of traffic negotiating the bends. Once up there you can visit the military ruins (free) and enjoy the views back down to Castries – an impressive sight when there are up to four super-sized cruise ships in port.

Government House with its curious metalwork crown can be seen from the road. It dates from 1895 and is the official residence of the Governor-General of Saint Lucia. The house is not open to the public but there is a small museum called **Le Pavillon Royal Museum** ① *T758-452 2481, Tue and Thu 1000-1600, by appointment only, donations welcome*, which contains a collection of historical documents, photographs and artefacts that chronicle the history of Government House and the successive governors and governors-general who have administered from the early 17th century. **Howelton Estate 1896** ① *T758-452 3785, see Facebook, Mon-Sat 0800-1600, Sun if a cruise ship is in port*, is just past Government House on Old Victoria Road. Formerly known as Caribelle Batik, you

BACKGROUND

Castries

The first settlement and fortification on St Lucia was built by the French in 1650 at Vigie and was known as Carénage, meaning 'safe anchorage', in reference to the deep-water harbour. It was renamed in 1756 after Charles Eugène Gabriel de La Croix, Marquis de Castries, and the commander of a fleet of French ships. However, after a devastating hurricane in 1780, the main fort was moved up to Morne Fortuné and the government buildings, including Government House, followed.

By 1814, after a prolonged series of destructive battles, the island had gone to the British, who made Castries a major naval port in the region as the harbour could accommodate their largest warships. In the second half of the 19th century Britain decided to develop the port for coal bunkering too, and Welsh coal was brought to St Lucia and sold on to passing steam ships. By the turn of the century Castries was the 14th most important port in the world in terms of tonnage handled. However, by the 1930s oil had superseded coal and the port declined.

During the Second World War two ships in the harbour were torpedoed by a German submarine. A third torpedo missed its target: an Alcoa ship carrying a full cargo of TNT which might have blown the whole of Castries to smithereens. Castries has been rebuilt many times, following major fires in 1796 and 1813, and most notably after June 19, 1948 when about 75% of the town was destroyed after a fire started in a tailor's shop (fortunately there was no loss of life). Castries officially became a city in 1967; today it covers about 80 sq km and has a population of some 70,000. Buoyed by tourism, the port is again thriving, receiving some of the largest cruise ships in the world.

can visit the batik studio and print shop, see how the fabric is printed on sea-island cotton and then made into vibrant clothes and furnishings full of tropical colour. There's also a bar/restaurant and the shop is a treasure trove of souvenirs including bags, jewellery, chocolate and items made from coconut husks.

Military sites on Morne Fortuné There are six historical military sites on Morne Fortuné under the control of the **St Lucia National Trust** ⓘ www.slunatrust.org. They were built for obvious strategic reasons as you can see most of the northwest coast and the town from the top of the 260-m hill. The fortifications were started by the French in 1768, but expanded and completed by the British. Most of the buildings and the ruins are used for housing or educational purposes.

Fort Charlotte, the old Morne Fortuné fortress, is now the Sir Arthur Lewis Community College. The **Morne Battery** (1888-1892) is situated above the eastern side of Morne Road at the north side of its junction with Henry Dulieu Road. Also known as the Apostles Battery, it was built by the British long after the threat from France had gone, but at a time when the port was important as a coaling station and the harbour needed protecting. It was built at ground level so you couldn't see it from the sea, and once had four cannons, each weighing four tons. Nearby the **Powder Magazine**, the **Guard Cells** and the stables next to them were constructed by the French in 1763-1765 and are probably the oldest buildings on the Morne. The walls of the Powder Magazine are thick enough to contain any accidental explosion from the gunpowder and ammunition stored there. **Provost's**

Redoubt (1782) was a lookout point and from here you can see as far as Martinique on a clear day. The French and British **cemeteries** are beside each other in a residential area. Five British and one French governor are buried here, as well as military personnel and civilians, many of whom died of cholera and yellow fever.

The most spectacular view is from the **Inniskilling Monument** at the far side of the college (just beyond the old Combermere barracks) where you get a fine panorama of the town, coast, mountains and Martinique. It was here in 1796 that General Moore launched an attack on the French who, together with the Brigands, had gained control of the island after defeating the British at Vieux Fort and Rabot. The steep slopes give some idea of how fierce the two days of fighting must have been. As a rare honour, the 27th Inniskilling Fusiliers were allowed to fly their regimental flag for one hour after they took the fortress before the Union Jack was raised. The monument was built at the eastern end of Fort Charlotte in 1932 to commemorate the event. Both Sir Arthur Lewis, Nobel Laureate in Economics, and Derek Walcott, Nobel Laureate in Literature, are buried in front of the monument.

Vigie

Castries harbour is protected on three sides by hills, of which the **Vigie Peninsula** is the northern promontory. The word Vigie comes from the French term for having someone posted as lookout, and both the French and the English saw its strategic advantage and built defensive military positions there, making the entire peninsula a military stronghold. **Vigie Lighthouse** on Beacon Road is a white cylindrical tower with a red dome. Built in 1914, it was originally a wooden structure but was rebuilt in stone in 1989, and the now 10-m tower overlooks the ruins of 18th- and 19th-century military barracks – a lookout of sorts was used here as far back as 1768. **Vigie Beach** is 2-3 km north of the centre of Castries and runs parallel with the George F L Charles Airport runway (the smaller of the two airports on St Lucia); but, as the airport is only used for inter-island flights with small aircraft, planes don't take long to take off or land and the noise soon passes. The beach is a lovely long strip of sand with plenty of shade, popular with locals at the weekend, cleaned regularly, and opposite are a few small food kiosks serving the airport departures area. There is only one resort here (**Rendezvous**, see page 62) which lies at the eastern end. To get there from town, go north and east on John Compton Highway and take a left at the roundabout as you pass the airstrip on to Peninsular Road which follows the shoreline (it's a good idea to get a taxi from town as the walk is longer than it looks around the airstrip). If driving, there's plenty of parking under the trees.

★ Rodney Bay and the north

the place to come for an action-packed beach holiday and nightlife

North of Castries is the principal resort area, where the best beaches are. The Rodney Bay and Gros Islet region supports a mass of tourist facilities including watersports, shops, restaurants and nightlife, and the horseshoe-shaped bay itself is always full of yachts. Rodney Bay Marina is one of the best anchorages in the Caribbean, impressive homes dot the hills surrounding the bay, there is a lovely beach at Reduit and Pigeon Island makes an interesting excursion.

North of Castries

Beyond Vigie, at the roundabout near the runway of George F L Charles Airport, John Compton Highway becomes the Castries–Gros Islet Highway and heads north. Passing the **Gablewoods Shopping Mall** on the right, and then, on the left, the all-inclusive **Sandals Halcyon Beach Resort & Spa** ⓘ *T758-4530222, www.sandals.com*, the highway

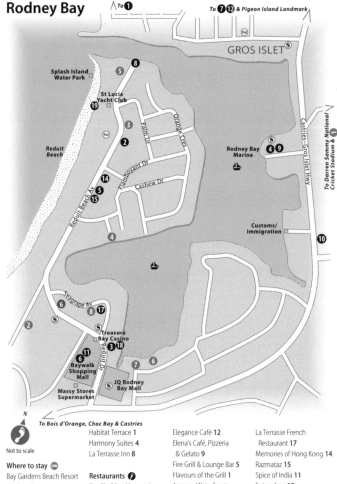

Rodney Bay

To ① To ❼ ❿ & Pigeon Island Landmark

GROS ISLET ⓢ

Splash Island Water Park ❽ ❺

St Lucia Yacht Club ⓵❾

Reduit Beach

❸ Palm Dr

Orange Cres

Rodney Bay Marina ⓢ ❹❾

Flamboyant Dr

Cashew Dr

❶❹ ❺ ⓵❺

Castries-Gros Islet Hwy

To Darren Sammy National Cricket Stadium & ⓘ

❹

Customs/ Immigration ❿

Seagrape Av

❻ ❽ ⓵❼

❷ ⓢ

ⓢ Treasure Bay Casino

❸ ⓵❽

Reduit Dr

❻ ❻ ⓵❶ Baywalk Shopping Mall

❼

JQ Rodney Bay Mall ⓢ

Massy Stores Supermarket

N

Not to scale

To Bois d'Orange, Choc Bay & Castries

Where to stay 🛏
Bay Gardens Beach Resort & Spa **5**
Bay Gardens Hotel **6**
Bay Gardens Inn **7**
Coco Palm **2**
The Ginger Lily Hotel **3**

Habitat Terrace **1**
Harmony Suites **4**
La Terrasse Inn **8**

Restaurants 🍴
Big Chef Steakhouse **3**
Blue Olive Restaurant & Wine Bar **6**
Buzz Seafood & Grill **2**
Café Olé **4**

Elegance Café **12**
Elena's Café, Pizzeria & Gelato **9**
Fire Grill & Lounge Bar **5**
Flavours of the Grill **1**
Jacques Waterfront Dining **8**
Jambe de Bois **7**
Il Pappa Trattoria Pizzeria Gelataria **10**

La Terrasse French Restaurant **17**
Memories of Hong Kong **14**
Razmataz **15**
Spice of India **11**
Spinnakers **19**
Tapas on the Bay **18**

Bars & clubs 🍴
Delirius **6**

runs alongside the beach at **Choc Bay**. This has placid waters and is lined by particularly tall coconut palms (the units at **Villa Beach Cottages**, see page 63, sit right behind the beach and Sandals is at the southern end) but there are no other facilities for casual visitors except for a car park. However, there are shops and restaurants on the main road and again a day pass is available at **Sandals** (over 18s only, 1000-1800 US$100, 1000-0200 US$200), which includes non-motorized watersports and use of sun loungers and umbrellas on the beach, as well as unlimited food and drink in the six restaurants/bars, one of which, **Kelly's Dockside**, is on an attractive pier that juts into the bay. Offshore is a mysterious undeveloped island (no more than a wooded outcrop of rock) called **Rat Island**. Its name is thought to have derived from when early ships deposited their dead rats (rodent stowaways) here; it was once a quarantine centre for smallpox victims and a French family lived there for a while after the Castries fire of 1948. Just north of Choc Bay at the next roundabout, is the turning to **St Lucia Megaplex 8** cinema, **Massy Stores Mega Store** and other shops, while on the left the highway passes another large all-inclusive resort, **St James's Club Morgan Bay**, and then heads up to the busy junction at Rodney Bay Village.

Lushan Country Life
T758-451 6091, www.lushancountrylife.com, Mon-Fri 0830-1600, US$15 per person.

Just over 3 km inland from Choc Bay at Union, and on the way to Babonneau (see page 44), the Anthony family have turned their 7 acres (2.8 ha) of gardens, forest and farmland into a charming tourist attraction. Visitors are guided along trails through the grounds, while the guides point out the different types of trees, plants and herbs and teach bird calls. There are also various food-tasting stops such as sugar cane, coconuts, guavas and star fruits picked from the trees, and local drinks and home-made snacks are included: fishcakes and bakes, prepared by Mama Wanita who will also give some explanation about local cooking methods. You can also buy their own packaged spices and hot sauces from the shop. The family are very friendly and take great pride in showing you around their home. Allow about one hour for the visit.

Rodney Bay Village and Reduit Beach
About 10 km north of Castries, the turn-off from the Castries–Gros Islet Highway to the centre of **Rodney Bay Village** is unmistakable, as it's flanked on both sides by modern shopping malls, banks, restaurants and bars. Enclosed to the south by Labrellotte Point and to the north by Pigeon Island National Landmark, Rodney Bay is named after British naval officer George Brydges Rodney who arrived in 1778. He won many battles against the French by using the fort built on Pigeon Island to view movements at France's naval base in Martinique. From 1941 until 1947 Rodney Bay was the site of the US Naval Air Station of Reduit, the first of a chain of bases established to protect the Panama Canal; it supported a squadron of sea planes during the Second World War. Today the village is home to many resorts, shops and lively nightlife and it's a thriving hub of activity.

Soon after the Castries–Gros Islet Highway turn-off is Baywalk Shopping Mall ① *T758-452 6666, www.baywalkslu.com, Mon-Thu 0900-1900, Fri-Sat 0900-2000, Sun 0900-1400*, the largest mall on St Lucia with over 60 shops (many of them duty-free), several restaurants, the **Treasure Bay Casino** (see page 74), a branch of **Massy Stores Supermarket** and a multi-storey car park. Across the road is JQ **Rodney Bay Mall** ① *T758-458 0700, www.shopjq mall.com, Mon-Thu 0900-2100, Fri-Sat 0900-2000, Sun 1000-1400*, with more shops, banks, a post office and fast-food places. From here Reduit Beach Avenue goes past restaurants, bars and resorts (including the four all-inclusive **Rex Resorts** sharing the same large property on the left) to the public access to **Reduit Beach** (pronounced red-wee). With fine white sand that shelves fairly gently and is excellent for safe swimming, this is one of the best (if busiest) beaches on the island with lovely views across the bay to double-hilled Pigeon Island. Popular with guests from the low-rise resorts that line much of the beach, it's also a favourite spot with local families enjoying picnics and the beach bars at the southern end at the weekend. There are loads of vendors so be prepared for a bit of hassling to buy things and to book watersports, such as inflatable banana boat and doughnut rides, windsurfing and water-skiing, and there are sun loungers and umbrellas to rent.

The stand-out beach bar here is **Spinnakers** (see page 70), which is towards the northern end of the beach and next door to St Lucia Yacht Club. At the far northern end of the beach, beyond Bay Gardens Beach Resort & Spa, is the colourful **Splash Island Water Park** ① T758-457 8532, www.saintluciawaterpark.com, daily 0900-1800, last ticket 1700, US$13 per person per hr, half-day pass US$34.50, full-day pass US$57.50. This is the Caribbean's first floating, inflatable water park featuring over a dozen activities including a trampoline, climbing wall, monkey bars, a swing, a slide, hurdles, and water volleyball court. All users of the park must be over six years of age and are required to wear lifevests, irrespective of their swimming abilities. **Bay Gardens Beach Resort & Spa** ① T758-457 8006, www.baygardensresorts.com, also see page 63, offers a day pass that includes a two-course lunch, drinks, and a choice of either a 20-minute massage, two non-motorized watersports, or a half-day pass to Splash Island Water Park; US$85, children (under 12) US$45. The inland side of Rodney Bay Village backs on to the man-made lagoon constructed in the 1970s for the later building (in 1985) of the **Rodney Bay Marina** ① T758-572 7200, www.igy-rodneybay.com. This has first-class facilities for yachts, including 253 slip berths and 32 mega-yacht docks as well as a wide range of ancillary services. The lagoon is well protected and many yachts shelter here during hurricane season; it's also an official Port of Entry to St Lucia so has customs and immigration offices. Situated on an attractive boardwalk with wonderful views overlooking the marina and the sleek boats, are a number of restaurants/cafés and shops. Landlubbers can get here from the Castries–Gros Islet Highway.

Gros Islet and Cap Estate

Just half a kilometre north of Rodney Bay Marina on the highway is the once-sleepy fishing village of **Gros Islet**, which lies on the northern shore of the lagoon. It is not a glitzy tourist destination like Rodney Bay Village, but it has a few guesthouses and cheap and cheerful bars along the beach and in the

> **Tip...**
> Inland from Gros Islet is the Darren Sammy National Cricket Stadium, St Lucia's flagship cricket ground that can accommodate 15,000 spectators. See page 77 for information.

village of colourful wooden Caribbean homes. Each Friday night it holds a popular 'fish fry' or 'jump up', with music and dancing, and drink and barbecue stalls are set up all along the main street serving plates of steamed fish, grilled pork and chicken, and lambi (conch) with all the trimmings; things start to get lively and loud from about 2200 (don't take anything valuable and stay in the busy and well-lit areas).

Just north of Gros Islet, the main road goes a few kilometres to **Cap Estate**. Once a 1500-acre (607 ha) sugar plantation covering the entire northern tip of St Lucia, it is now the island's most exclusive residential development with luxury villas on large plots all the way up to Pointe du Cap (some of them are available as holiday rentals). The **St Lucia Golf Club** (see page 78) is also on the property.

Pigeon Island National Landmark
Daily 0900-1700, US$7, children (5-12) US$1, under 5s free.

Across the bay from Rodney Bay Village and 3 km northwest of Gros Islet by road, Pigeon Island is a 44-acre (18-ha) islet which was artificially joined to the mainland in 1972 by a man-made causeway built from dirt excavated to form the Rodney Bay Marina. It is of considerable archaeological and historical interest. The Caribs arrived around AD 1000, and it is assumed they would have lived in the caves and caught fish, birds and small animals as well as foraging for plants and fruit. When

Tip...

To reach Pigeon Island, you can drive across the causeway (there's a big car park right outside the entrance); you can walk across the causeway past Sandals Grande St Lucian Spa & Beach Resort; or you can get a water taxi from Reduit Beach in Rodney Bay for around US$15 per person return.

French pirate François le Clerc (aka Jambe de Bois) settled on the island in the 1550s and made it his base for preying on Spanish galleons, the Caribs forged a peace treaty with him. The Duke of Montagu tried to colonize the island in 1722 (but abandoned it after one afternoon), and in 1778, British Admiral George Brydges Rodney arrived and built a fort on the hill called Fort Rodney. He expelled the remaining Caribs and had all the trees on the island cut down. This gave him clear sight lines for spying on the French naval base at Martinique before he defeated them at the Battle of Saints in 1782. The islet was captured again in 1795 by the Brigands but was retaken in 1798 by the British. It was later used as a quarantine centre from 1842 to 1904, and then in 1909 a whaling station was established on the island but legislation to control whaling in 1952 put an end to this operation. It became a US observation post and signal station during the Second World War, and finally became the home of Josset Agnes Huchinson, a member of the D'Oyly Carte Theatre, who leased the island from 1937 to 1976. The bay became a busy yacht haven and 'Joss' held large parties to entertain the crews. Her abandoned house can still be seen on the south shore of the island. Pigeon Island was designated as a National Park in 1979 and as a National Landmark in 1992.

Today it is managed by the St Lucia National Trust and is a lovely spot to spend a few hours. The Interpretation Centre near the entrance exhibits the island's fascinating history and adjacent is a gift shop. Visitors can then explore the island on foot along marked trails; there are two peaks which are joined by a saddle with a spur to the northeast

Tip...

Another day pass option in the area is at Sandals Grande St Lucian Spa & Beach Resort (T758-455 2000, www.sandals.com), which is on the causeway over to Pigeon Island; over 18s only, 1000-1800 US$100, 1000-0200 US$200, which includes unlimited food and drink in the 12 restaurants and nine bars, use of the five swimming pools and non-motorized watersports.

running into the sea. The higher peak, **Signal Hill**, rises to about 110 m, while the second hill is occupied by **Fort Rodney**; the original barracks were destroyed by a hurricane in 1817 and were rebuilt in 1824. Paths now wind around the remains of the batteries and garrisons. From the top of these hills are 360-degree views of St Lucia's northwest coast and on a clear day you can see Martinique.

Finally, while most of the coastline is rocky, on the southern side of Pigeon Island, just inside the entrance, are two sheltered, shaded and extremely picturesque little strips of golden sand with beautifully clear water for swimming and snorkelling; sun loungers and umbrellas can be hired and there's a changing facility with toilets and showers. Follow the shore along from the second beach and you'll get to **Jambe de Bois Restaurant & Bar** (see page 71), which is named after the infamous pirate. You can go for dinner even when the Pigeon Island main gate is closed – just tell security you're going for a meal.

Cas-en-Bas Beach

A 4-km or a 10-minute drive east of Gros Islet on Cas-en-Bas Road on the south side of the golf course takes you to the Atlantic beach at Cas-en-Bas. It lies deep within a cove, protecting it from the rough waters you will find elsewhere on the northeast coast, and is shallow for a long way out and protected by offshore reefs making it good for good swimming and wading. It's a popular bay for kitesurfing; **Aquaholics** kitesurfing school and **Kitesurfing St Lucia** are based here (see page 79). Unfortunately, however, large quantities of seaweed are regularly deposited on the beach and it is also used by horse riding tour parties, so the sand is not always clean. **Marjorie's Beach Bar** ① T758-450 8637, see Facebook, daily 0800-1800, has picnic benches on the sand or tables under cover and offers tasty local food for lunch, rents out sun loungers and staff can advise on hiking in the area.

> **Tip...**
> There are good walks along the coast from Cas-en-Bas Beach; a rocky track goes north and it takes about half an hour to walk to the secluded and tiny strip of sand at Donkey Beach; to the south, the path also takes about half an hour to the deserted and windswept beach at Anse Lavoutte where turtles nest.

Inland to Babonneau

About 500 m south of the junction to Rodney Bay Village on the Castries–Gros Islet Highway, is Monchy Road, which takes you on a pleasant drive inland through several small villages in St Lucia's northern heartland, most of them unaffected by tourism. You gradually leave the dry northern part of the island and climb into forest, and the ridge between Mount Monier and Mount Chaubourg gives particularly impressive views over the east coast. There are no road signs; watch out for the names on schools and if in doubt bear west at the junctions. Once in the larger village of Babonneau (a Catholic church and a couple of small shops), you can turn right to go back down to the coast at **Choc Bay** and re-join the Castries–Gros Islet Highway, or go straight on to **Fond Cacao** where a west turn will take you back to Castries.

Rainforest Adventures

Castries Waterworks Forest Reserve, Chassin, T758-458 5151, www.rainforestadventure.com/st-lucia, opening times vary; often dependent on cruise ship schedules, online prices US$45-95 depending on activity, hotel transfers available from US$16 per person. Pre-booking essential, either online or through a hotel.

At Chassin, 6.3 km southwest of Babonneau via Fond Assua, Rainforest Adventures is based in the 1250-acre (506-ha) Castries Waterworks Forest Reserve; it is particularly popular with cruise ship visitors and resort guests from Rodney Bay. There are a number of things to do: you can be taken up the side of La Sorcière hill in an eight-seater gondola; it ascends at one level and descends at a higher level through the forest canopy, so you see two layers of rainforest and the informative guide will point out the giant ficus trees, dazzling heliconias and hummingbirds. There are great views of both sides of the island and across to Martinique in the distance. If the ride sounds too sedate, you can also go zip-lining down the mountainside along a series of cables linking 18 platforms high up in the tree canopy, or you can hike the **Jacquot Trail** (four to five hours) with a naturalist guide during the day or at 0600 to see birds. You can combine activities for a discount and fun day out.

Des Barra and Grand Anse

An alternative road from Babonneau leads east to **Des Barra** and St Lucia's isolated mountainous east coast, far removed from the island's tourist spots in the northwest. **Grand Anse** (meaning 'Grand Cove' in French – there are a number of Grands Anses around the Caribbean) is 10 km from Babonneau and is one of the island's longest beaches and it is completely undeveloped. Just getting there is an adventure. From, Castries, the road climbs out of the city, going up to the cool heights of Babonneau in the centre of the island and then twists and turns its way down into the fertile green valley of the Marquis River; then it climbs again to the high village of Des Barra. At this point, the road deteriorates dramatically and only 4WD vehicles can continue for the last 4 km or so; otherwise you can continue on foot. The beach is one of the most important sites on the island for leatherback turtles to nest and later hatch (between March and August). They do this at night, but unfortunately there are currently no established turtle watching excursions; do ask at hotels, however, to see whether tours can be arranged.

Forestiere Trail

T758-451 6168, Mon-Fri 0830-1400, US$10.

About 10 km south of Babonneau, or 9 km southeast of Castries (both roads go via Fond Cacao) is the village of Forestiere. Follow the road and, where the houses end, there is a Forestry Department rangers' station and the start of the 5-km Forestiere Rainforest Trail (also known as the **Piton Flore Nature Trail**), which in parts follows a 200-year-old French-built road that connected Castries with Dennery. This is a circular path around the base of Piton Flore (570 m high) through a deep and shady rainforest with fig trees, epiphytes and ferns. Most sections are fairly flat but at one point, about midway along, you have the option of a fairly long climb on steps made from tree trunks up to a viewpoint at the top of Piton Flore; on a clear day you can see both the Atlantic on the east coast and the Caribbean Sea on the west coast. The circular route takes a couple of hours and you should allow for another hour for the strenuous Piton Flore return (how difficult it is will depend on how slippery conditions are). Guides are not necessary but are available at the rangers' station.

East coast to Vieux Fort

dramatic Atlantic coast dotted with beaches and fishing villages

The beaches along St Lucia's less densely populated east coast, or windward side, face the Atlantic Ocean. The choppy waves here aren't always suitable for swimming, but are great for ocean views and isolated walks. South of Castries, the transinsular road begins near the Hess Oil Terminal and goes through extensive banana plantations before climbing steeply over the Barre de l'Isle, the mountain barrier that divides the island into eastern and western halves. It then descends to Dennery and continues down the east coast as the Micoud Highway as far as Vieux Fort and the Hewanorra International Airport. The highway is good, although a little twisty and hilly in parts, and this is the usual route between the airport and Castries and Rodney Bay as it's quicker than going around the west coast.

Barre le l'Isle Rainforest Trail
T758-453 3242, Mon-Fri 0830-1400, US$10.

At the top of the Barre de l'Isle ridge at the high point on the road, about a 30-minute drive from Castries and 15 minutes before Dennery, this 1.6 km out-and-back rainforest self-guided trail takes about one hour and affords good views of Cul-de-Sac River valley and the Caribbean Sea to the west, and of the Mabouya Valley and Fond d'Or beach on the Atlantic to the east.

The final ascent to **Mount La Combe** (438 m), which would have taken an extra hour, has been closed for a few years now due to mudslides. Nonetheless, it's a pleasant walk through the lush green foliage and you may hear, even if you don't see, the St Lucia parrot, as well as many other birds such as the St Lucia oreole and St Lucia warbler. There are mosquitoes so take insect repellent. The Forestry Department's hut is on the right of the road (going towards Dennery) where you can park and pay the entrance fee; buses also drop off here.

Dennery
The road descends from the ridge with spectacular Atlantic views through Grande Rivière down the Mabouya Valley to Fond d'Or Bay, framed by scenic cliffs and the Fond d'Or River, which has its mouth in the bay. There are patches of mangrove and estuarine forest here and trails through dry scrub woodland lead down to a sandy beach. Beyond and just south of here and about 25 km from Castries, Dennery is set in a sheltered bay about halfway along the Atlantic coast; it was named after Count d'Ennery, Governor General of the French Windward Islands from 1766 to 1770. The main east coast road, the Micoud Highway, hugs the hillside bypassing the town below, but you can drive or walk down and wander along Mole Road by the shoreline. These waters are choppy and rough, and not generally suitable for swimming, but you can see the distinctive St Lucia fishing boats pulled up on the beach. The rocky uninhabited **Dennery Island** guards the entrance of the bay and the town is dominated by the late 18th-century, white and rust-coloured Saint Peter Catholic Church, which is perched on a hill on (not surprisingly) Church Street. The **Fish Fiesta** takes place every Saturday night from 1800 and stalls serve up grilled fish and lambi (conch), while music is provided by a DJ; but this is a local community event and much more low key than the Fish Fry at Gros Islet or Fish Friday at Anse La Raye, so don't expect a big street party.

Treetop Adventure Park and Errard Falls
Errard Estate, T758-452 0808, www.adventuretoursstlucia.com, Mon-Sat 0800-1600, daily for cruise passengers, everything must be pre-booked, hotel transfers available.

Inland from Dennery along the Dennery River (turn off the highway beside a small bridge and bus stop just south of Dennery), this adventure park has a zip-line connected to 12 forest canopy platforms (US$59 per person, minimum age eight). There's also a mini playground-type zip-line for children from the age of three. This can be combined with a short hike to Errard Falls (also known as Sault Falls or Dennery Falls), and an open-top jeep safari through the rainforest (US$99); other options include mountain biking to the falls (US$42). There's a welcome centre where guests are given drinks on arrival. The park is often included on tours of the east coast; otherwise groups are shuttled in from cruise ships and resorts.

You can make your own way to Errard Falls: just after Treetop Adventure Park, veer left through the banana trees at the next fork where there is a shack on the side of the road that marks the path. The falls are part of the **Errard Estate**, so there maybe someone there to collect a US$5 entrance fee. It is only a short walk but requires a bit of a downhill scramble and a splashy walk across the Dennery River; the waterfall is very scenic and drops about 15 m over a rounded cliff and you are able to wade in the pool below and stand under the cascade. It's usually quiet unless a tour group is there.

Praslin Bay

Just after Dennery, Praslin Bay is a deep, picturesque bay divided by a small promontory that stretches out to tiny Praslin Island. In the southern part, the village of Praslin is a fishing community with an unhurried atmosphere, known for its traditional local boat builders who still fashion fishing boats from gommier trees (Dacryodes hexandra), in what is believed to be the same style as the dugout canoes used by the Caribs. The village was originally named Les Trois Islets but was renamed in 1780 to honour the Minister of the Navy to Louis XIV of France, the Duc de Praslin. **Praslin Island** is one of only three islands where St Lucian whiptails live. This endemic lizard (*Cnemidophorus vanzoi*) had its population decimated by introduced cats, rats and mongooses and used to live only on Maria Major Island until being successfully introduced here in 1995 to prevent extinction and then in 2008 to Rat Island off Castries. The only whiptail found in the eastern Caribbean, the males patriotically wear the colours of the St Lucian flag: black, white, blue and yellow.

Mamiku Botanical Gardens

Micoud Highway, between Praslin and Mon Repos, T758-455 3729, www.mamikugardens. com, daily 0900-1700, US$8, with a guided tour US$10, per person.

Set back from the east coast, this lovely 12-acre (4.8-ha) botanical garden is a scenic and tranquil spot with hummingbirds and butterflies, scented flowers and aromatic plants. paths meander through the grounds to the ruined estate house and a stream tumbling down a wooded hillside. The estate was originally acquired in 1766 by the Baron de Micoud, a colonel in the French army and a former governor of St Lucia. The name 'Mamiku' is an adaptation of the title of the Baron's wife, who was known as Madame de Micoud and, in true Creole fashion, the estate would have been known as Ma Micoud's estate. By 1796 the estate house became a British military post under the charge of General Sir John Moore; in the same year a famous battle with the Brigands resulted in 15 British soldiers being killed and the Micoud house being burnt down and left as a ruin. Mamiku Estate was then abandoned until the Shingleton-Smith family took it over in 1906, and today it produces bananas and tropical flowers for export. The botanical gardens surrounding the hilltop ruins were opened to the public in 1997 and were created by keen horticulturist, Veronica Shingleton-Smith. There are several different types of gardens to see, including an orchid garden and medicinal herb garden; a booklet will help you to identify the 300 numbered trees and plants or you can wander around with a guide. Drinks and snacks are served on the lovely terrace at the café, the **Brigand's Bar**, or there are picnic tables if you want to take your own food, and the **Garden Gate Shop** sells gifts.

Micoud

Also named after Baron de Micoud, this has long been an important agricultural area on the island. By 1775 when more than one-sixth of Saint Lucia was under cultivation of sugar cane, the area around Micoud alone had 84 estates. Micoud is also rich in Amerindian history and evidence of cooking pits, stone and shell tools, pots and ornaments have been found by archaeologists at several locations in the region. Today the local farms produce bananas, guavas, pineapples and ginger, and the tightly packed (and somewhat non-descript) village lies close to the shore, while the Micoud Highway passes further inland up the hill. As you are approaching the village from the north, there is a road to the right; turn up here for about 1 km (it's signposted) to **La Tille Waterfalls** ① *T758-489 6271, see Facebook, daily 0800-1700, US$5 per person*. This lovely garden and waterfall is right on the edge of the rainforest on land owned by John Selie, a friendly Rastafarian retired teacher, now farmer, who grows organic fruit, flowers and herbs and has fish ponds for carp. It's a beautiful and peaceful spot and John or his son will show you around, there are hammocks in the trees to relax in, toilets, and with any luck you might be offered a glass of lemongrass juice. The 6-m-high waterfall itself cascades into a deep pool where you can swim and there are other pools downstream to splash around in.

Des Cartiers Rainforest Trail
Mahaut, T758-454-5589, Mon-Fri 0830-1400, US$10.

About 9 km inland from the Micoud Highway, west of Mahaut and up the same road as the La Tille Waterfalls, is the Forestry Department's rangers' station at the start of Des Cartiers Rainforest Trail. It is signposted from the main road, but unfortunately after this the road inland regularly splits; the best advice is to keep heading west and ask directions. This moderately easy and enjoyable hike follows a figure-of-eight loop of about 4 km and takes 1½ to two hours; the guides are usually there but if you find the office empty it means they are all out on the hike so you may have to wait. The high-canopied rainforest here is thick and lush with tall and mature trees that have Tarzan-sized vines hanging from their branches. It is perfect for birdwatching, with many of the endemics found here, including the St Lucia parrot and St Lucia oriole. It is also part of the **Edmund Forest Trail**: a more strenuous 10-km guided hike that takes 3½ to four hours from the Edmund Forest Reserve just outside Soufrière on the west coast (see page 56 for details) through the Quilesse Forest Reserve and ending at Des Cartiers Rainforest Trail.

> **Tip...**
> Located about 550 m above sea level, this hike goes through moist tropical and montane forest where it rains a lot; the leaves on the trail are slippery in the wet so come prepared with sturdy closed shoes and wet weather gear.

Anse des Sables Beach
The Micoud Highway continues south past Savannes Bay and its villa developments, and then past the popular 85-acre (34-ha), all-inclusive **Coconut Bay Beach Resort & Spa** ① *T758-459 6000, www.cbayresort.com, see also page 65*, where day passes are available (1000-1700, US$125, children, 13-17, US$68, 3-12, US$56), which includes a buffet lunch, all drinks, access to the beach and the waterpark area with its multiple pools, slides and lazy rivers. The highway then reaches Hewanorra International Airport, which is 15 km south of Micoud. As the highway curves around the eastern end of the runway and turns towards Vieux Fort, you'll see on the ocean side the longest stretch of white sand on the island, Anse des Sables Beach (the name means 'Sandy Beach'). Almost 2 km long, it opens out into a shallow, reef-enclosed bay with a fantastic view over the Maria Islands, but it's on the Atlantic at the southern end of the island so can be windy and choppy at certain times of year; it is a popular spot for windsurfing and kitesurfing. The beach attracts many day-trippers for sunbathing, picnics and long walks, and at the northeastern end is the **Reef Beach Café** ① *T758-454 3418, www.slucia.com/reef, daily 1000-2100*, which has a car

park, offers good food (see page 72) and rents out sun loungers, kayaks and stand-up paddleboards; it also operates the **Reef Kite & Surf** windsurfing and kitesurfing school (see page 79).

Maria Islands Nature Reserve

St Lucia National Trust, T758-454 5014, www.slunatrust.org, entry by prior reservation only, preferably a few days in advance as they have to find a boat and captain, US$125 for up to 4 people, which is the minimum price for boat and guide; able swimmers only.

Offshore from Anse des Sables Beach these two islands were declared a nature reserve in 1982 to protect the unique flora and fauna. The 25-acre (10-ha) Maria Major and the 4-acre (1.6-ha) Maria Minor support over 80 plant species and five endemic reptile species; the Kouwés snake,

> **Tip...**
> Bring water, snacks, snorkelling gear, sunscreen and two pairs of shoes: flip-flops for getting in and out of the boat, and trainers/sneakers for the hike.

the worm snake, the whiptail lizard, and a couple of geckos, who share their islands with frigate birds, sooty and bridle terns, red-billed tropicbirds and ground doves. A three-hour guided excursion to Maria Major can be organized through the St Lucia National Trust. You take a boat from Savannes Bay with a local fisherman (or they'll pick you up from **Coconut Bay Beach Resort & Spa** if you happen to be staying there); the journey takes about 15-20 minutes. What follows is a hike up to the top of the island; it's quite steep with lots of cacti to negotiate and takes about 45 minutes. From the top you can look down on Maria Minor and there are clear views across to Vieux Fort and the airport. After the guided walk there is time to relax on the nice sandy beach and snorkel. It's a unique excursion and you will have the whole island to yourself (even the fisherman goes away to do a spot of fishing). From May to August access is restricted or prohibited while migrating seabirds are nesting in their hundreds on the cliffs and on the ground.

Vieux Fort

The old fishing port of Vieux Fort lies on flat, fertile ground on a headland that cuts into the Atlantic Ocean to the east and the Caribbean Sea to the west. There is evidence that the Amerindians had many settlements in the southern part of the island and cultivated crops; archaeologists have found remains of houses and petroglyphs all around the area. It is believed that the Dutch were the first Europeans to try and settle in the south (around 1600) but later it became an important sugar cane area with both the French and British using imported slave labour on the plantations and it was the site of St Lucia's first sugar works (1765). The name of Vieux Fort ('Old Fort') is probably a reference to a 17th-century fort that used to look south towards Saint Vincent. The airbase built here by the Americans during the Second World War has now become the island's main airport. Their presence brought prosperity, giving local people and immigrants from other islands jobs and a market for their produce. Rum shops, nightclubs and dance halls flourished, as did typhoid, tuberculosis and venereal disease until the base was dismantled in 1949.

Today Vieux Fort is St Lucia's second and most southerly town and the island's most industrialized area with warehouses, factories and the Windward & Leeward Brewing Ltd brewery, which produces Piton beer. It's divided into two distinct sections: the old town centre near the harbour, which features traditional wooden housing and is dotted with churches; and a newer area consisting of a proliferation of small malls and commercial buildings strewn untidily along the main road as it passes the edge of town and the

Hewanorra International Airport. The bus terminal is at the end of Clarke Street near the airport. It is an active town with a good fish market and supermarkets, although there is not much else to hold your attention for too long.

Cap Moule à Chique

Cap Moule à Chique is the tip of the headland and is the most southerly point on the island. You can wind your way up from town through the residential area to the 9-m-tall **Moule à Chique Lighthouse** (also known as the Vieux Fort Lighthouse and built in 1901), which has good views north over Vieux Fort and the airport (with planes coming into land), the Maria Islands offshore, St Vincent to the southwest, and the Pitons to the northwest.

West coast to Soufrière and the Pitons
the beautiful Caribbean coastline with some of the island's top natural attractions

From central Castries, follow Brazil Street and Government House Road to La Toc Road which heads southwards past the University of the West Indies on the left and the Hess Oil Terminal on the right to Marigot Bay. Beyond, it becomes the West Coast Road (also known as the Castries–Soufrière Highway), which is in excellent condition with good signposting. It is a curvy but spectacular drive down to Soufrière, backed by stunning mountain scenery and dozens of pretty bays lapped by the calm waters of the Caribbean. This is the most beautiful part of the island with plenty of natural attractions, resorts and restaurants; the highlight being the views of the magnificent Pitons, a UNESCO World Heritage Site since 2004.

★ Marigot Bay

Fringed with mangroves and surrounded by lush, steep hills, this beautiful inlet and natural harbour is 11 km south of Castries. On reaching the Roseau Valley, take the signposted road to Marigot Bay, which is simply called **Waterfront**, and follow that all the way to the southern side of the bay. The harbour is so deep and sheltered that it's been said that French ships would sail far into the bay and hide from the British fleet by covering their masts with palm fronds. Today it supports the large **Capella Marigot Bay Resort and Marina** ① *T758-458 5300, www.capellahotels.com*, and, not surprisingly, a large number of yachts berth here to restock with supplies and to shelter in the so-called hurricane hole in the inland portion of the bay. It is a Port of Entry to St Lucia and the marina has customs and immigration facilities. Marigot Bay was also the setting for the 1967 film *Dr Doolittle*; scenes of the shipwreck, Great Pink Sea Snail, and the construction of the harness for the Giant Lunar Moth were filmed in the bay. On the south side where Waterfront ends and close to the water taxi and ferry jetty, there is parking, a small supermarket, bank with ATM, bars and restaurants. Part of the marina, **Marina Village** ① *T758-451 5950, daily 0830-2000*, has a number of high-end souvenir and clothing shops and the Bayside Café that has a pleasant wooden deck overlooking the yachts. A small palm-studded sand spit juts out into the bay and has a little beach, reached by water taxi, while a little goes-on-request ferry takes people across the bay to the hotels on the north side. The lights of restaurants and bars shimmering on the water make Marigot Bay enchanting after dark.

Roseau Valley

From the turn-off to Marigot Bay, the West Coast Road continues south through the Roseau Valley, which is the principal banana-growing area on the island. The Roseau

River runs through the valley and enters the sea at Roseau Bay and is the longest river in St Lucia. Originally the valley was used for the cultivation of sugar and there was a railway to transport the sugar from further up the valley to a processing plant at Roseau. Thanks to this sugar heritage, there is a rum distillery here. **St Lucia Distillers** ① *T758-456 3148, www.saintluciarums.com, 1-hr tours on the hour Mon-Fri 0900-1500, reservations mandatory, call 24 hrs in advance, US$10 per person*, offers a **Rhythm of Rum** tour of the factory, which begins with a short video in a reconstructed ship's hold that explains rum production and then proceeds to the main distillery to see the molasses vats, copper stills and oak barrels and ends with a tasting of some of their 25 different brands of rum, which naturally you can also buy.

Roseau Beach in the bay of the same name is a secluded little stretch of soft sand, which is completely undeveloped, lined with palms and backed by steep green hills, and the water is clear and good for swimming. It's easy to get to for yachts mooring at Marigot Bay, but a bit more of a challenge to get to by land; take the first right on the small track after Roseau and follow it to the shore but a 4WD is essential, or you could walk (about 2 km from the distillery). Alternatively, a number of operators including the dive shop at **Marigot Beach Club** (see page 66) and **DFH Kayaking** (see page 78) offer three-hour guided kayaking trips around Marigot Bay for US$75; you'll also paddle up the Roseau River, where the guide tells you about the birds, crabs, fish and plants in the estuary.

Millet Bird Sanctuary Trail

The Forestry Department's rangers' station is at the end of the road after the village of Millet where there is a car park and toilets, T758-451 1691. Mon-Fri 0830-1500, US$10, weekends by prior arrangement with higher prices, or phone the Forestry Department, T758-519 0787/758-716 1430, to pre-book 4-hr birdwatching tours starting early in the morning, US$30.

This area of secondary rainforest in the heart of the island and 300 m above sea level is one of the best places for birdwatching. The land was acquired by the Forestry Department to protect the John Compton Dam (formerly known as Roseau Dam) and its watershed; the dam was built in the 1990s and its 2-km-long reservoir is the largest stretch of freshwater in the Eastern Caribbean. The well-maintained, 2.8-km loop trail takes about two hours to walk with only one steep section up to the panoramic viewpoint of **Morne Gimie**, the forest and dam. There is a high biodiversity with many fruit trees as well as forest and over 30 species of bird can be found here, including five endemics: the St Lucia parrot, St Lucia black finch, St Lucia oriole, St Lucia pewee and St Lucia warbler. If you want to see parrots it is best to arrange a tour at dawn, but you can see birds at any time of day. Bring mosquito repellent and perhaps bananas to replenish your energy after the walk.

Anse La Raye

The main road continues to Soufrière and passes through Anse La Raye about 5 km southwest from Roseau. This is an attractive traditional fishing village, which derives its name from the rays (or skates) that are found in the bay of L'Anse la Raye (The Bay of Rays). Many of the old wooden cottages have pretty verandas and decorative details. Colourful fishing boats line the beach, with nets hung out to dry

Tip...

To get to the Millet Bird Sanctuary Trail, either turn east on to Morne d'Or Road opposite the turning to St Lucia Distillers and then right at Vanard to the village of Millet (about 10 km), or go from Anse la Raye further south by turning east on the road past La Sikwi to Millet (about 11 km).

and cleaning tables still bearing the residue of the day's catch, and a pier juts out into the middle of the bay. The Catholic **Church of the Nativity of the Blessed Virgin Mary** was built in 1907, but records show that a chapel has existed here since 1762.

Anse La Raye is popular for its Fish Friday event from about 1900 when tables and stalls are set out along the seafront road. Make sure you come early to watch the sunset given that the village faces due west. It attracts many people on excursions from resorts in Marigot Bay to eat grilled and steamed fish, lobster in season, crab cakes and claws, with local accompaniments such as breadfruit salad and bakes, and there's drinking, music and dancing.

Anse Cochon

This lovely deep cove with a 200-m-long strip of dark sand is overlooked by the **Ti Kaye Resort & Spa** ① *T758-456-8101, www.tikaye.com, see also page 66*, which is dotted around the wooded hillside above. It's also popular with party boats and day-trippers on snorkelling excursions. To get there from the West Coast Road, turn off at a hairpin bend 3.6 km south of Anse La Raye; after that it's another 2 km along a rough road, although it is manageable in a normal car if you take it slowly over the bumps. When you get to the resort gate, there is a fee of US$10 per person, which covers parking and is redeemable at the resort's **Ti Manje** beach bar/restaurant (daily 1000-1700). To get to the beach itself, it's a descent down 166 wooden steps. Note that as all beaches on St Lucia are public, you can park some way back on the road to avoid the entrance fee, but it will be a bit of hike down and unnecessary if you intend to eat/drink at Ti Manje. The reef is very close to shore and the best snorkelling is on the right-hand side furthest from the restaurant. Visibility is excellent and you might see angel fish, seahorses, sting rays, black beauties and spotted eels. Ti Kaye rents out snorkelling equipment, and vendors on the beach hire out sun loungers.

Canaries

The road heads south, and just before Canaries on one of the curves where the road widens, in a wooden structure that doubles as a factory and café, is **Plas Kassav** ① *T758-459 4050, daily 0900-1800*. It is a favourite stop with St Lucians and tourists alike on the way to Soufrière, and in Patois Creole (Kwéyòl) the name means Cassava Place. This family-run bakery makes *farine* (cassava flour) to produce delicious cassava bread in many flavours, both sweet and savoury: salt, saltfish, smoked herring, peanut butter, cinnamon, coconut, chocolate, cherry and raisin. A long, starchy root vegetable, cassava featured prominently in the diets of the Amerindian people and is today a mainstay in Caribbean cuisine. The shop also sells hot pepper sauces, honey and other local products. Canaries itself is a quiet fishing village which, according to records, has existed since 1763. The original French settlers came from Martinique and it once had a large sugar plantation that ran inland up the valley. In many ways it has changed less than any other community on the west coast. Until the 1960s there was no road transport to the village and it was only accessible by boat. Even today the streets in the centre are extremely narrow and, although vehicles go both ways, gridlock may occur with only three or four cars on the road.

Soufrière

After Canaries the road goes inland and skirts Mount Tabac (693 m) before descending into Soufrière, a distance of 11 km. Wrapped around a beautiful bay, this is the most picturesque and interesting town on the island. Soufrière dates back to 1713 and the name is a French term used to describe any volcanic area, literally translated to mean

BACKGROUND

Soufrière

After the Amerindians, the first permanent settlers were the French who were lured to Soufrière by the rich fertile soil that was ideal for farming. In 1713, Louis XIV of France granted 2300 acres (930 ha) to the Devaux family in recognition of service to crown and country. The land extended from Soufrière Bay to Ravine Du Val and south from the Soufrière River to a parallel line with Petit Piton. Three of the Devaux brothers migrated from Martinique in the 1740s, divided the land into three estates and subsequently produced cotton, tobacco, coffee and cocoa, and later moved over to sugar. The town of Soufrière was laid out in 1746 as the island's first capital. In 1784 the road between Soufrière and Roseau was built by the French Artillery, and around the same time, Baron de Laborie ordered the construction of a mineral bath at Diamond for use by His Majesty's troops. The effects of the French Revolution (1789-1797) were felt throughout the French-held islands of the Caribbean. In 1795, a ship carrying a guillotine sailed into Soufrière Bay and set up in the town square in front of the church and many Royalist plantation owners (who had been given their lands by the king) were beheaded. The fortunate Devaux family were protected by loyal slaves and managed to escape.

The British moved the capital to Castries in 1803, but Soufrière continued to grow and prosper from the cultivation of cocoa, sugar, coffee and even grapes for the production of wine. There was more need for shops and other services and, after emancipation in 1834, many former slaves became merchants or fishermen. Even after the island became British, the descendants of the French families continued to speak French-based Patois Creole (Kwéyòl) and overall Soufrière kept its French character.

'sulphur in the air'; the same name was used by the French for other volcanic areas in St Vincent, Dominica, Guadeloupe and Montserrat.

The town is dominated by a square, overlooked by the **Church of the Assumption of the Blessed Virgin Mary** (1953) and a number of French **colonial houses** with shutters and overhanging balconies with gingerbread fretwork that create shady walkways. The **waterfront area**, a block east of the town square, is the centre of action, where the pier is the stopping point for sightseeing cruises, vendors sell straw hats, crafts, spices and T-shirts and, on Saturday mornings, there's a colourful fruit and vegetable market. A dark sand beach to the north of the bay in front of the **Hummingbird Beach Resort** has lots of colourful wooden fishing boats pulled up on the shore. The town has a few souvenir shops and cafés, but it also has a reputation for hassling; tour parties are usually whisked through fairly quickly to avoid unwanted attention.

Anse Chastanet and Anse Mamin beaches

Along the coast just to the northwest of Soufrière, the lovely 150-m-long beach at Anse Chastanet has dark, silvery sand and is dotted with palms and surrounded by steep, forested hillsides with beautiful views of the Pitons. Thanks to a thriving reef just offshore, it offers some of the best snorkelling and diving in St Lucia and is protected as part of a marine reserve administered by the **Soufrière Marine Management Area** (SMMA; www.smma.org.lc). The SMMA preserves the coastal environment between Anse Jambon, north of Anse Chastanet, and Anse L'Ivrogne to the south. Anchoring is prohibited so yachts and sightseeing boats are required to use allocated moorings, with charges based on the size of the boat, and divers also have a marine park fee included in the cost of a dive.

Set on a 600-acre (243-ha) estate, the **Anse Chastanet Resort** and super-luxurious **Jade Mountain** (see page 66) are here, with rooms tucked in behind the coconut palms that line the beach or climbing up the flower-decked hillside. But the beach is also visited by day-trippers and boat excursions stop off in the bay. This is one of the best beach-entry dives in the Caribbean and an absolute must if you enjoy snorkelling (the south end near the jetty is superb but keep within the roped-off area; the north end is also good with some rocks to explore, but avoid the middle where boats come in). The bay harbours a treasure trove of sealife across varying depths. On a plateau of 2-8 m, you can see coloured sponges, soft, boulder and brain corals, and fish including parrotfish, goatfish, wrasse, chromis and barracuda. The edge of the plateau is a wall that drops 46-m to a lace coral ecosystem inhabited by lobsters, crabs, and eels. Anse Chastanet's dive centre can organize dives and rents out snorkelling gear. The resort rents out sun loungers to non-residents and has an excellent bar/restaurant right on the beach, **Trou Au Diable** (open daily 1000-2200).

Anse Mamin, a quieter beach that is also part of the resort's estate, is a 10-minute walk north on a coastal track from Anse Chastenet or a five-minute boat ride from the dive centre. Again the resort rents out sun loungers and operates the casual **Jungle Grill and Bar** (Sunday to Friday 1000-1600). Behind this beach you can explore a 13-km network of trails through the rainforest and tropical vegetation on mountain bikes with **Bike St Lucia** (see page 77).

Tip...
Getting to Anse Chastanet from Soufrière involves a 20- to 30-minute drive along a very steep and bumpy track – take it slowly and don't attempt it if you are a nervous driver (taxis sometimes refuse to go down); the best and most enjoyable way to get there is to take a water taxi from Soufrière; around US$15 per person return.

★ Diamond Falls Botanical Gardens and Mineral Baths
Soufrière Estate, Diamond Rd, T758-459 7155, www.diamondstlucia.com, Mon-Sat 1000-1700, Sun 1000-1500, US$7, children (under 12) US$3.50, US$6 to use the public outdoor hot baths, US$7 for a private bath; only official guides on tours are allowed in, if you are not on a tour, you do not need a guide so do not accept offers from those at the gates. To get there from the town square in Soufrière, take Sir Arthur Lewis St east past the church and look for the right turning to Diamond Rd to reach the entrance gate and car park to Diamond Falls. If you walk it's about 1.6 km uphill from the town square.

Covering 6 acres (2.4 ha), there are three attractions in one here: lovely, well-maintained gardens, an impressive waterfall coloured by mineral deposits, and historic mineral baths that you can bathe in. The land was once part of the 2300-acre (930-ha) Soufrière Estate granted to the Devaux family by King Louis XIV of France in 1713. An old mill and waterwheel on the property date back to 1765 when the estate grew sugar cane, and later, after the decline of sugar, it went into lime oil production (the old vats

Fact...
British sailors on board ships travelling between the West Indies and Europe used to drink a daily spoonful of vitamin C-rich lime oil to combat scurvy and for that reason they became known as 'limeys'.

can still be seen). Later still, the waterwheel was used to generate the first electricity to Soufrière village when each house was permitted to have two light bulbs and the price for electricity was one shilling a month. The mill and waterwheel are now part of the **Old Mill Restaurant** which serves buffet lunches to tour groups and an à la carte menu for independent visitors.

The baths were developed in 1784 after Baron de Laborie sent samples taken from sulphur springs near the Diamond River to Paris for analysis. They were found to contain minerals which were equivalent to those found in the spa town of Aix-la-Chapelle and were said to be effective against rheumatism and other complaints. King Louis the XVI of France had a building with 12 stone baths erected so his troops could take advantage of the water's therapeutic powers. The baths were destroyed in the French Revolution but were later rebuilt and are now open to the public with modern bathroom and changing facilities. The three tiled open-air pools, fed by hot springs, each one slightly warmer than the next, are nicer than the rather claustrophobic private covered ones.

A path winds its way from the mineral baths through ferns and banana trees to the spot where the Diamond River drops down the picturesque 17-m-high **Diamond Waterfall** into a calm pond below. The water is black from volcanic mud and rich in minerals such as copper sulphate and manganese, staining the rock face behind with many metallic colours. The botanical gardens were established in 1983 by Mrs Joan Devaux beneath the existing coconut, cocoa, mahogany and red cedar trees. The magnificent flowering hibiscus, heliconia and anthurium bushes provide a riot of colour and there are also displays of local fruits and vegetables such as christophine, soursop and dasheen. Everything is well labelled.

Toraille Waterfall and Gardens
Diamond Rd, Fond St Jaques, T758-459 7527, US$3 per person, daily 0930-1530.

Close to Fond St Jaques and about 1.5 km further up Diamond Road from Diamond Falls, there is a sign near a bridge to the car park for this pretty waterfall. It's an attraction that's often combined on the same organized tour and offers a cooling dip after the warmer mineral baths. Surrounded by palms and ferns, the falls drop 15 m into a pool that has been widened with concrete to enable people to get in and splash around; if the water pressure's not too strong, you can enjoy a natural massage as the falls tumble over your head and shoulders. The falls sit in a garden with a short nature trail and there are changing rooms and a seating area for picnics. Just beside the bridge outside are several roadside vendors selling souvenirs and handicrafts.

New Jerusalem Mineral Baths
Diamond Rd, Fond St Jaques, T758-518 9802, US$3.70 per person, daily 0930-1600.

Just after the bridge and the entrance to Toraille Waterfall, and on the opposite side of Diamond Road, this more rustic hot spring experience, which is privately owned (and inexplicably named), again harnesses the naturally warm water that is filtered through volcanic rock. Tucked away in a pretty tract of rainforest and not a major tourist attraction (so veryu peaceful and rarely crowded), there are three baths with seating areas on the hillside. They have three different temperatures of water (hot, warm and cold) gushing from hollow bamboo stems above – if you sit beneath, the pressure creates an invigorating massage. There are changing facilities and a sheltered area to leave clothes and bags. Park along the road, and from the entrance it's a 10-minute hike across a tiny river; but it's not difficult and a very pretty path surrounded by giant trees.

Enbas Saut Forest Trail

Edmund Forest Reserve, T758-457 1427, Mon-Fri 0830-1600, US$10, with or without a guide.

Through Fond St Jacques and up a poor and deeply rutted road that requires a high-clearance vehicle, is the Forestry Department rangers' station for the Enbas Saut Forest Trail. It's at the foot of the island's highest mountain, **Morne Gimie** (950 m) in the Edmund Forest Reserve, part of the 19,000 acres (7690 ha) of St Lucia's central rainforest. Remote, wild and unbelievably scenic, the 4-km loop trail goes through cloudforest and elfin woodland with glorious views of Morne Gimie and other nearby peaks. Birds common to the area include the St Lucia parrot; St Lucia black finch, blue-hooded euphonia and mountain whistler. Enbas Saut is loosely translated from French as 'below the falls' and the trail has been cut down to the Troumassee River, where there are a couple of small waterfalls and a pool where you can bathe. There are picnic tables and a screen behind which you can change and toilets at the rangers' station at the start of the trail. It is a moderate to strenuous hike as there are 2112 steps down to the waterfall (and back up again).

> **Tip...**
> Allow 1½-2 hours to walk the Enbas Saut Forest Trail and 20-30 minutes each way for the slow drive from Fond St Jacques; there are good views of the Pitons from this road.

Edmund Forest Trail

Book a guide through the Forestry Department, T758-468 5649/5645/5648, US$10.

From the Enbas Saut rangers' station (above) you can (with prior arrangement) continue along the track to hike the Edmund Forest Trail through the **Edmund Forest Reserve** and the **Quilesse Forest Reserve** to the east side and down to the **Des Cartiers Rainforest Trail** (see page 48). In the company of a Forestry Department guide, it covers 10 km and takes 3½ to four hours each way, so an option would be to arrange transport at the end of Des Cartiers Rainforest Trail, which is 9 km inland from Micoud. You don't have to walk the full length of the trail although you will have to retrace your steps if only going part way. The route takes you into the very heart of the central rainforest, through lush green valleys of giant ferns and orchids, and past waterfalls and towering trees, and occasionally there are long-distance views to the Caribbean Sea. The trail is flat much of the way with foot bridges for crossing the odd stream, but as this is the rainforest and the interior of the island is often cloaked in cloud, expect to get damp and go prepared.

Morne Coubaril Estate

On the Vieux Fort road, opposite the turning to Stonefield Estate Resort, T758-459 7340, www.stluciaziplining.com, daily 0830-1700, everything must be pre-booked.

Another former Devaux plantation and 2 km south of Soufrière on the Vieux Fort road, Morne Coubaril Estate was bought in 1960 by Donald Monplaisir and is a 280-acre (113 ha) working farm producing cocoa, coffee, copra, coconuts, orange, grapefruit, lime, bananas and other fruit. Popular with tour groups, there are a number of things to do here. The 30-minute guided **Historical Estate Tour** (US$11 per person) goes to the plantations, its tropical gardens, and a replica workers' village where the guides demonstrate the processing of coconut for food products and show how sugar cane syrup, cocoa, coffee and cassava are produced. The tour does not include the plantation house itself as this is the family home, but you can see it from the outside. You can also do a similar tour of

IN THE WATER

Coral reef

A diving or snorkelling trip over a tropical reef allows a first-hand experience of this habitat's diversity of wildlife. There are a number of good field guides to reef fish and animals; some are even printed on waterproof paper. Among the most common fish are the grunts, butterfly, soldier, squirrel and angel fish. Tiny damsel fish are very territorial and may even attempt to nip swimmers who venture too close to their patch (more surprising than painful).

There are over 50 species of hard coral (the form that builds reefs) with a variety of sizes and colours. Among the most dramatic are the stagshorn and elkhorn corals, which are found on the more exposed outer reefs. Brain coral forms massive round structures up to 2 m high and pillar coral forms columns that may also reach 2 m in height. Soft corals, which include black corals, sea fans and gorgonians, colonize the surface of the hard coral adding colour and variety. Associated with these structures is a host of animals and plants. Spiny lobsters may be seen lurking in holes and crevices along with other crustaceans and reef fish. The patches of sand between outcrops of coral provide suitable habitat for conch and other shellfish. The islands now restrict the collection and sale of corals (especially black corals) and there are legal restrictions on the sale of black corals under CITES. Overfishing has also affected conch and lobster in places.

The delights of swimming on a coral reef need to be tempered by a few words of caution. Many people assume the water will be seething with sharks; however, these animals are fairly uncommon in nearshore waters and the species most likely to be encountered is the nurse shark, which is harmless unless provoked. Other fish to keep an eye open for include the scorpion fish with its poisonous dorsal spines; it frequently lies stationary on coral reefs. Moray eels may be encountered, a fearsome looking fish, but harmless unless provoked at which point they can inflict serious bites. Of far more concern should be the variety of stinging invertebrates that are found on coral reefs. The most obvious is fire coral, which comes in a range of shapes and sizes but is recognizable by the white tips to its branches. In addition, many corals have sharp edges and branches that can graze and cut. Another common group of stinging invertebrates are the fire worms, which have white bristles. As with the fire coral, these can inflict a painful sting if handled or brushed against. Large black sea urchins are also common on some reefs and their spines can penetrate unprotected skin very easily. The best advice when observing coral reefs and their wildlife is to look and not touch.

the estate on a one-hour gentle horse ride (US$75, suitable for novices, no children under five). Before or after the tour, you can opt for the Creole Buffet Lunch (US$15 per person) in the restaurant where there is also a clutch of mock gingerbread cottages with a bar and a gift shop. There's also one-hour of **zip-lining** (US$75, no children under eight), which whizzes between eight platforms high up in the trees; if you're able to keep your eyes open, the views of Soufrière and the Pitons are impressive. Another horse-riding option is the two-hour **Ride-In Volcano Tour** (US$120, suitable for novices, no children under five), which goes from the stables on the estate to the Sulphur Springs Park (see below).

Sulphur Springs Park

Sulphur Springs Access Rd, T758-459 7200, www.soufrierefoundation.org, daily 0900-1700, US$15, children (under 12) US$7.50, compulsory tour with guide takes about 30 mins, after which you can spend time at the baths.

From Morne Coubaril Estate, it's another 1.6 km to the Sulphur Springs Park; buses to Vieux Fort pass the entrance, from where it is a five- to 10-minute walk up Sulphur Springs Access Road. These springs are the big attraction in the area (you will be able to smell them well before you reach them), and it is believed to be the hottest and most active geothermal area in the Lesser Antilles. The park covers 111 acres (45 ha) and is billed as the Caribbean's only 'drive-in volcano' (although actually you have to stop at a car park). Originally measuring a massive 4.8 km in diameter, the volcano collapsed some 40,000 years ago leaving the west part of the rim empty (where you drive in). This volcanic pit continues to vent sulphur into the air and visitors can view the bubbling pools of rich, grey-black mud and hissing fumaroles from observation platforms. Many fumaroles have temperatures of 100°C or hotter, and temperatures of up to 172°C have been recorded; the Caribs called it Qualibou, 'the place of death'. There are two pools you can bathe in: **Black Water Pool** is the hotter at 38.7°C, and here buckets of volcanic mud are provided which you can paste onto yourself (or significant other), while the smaller and clearer **Pool of Love** reaches 31.3°C. The idea is to cake yourself in the black mud in the first pool and then wash it off in the second one (there are also showers and changing rooms) – it's not a good idea to wear expensive swimwear. There are also souvenir stalls, an interpretation centre and a short nature trail. Try and go earlier in the morning as cruise ship and other tours start showing up in the middle of the day and the pools are not that big and can get crowded.

Rabot Estate

Boucan by Hotel Chocolat, T758-572 9600, www.hotelchocolat.com, tours Mon-Sat, US$88 per person, must be pre-booked.

From the turn-off to the Sulphur Springs Park on the Vieux Fort road, it's another 1.5 km south to the turn-off to Rabot Estate on the left. This 140-acre (56-ha) cocoa plantation dates back to 1745 and is the oldest cocoa plantation on the island; today it is owned by the British chocolatier, Hotel Chocolat, which has over 70 shops in the UK. It is also the location of the modern, 14-suite luxury hotel, **Boucan by Hotel Chocolat** (see page 67), for total immersion in all things chocolate (especially in the restaurant and spa), although it also has its own speedboat at Soufrière to take guests to the local beaches. For non-guests, a pre-booked two-hour 'Tree-to-Bar Experience' tour can be organized, which is interesting, fun and unique although somewhat expensive. In two parts (visitors usually arrange lunch at the restaurant in between), the Tree-to-Bean is a walk through the estate's cocoa groves with a chance to harvest the pods, then see the sun-drying and fermenting processes, while the second Bean-to-Bar part involves grinding cocoa nibs and other ingredients in a giant pestle and mortar and pouring into a mould to set. Finally, your very own chocolate bar is packaged for you.

Fond Doux Plantation and Resort

Château Belair, T758-459 7545, www.fonddouxestate.com, daily 1100-1400 for tours, US$20 per person with snacks and drinks, US$30 with buffet lunch; must be pre-booked.

It is another 1.5 km to this 135-acre (55-ha) historic plantation in the hills and set back from the road down its own lane. Dating back to 1745 when it cultivated cocoa and coffee, then sugar, it is still producing cocoa at the same time as embracing tourism. There are 15 charming cottages where you can stay (see page 68) and the estate is open for a plantation tour that takes about 40 minutes followed by either snacks and fresh fruit juice or a buffet lunch in the restaurant. The guide shows traditional methods of drying and grinding cocoa beans and how cocoa grows, and identifies flowers and fruit trees. The 1864 plantation house, which today acts as reception, is a typical single-storey wooden construction with a veranda and outside kitchen, surrounded by pleasant gardens. You can follow the tour with a 20-minute hike through the nutmeg and breadfruit trees and thick swathes of palms to a high point on the property from where there is a wonderful view of Petit Piton.

Tet Paul Nature Trail
Château Belair, T758-459 7200, daily 0900-1700, US$9, children (under 12) US$4.50.

A short drive further up the road from Fond Doux is this community tourism project which sits on 6 acres (2.4 ha) of farmland. The easy-to-moderate loop trail is guided and you are shown traditional farming and cooking methods as well as medicinal plants, fruit trees such as guava, avocado and soursop, and there's a bit of information on Amerindian history. The highlight of the 45-minute trail, however, is the ascent on wooden steps – the 'Stairway to Heaven' – to a lookout platform and the 360-degree view of the Pitons, Jalousie Bay, Morne Gimie and the whole of the southern part of the island to Vieux Fort and the Maria Islands; on a clear day you can see all the way to Martinique and St Vincent. Note that if you are coming by bus along Vieux Fort road, it's quite a long walk uphill to the start of the trail.

★ The Pitons
Gros Piton (771 m) and **Petit Piton** (743 m), St Lucia's twin pyramid-shaped volcanic spires, soar magnificently out of the Caribbean Sea on the southwest coast between Soufrière and Choiseul, and since 2004 have been a UNESCO World Heritage Site. Meaning 'peaks' in French, they were formed by volcanic activity about 200,000 to 300,000 years ago and, covered in emerald-coloured vegetation, they are the focal point of all views around Soufrière. Despite what you make be told locally, climbing Petit Piton is not encouraged as it is an extremely steep and challenging ascent and there is no marked trail, so is both dangerous and causes damage to the mountain. Although it is the higher of the two Pitons, Gros Piton is the one that can be climbed on a proper trail, but the gain in altitude is almost 500 m and the final ascent to the summit is steep, so it is still strenuous and you must be in good physical condition.

The trailhead for the **Gros Piton Nature Trail** ① *T758-459 3965/ 729 9277, 0700-1400, US$35 per person, discounts can be negotiated for groups,* is in the village of **Fond Gens Libre** at the base of the mountain. Turn off the Vieux Fort road at Etang, a hamlet 500 m south of Fond Doux Plantation & Resort, and look for the Gros Piton signs. From here, it's about a 10-minute drive on a quiet lane to Fond Gens Libre. This small settlement, which has been here since the 1700s, played a large part in the island's Brigands rebellion in 1748, when many slaves hid in the Pitons. Guides can be organized at the Interpretative Centre, and from here the hike begins on a volcanic stone

Tip...
The hike up and back takes a minimum of four hours; start early when it's cool, wear comfortable footwear and take a small backpack with some snacks, sunscreen and at least 2 litres of water.

ON THE ROAD

Forest birds

Blue-hooded euphonia (perruche; jacquot carim) (*Euphonia musica*) 12 cm long with a yellow forehead and blue head while the body is mostly green above and yellowish green underneath.

Pearly-eyed thrasher (gwo grieve) (*Margarops fuscatus*) Rather like a thrush, the 28-cm thrasher has a heavy brownish yellow bill, its upper parts are dark greyish-brown and its underparts are white with greyish-brown markings.

Purple-throated carib (kilibri rouge) (*Eulampis jugularis*) A sturdy 13-cm hummingbird with dark plumage and purplish red throat but noticeable for its metallic green wings.

Rufous-throated solitaire (siffleur montagne) (*Myadestes genibarbis*) Mostly grey, about 19 cm, with a rufous throat, foreneck and posterior underparts.

St Lucia Amazon, also known as the **St Lucia parrot** (*Amazona versicolor*) Now around 500 parrots in the wild, and a national symbol, they are mostly green with a bluish head, a touch of maroon on the underparts, red on the foreneck and a red patch on the wing.

St Lucia black finch (moisson; pyé blan) (*Melanospiza richardsoni*) 13-14 cm, the male is black with pink feet, the female is greyer.

St Lucia oriole (carouge) (*Icterus laudabilis*) Measuring 20-22 cm, mostly black with orange patches on the upper wing-coverts, under wing-coverts, rump, abdomen, flanks and under tail-coverts.

St Lucia pewee (pin caca) Formerly lesser Antillean pewee (*Contopus latirostris*) but reclassified because of colour differences. A flycatcher about 17 cm with rufous coloured underparts and olive-grey upper parts.

St Lucia warbler (sikwi barbade; petit chit) Formerly Adelaide's warbler (*Dendroica adelaidae*) but reclassified because it has black round the eyes, not white. The upper parts are grey and the underparts bright yellow.

Trembler (twanblè) (*Cinclocerthia ruficauda*) A dark brown to olive-grey bird measuring 23-25 cm with greyish-white underparts and a long, slender bill. It *really* does tremble.

---

staircase and then winds around the mountain at a gradual slope. About a quarter of the way up, the views of the Caribbean Sea and across to St Vincent start to open up, and at the halfway point there are wonderful views of Petit Piton. From here the trail follows a steeply rising ridge to the summit, of which there are actually two: turning right takes you to the higher south peak, which has a nice view across the rolling southern end of St Lucia. But the prime reward is the scramble to the left and north peak, where there is a tremendous 360-degree view of the island: Soufrière, Vieux Fort, Choiseul and the Maria Islands, the rooftops of the fishing villages and the island's many coconut groves, all blending together seamlessly.

Anse des Pitons

This astonishingly beautiful crescent-shaped beach on Jalousie Bay occupies a dramatic location in the 'cleavage' of the two Pitons and the view is absolutely breathtaking. Unlike the grey-black sand on the other beaches in this volcanic region, the sand here is gloriously white – it was in fact imported from Guyana for the benefit of guests at Sugar Beach, a **Viceroy Resort** (see page 67), the very stylish resort behind the beach. As all beaches in St Lucia are public, anyone can visit (guests from other nearby hotels are shuttled in each day) and it's a lovely spot with clear water and good snorkelling. It's also very popular with boat excursions, which stop at the little pier in the bay so tour groups can have a break on the beach, an hour of snorkelling and take photographs of the peaks. From Soufrière, follow the signs to the hotel – the turn-off from the main road is opposite the Morne Coubaril Estate (above) – and inform the security guards at the gate that you're visiting the beach; they will tell you where to park and then there is a shuttle by motorized tuk-tuk down the long windy road to the beach (you are expected to show a receipt from the beach bar or restaurant to get the tuk-tuk ride back up to the car park, otherwise it's a hot steep walk). You can also reach Anse des Pitons by water taxi from Soufrière; about US$20 per person return and it is a beautiful journey. You can pay to use the resort's luxurious sun loungers (or there's a cheaper vendor near the jetty) and rent kayaks and snorkelling equipment. Right behind the beach is **Bayside Bar** (daily 0900-2300), with hammocks in the shade of almond trees, which does sandwiches, pizzas, burgers and salads, and the elegant but pricey **Bayside Restaurant** (daily 1230-1500, 1800-2200), with a gourmet menu and attractive thatched terrace on the sand.

The Pitons to Vieux Fort

The rest of the road south of the Pitons is windy but in reasonable condition and it is 25 km from Etangs to Vieux Fort. The road rejoins the coast again at **Choiseul**, a small fishing town with ruined fortifications and petroglyphs in the area. It was once known as Anse Citron (Lime Bay) because of the abundance of lime trees growing in the area, but was later named after French military officer the Duke of Choiseul. **Sab Wee-Sha Beach** is a black-sand beach just north of Choiseul with a large grassy area shaded by palm trees and spectacular views of Gros Piton as well as St Vincent. At the time of writing it had been earmarked for the construction of a 25-acre (10-ha) resort to be called **Sunset Bay Saint Lucia**. After Choiseul the road descends from the hilly west coast into the relatively flat agricultural area of the south.

The road then passes though **Laborie**, 8 km northwest of Vieux Fort, which is worth a detour. Another small fishing community set in a lovely bay with a picturesque arc of beach, where fishermen under the almond trees maintain their nets and colourful boats moor at the pier. The centre of the town has a market square, many wooden colonial buildings and some local restaurants and rum shops. A market is held on Saturday mornings when vendors come in from the countryside to hawk fruit and vegetables such as yams and bananas and you might pick up home-baked cassava breads. At the northern end of the beach, **Rudy John Beach Park** is a small park (just off the main road where the Laborie road rejoins the main road on the west side), which has a few trees, a beach bar and a little strip of sand. Prior to 1758 the village was referred to as Islet a Caret (Turtle Island), probably in reference to a sandbar, no longer visible today, where turtles nested. In 1758 a devastating hurricane destroyed most of the churches on the island, including the Islet a Caret parish church. The village later became known as Laborie in honour of Baron de Laborie (Governor of Saint Lucia from 1784 to 1789) after he contributed to the rebuilding of the church. However, Laborie's church didn't survive either and the present church was built in 1907.

Tourist information

St Lucia Tourist Board
Sureline Building, Vide Boutielle, Castries, T758-452 4094, www.stlucia.org. Mon-Fri 0800-1700.

There are tourist information desks at George F L Charles Airport and in the shopping centres at Pointe Seraphine and Place Carenage, where the cruise ships come in.

Where to stay

Unless otherwise stated, all hotel rooms have a/c, TV and Wi-Fi. Hotel VAT (10%) and service charge (10%) is charged by all accommodation options, usually as a single charge of 20%. Check if this has been included in quoted rates.

Castries

$$$$ Rendezvous
Malabar Beach, T758-457 7900, www.theromanticholiday.com.
All-inclusive 100-room resort at the eastern end of Vigie Beach and the best place to stay near Castries; however, it's for couples only and is a popular and romantic wedding and honeymoon venue and is expensive, although almost everything is included in the rates, including diving and spa treatments. Of the many facilities, there's a lazy-river pool, tennis, watersports, 4 restaurants, 3 bars and nightly entertainment.

$$ Auberge Seraphine
Pointe Seraphine, T758-453 2073, www.aubergeseraphine.com.
A white, modern, business-style hotel on the edge of the harbour but close to Pointe Seraphine and the cruise ship terminal and handy for the George F L Charles Airport. There are 22 plain but adequate rooms on 2 levels, terrace and pool with great views of the ships, very good and elegant restaurant (see page 69). Room-only or B&B.

$$-$ Casa del Vega
Clarke Av, south side of Vigie Peninsula, T758-459 0780, www.casadelvega.com.
On a little cove overlooking the harbour and accessed via Peninsular Rd, a cheap and useful option if you have an early/late flight from George F L Charles Airport (you can walk or there's a free shuttle). 9 self-catering units from studios to 3- to 5-bedroom apartments, some have balconies with great ocean views, 96 steps down to a little beach or walk to Vigie Beach, helpful owners. Room-only or B&B.

$$-$ Heritage House
Clarke Av, south side of Vigie Peninsula, T758-518 0428, www.heritagehouseslu.com.
High up on St Victor's View near the Vigie Lighthouse and again close to George F L Charles Airport, this simple but comfortable and immaculate guesthouse has 4 rooms, 2 share a bathroom so can be combined for families, 3 have kitchens and sofa beds, while the cheapest has fridge and kettle. Small splash pool and hot breakfast included and served on the airy patio with good views of the cruise ships in the harbour.

North of Castries

$$$$ Calabash Cove Resort & Spa
Bonaire Estate, Marisule, T758-456 3500, www.calabashcove.com.
Very attractive beachfront adults-only resort on a small cove and in tropical gardens full of flowers. This intimate and relaxing resort has 26 rooms in hillside and beachfront cottages, all with ocean and sunset views, some with plunge pools, jacuzzis and outdoor showers, gym, spa, pool and excellent service and food. B&B or full board.

$$$$ Windjammer Landing
Labrellotte Bay, T758-452 0913, www.windjammer-landing.com.
A lovely hillside setting but a little isolated (a 30-min walk to a bus route and a 15-min

drive to Rodney Bay Village), although it has everything you could need for a holiday with accommodation varying from standard hotel rooms to 2- to 4-bedroom villas with plunge pools, all white, with red-tiled roofs in a Spanish hacienda style. Shops, a number of swimming pools, watersports and dive centre, tennis courts, 5 restaurants, families well catered for with a kids' club that occupies children in the evening too. Room-only, B&B and all-inclusive.

$$$ Villa Beach Cottages
John Compton Hwy, Choc Beach, T758-450 2884, www.villabeachcottages.com.
On the busy road between Castries and Rodney Bay Village, but also tucked behind the row of palms on Choc Beach, the 20 units with 1 or 2 bedrooms have gingerbread fretwork, wooden shutters, sea-facing terraces or balconies, well-equipped kitchens and a pool. Kayaks and snorkelling equipment can be rented, there are 2 large supermarkets in walking distance and you can pre-order a grocery starter pack, but a car is useful to get to restaurants.

$$ Alize Inn
Mongiraud, T758-452 0960, www.alize-inn.info. Buses on the highway go to Rodney Bay Village (2 km).
On the inland side of the highway between Castries and Rodney Bay Village and up a short rocky road, this quiet and simple inn has 14 well-priced rooms, some with 2 or 4 beds and kitchenettes, spread across 2 blue-and-white buildings and most with fretwork balconies (ensure you ask for one), pool, and reasonable restaurant and bar. B&B with continental breakfast.

$$ The Boiled Frog
Choc Bay, T758-720 8843, www.theboiledfrog.net.
The hosts of this 1-room guesthouse are an engaging Canadian family who make you feel instantly welcome and you are free to be independent as you like or enjoy their company and join them for dinner. The huge

house was originally built by Caribbean shipping tycoon Jon Van Geest, owner of Geest Lines. Separated from the rest of the house, the unit has a kitchen, living room and beachfront access, and there's a supermarket, bank and buses on the other side of the road. US$110 with a basic continental breakfast.

Rodney Bay Village
Reduit Beach is dominated by the large **Rex** all-inclusive resorts: **Royal St Lucia Resort & Spa**, **Papillon** and **St Lucian**. **Bay Gardens Beach Resort & Spa** (below) is the other property on the beach and there are plenty of smaller and cheaper places in the village. While all-inclusive or full board is offered at many, there's such a good choice of restaurants nearby, you may prefer B&B or room-only.

$$$ Bay Gardens Beach Resort & Spa
Reduit Beach, T758-457 8006, www.baygardensresorts.com.
One of the most appealing places to stay in Rodney Bay Village on Reduit Beach next to popular beach bar **Spinnakers**, 6 orange- and lime-coloured blocks with 76 rooms set around well-kept grounds and a vast swimming pool. The suites have sofa beds and full kitchens. Room-only or B&B, and there's also a 'dine-around' option for several restaurants in the village. Also has 2 other properties on the lagoon side of the village: **Bay Gardens Hotel** and **Bay Gardens Inn**, both convenient and comfortable.

$$ Coco Palm
Rodney Bay Blvd, T758-456 2800, www.coco-resorts.com.
Great value and in the centre of the village among restaurants and nightlife, but set back from the main road so quiet, and just a few minutes' walk to Reduit Beach. The 101 rooms are in 2 attractive, modern, 4-storey buildings with balconies/patios, good for families or couples. There's a large swimming pool, and colourful, open-air bar/restaurant. Room-only, B&B and full board.

$$ The Ginger Lily Hotel
Reduit Beach Av, T758-458 0300,
www.gingerlilyhotel.com.
This small and inexpensive hotel has
11 spacious rooms with fridge, kettle and
sofa beds for children, most have hammocks
on the terrace/balcony. It is conveniently
located opposite **Spinnakers** and Reduit
Beach, there's a decent-sized swimming
pool surrounded by palms, pot plants
and sun loungers. B&B.

$$ Habitat Terrace
Old Military Rd, 2.8 km east of Baywalk
Shopping Mall, T758-(758)-452-0822,
www.habitatterrace.com.
In a brightly coloured block perched on
a peaceful hillside with great views over
Rodney Bay and Pigeon Island, the 12 studios
and apartments sleep 1-4, some have patio
doors on to the pretty garden and pool,
upstairs ones have Juliette balconies. It's
about a 10- to 15-min walk to Rodney Bay
Marina and is handy for the cricket ground;
a car's useful but taxis are available. Room-
only or B&B.

$$ Harmony Suites
Off Flamboyant Drive, T758-452 8756,
www.harmonysuites.com.
On the inland/lagoon side of the village, this
small, pleasant and well-priced hotel has
30 comfortable rooms with kitchenettes and
balconies/patios in 2-storey buildings around
tropical gardens with fountains and a pool.
There's a small deck area with sun loungers
over the lagoon, and the **Cockpit Bistro**
serves breakfasts and lunches daily except
Sun. Room-only, no children under 12.

$$ La Terrasse Inn
Seagrape Av, T758-572 0389,
www.la terrasestlucia.com.
Colourful 4-room guesthouse attached
to **La Terrasse French Restaurant** (see
page 70), 2 of the rooms share a bathroom,
2 have en suites and all are equipped with
fridge, kettle, cups and plates, etc and have
private terraces with table and chairs. Can

be noisy at weekends as it's in the hub of the
nightlife strip (take earplugs), but otherwise
friendly and cheap. Room-only, no children
under 15, minimum 2-night stay.

Gros Islet
The largest all-inclusive resort in this area
is **Sandals Grande St Lucian Spa & Beach
Resort**, which is on the causeway over to
Pigeon Island. There are several inexpensive
guesthouses in Gros Islet village.

$$$$ Cap Maison
Smugglers Cove Drive, Cap Estate,
T758-457 8670, www.capmaison.com.
In Cape Estate 3 km north of Gros Islet
village, a stylish and romantic hideaway with
fantastic views down the coast to Pigeon
Island, not on the beach but steps leads to
a small beach with beach bar, sun loungers,
kayaks and snorkelling gear. Accommodation
is spread over 10 2-storey, whitewashed
blocks with arches, courtyards and fountains,
and ranges from villas with kitchen, private
pool and rooftop terrace, to more modest
garden rooms, marvellous open-air clifftop
restaurant (open to all; see page 71), walk-in
wine cellar and spa. B&B or all-inclusive.

$$$$ The Landings Resort & Spa
Pigeon Island Causeway, T758-458 7300,
www.landingsstlucia.com.
Smart and modern and overlooking its own
yacht moorings and sandy beach on the
causeway just before Sandals and a short
walk to Pigeon Island, 70 1- to 3-bedroom
suites with kitchens, washer/dryers, some
have plunge pools, 3 restaurants and private
chefs are available, 3 pools, gym, tennis
courts, kids' club and watersports. B&B or
all-inclusive.

$ Bay Guesthouse
Bay St, T758-450 8956,
www.bay-guesthouse.com.
Set in gardens overlooking the water
and a short walk to a small beach, Bay
Guesthouse has 1 2-bedroom apartment
and 1 studio with kitchens, and 1 smaller

room with fridge and kettle which comes in at US$40 in low season, run by knowledgeable Will and Stephanie, an English/French couple, and their dogs. Room-only, 2-night minimum stay.

$ La Panache Holiday Apartments
Cas-en-Bas Rd, T758-450 0765, www.lapanache.com.
Simple self-catering accommodation in 2 studio apartments and a 2-bedroom apartment, all with balcony, bathroom, fridge, cooking facilities, no TV or a/c but insect screens and fans, lovely gardens with fruit trees and birds. On a hillside with good views of Rodney Bay and a 400-m walk downhill to the highway, buses and a small supermarket. Room-only.

$ Tropical Breeze Guest House
38 Marcie St, T758-450 0589, www.tropicalbreezeresorts.com.
Nothing fancy but a neat and clean modern white building with accommodating owners, Ruth and John, with 1- to 4-bedroomed apartments with kitchens and a couple of budget rooms, good for groups and families and within easy reach of buses on the highway, the Gros Islet fish fry and the cricket ground. Room-only.

East coast to Vieux Fort

$$$$ Coconut Bay Beach Resort & Spa
Eau Piquan, just before Hewanorra International Airport, T758-455 3271, www.foxgroveinn.com.
The only all-inclusive resort on the Atlantic coast, Coconut Bay covers 85 acres (34 ha) and has a superb range of facilities – everything you could want for a holiday with 5 restaurants, 6 bars, spa, tennis courts, a waterpark, several pools and nice beach lined with coconut palms. Accommodation ranges from standard hotel rooms split into 2 sections for adults and families to the newly built Serenity area with 36 super-luxurious, couples-only, plunge pool suites set in their own fenced gardens with butler service.

$$ The Fox Grove Inn
Mon Repos, T758-455 3271, www.foxgroveinn.com.
Between Dennery and Micoud and high up with wonderful views of Praslin Bay, this Swiss/St Lucian-owned hotel is just by Mamiku Botanical Gardens, and has 12 rooms, plus a 1-bedroom and a 2-bedroom apartment, ask for views to the front. It's nothing fancy but it's comfortable, has a large swimming pool, nature trails, tasty food in the restaurant (see page 72), and is a good and friendly base for exploring the east coast. B&B.

$$ Zamacá Bed & Breakfast
15 Fond Bay Drive, Micoud, T758-454 1309, www.zamacastlucia.com.
This pretty hillside white house has 5 comfortable and smart guest rooms with balconies, communal lounge and terrace with broad views over the Atlantic, Ellen and John offer excellent hospitality, good breakfasts and other meals on request and there are places to eat in the village. If you're not driving, it's a 20-min walk from buses on Micoud Hwy. B&B.

$$-$ Aupic Paradise
Eau Piquant, T758-454 5857, www.visitaupicparadise.com.
A 10-min drive from Hewanorra International Airport, plain, simple and cheap and useful for an overnight stay for early/late flights or delays. 15 units; rooms with fridge, kettle and microwave or fully equipped 1- to 2-bedroom apartments, continental breakfast but no restaurant so you need to go into Vieux Fort for food (5 mins by bus or taxi).

$$-$ Villa Caribbean Dream
Moule à Chique, T758-454 6846, www.caribdreams.net.
Pretty, Creole-style guesthouse on the Cap Moule à Chique south of Vieux Fort, with 4 rooms in the main house with shared bathrooms and communal kitchen, 1 self-contained apartment and a delightful double

Creole-style bungalow in the garden with kitchen and tremendous view up the coast to the Pitons. Room-only but breakfasts and other meals available.

Marigot Bay

$$$$ Capella Marigot Bay Resort and Marina
At the marina on the south shore, T758-458 5300, www.capellahotels.com.
Part of the marina so lots of yacht-watching. There's a pool and 124 rooms with wooden balconies and 57 multi-bedroom suites with kitchen (including washer/dryer), the higher ones have excellent views. **The Grill** at 14° 61° is the main restaurant, other restaurants/bars are down the boardwalk and the Marina Village has a grocery store and other shops. B&B.

$$$ The Inn On the Bay
Seaview Av, T758-451 4260, www.saint-lucia.com.
Only 5 spacious rooms in a lovely white West Indian-style building with wrap-around balconies up on the hill on the south side and overlooking the bay, no a/c but cool breezes, pool and deck, continental breakfast included with pastries, cereal and fruit, complimentary transport down to town.

$$$ Mango Beach Inn
North shore of Marigot Bay, T758-458 3188, www.mangobeachmarigot.com.
A homely B&B reached by water taxi, 5 comfortable rooms, 2 have private entrances and terraces, honesty bar, garden with small pool, the British owners Judith and John Verity are very hands-on and also own the excellent **Rainforest Hideaway** restaurant (see page 72) which is accessed via a gate at the bottom of the garden.

$$$-$$ Marigot Beach Club
On the north shore of Marigot Bay, T758-451 4974, www.marigotbeachclub.com.
Surrounded by palms, this waterfront option is accessible by water taxi and has 34 units; studios with kitchens and 2- to 3-bedroom villas with full kitchens, warmly decorated with balconies/terraces and bay views, pool with sundeck, **Doolittle's** restaurant/bar (see page 72), plus a pizzeria and juice bar. The offer lots of activities including sailing, kayaking and a PADI dive shop. Room-only or B&B.

$$ JJ's Paradise
La Croix Maingot, T758-451 4761, www.jjsparadise.com.
Budget-friendly spot, a bit worn but clean, friendly and quiet, 16 simple cabins on a hillside in lush gardens with fruit trees, some have kitchenettes and can accommodate families, decent-sized pool with sun loungers, rates are room-only but continental breakfast and sandwiches are available, a 15-min walk down into the bay below for meals.

Anse Cochon

$$$$ Ti Kaye Resort & Spa
T758-456 8101, www.tikaye.com.
Romantic and popular with honeymooners, and in a stunning location overlooking Anse Cochon beach, 33 white, very private, hillside cottages with 4-poster beds, decorative fretwork, open-air showers, large terraces furnished with a hammock and rocking chairs, and some have plunge pools (no TVs). Open-sided restaurant and bar by the main swimming pool, another beachside restaurant/bar, open-air treatment rooms in the cliff-edge spa, and snorkelling and diving can be arranged. No children under 12. Room-only or half-board.

Soufrière and the Pitons

$$$$ Anse Chastanet Resort and Jade Mountain
Anse Chastanet, northwest of Soufrière, T758-459 7000, www.ansechastanet.com, www.jademountainstlucia.com.
Set on a 600-acre (243-ha) tropical estate with both Anse Chastanet and Anse Mamin beaches on the property, 49 hilltop, hillside

and beachside suites, each different but all really special, including the super-luxurious, architecturally inspiring Jade Mountain suites which are suspended on platforms linked by sky bridges with every facility including an infinity pool and extraordinary views of the Pitons – ranked as one of the best places to stay in the whole of the Caribbean. There are 4 restaurants behind the beaches and up the hillside, spa, dive shop and watersports, mountain biking with **Bike St Lucia**, walks and excursions available. More a place for romantics than families, but children over 10 (or over 6 in the summer low season months) are accepted. Room-only and rates vary enormously depending on accommodation.

$$$$ Boucan by Hotel Chocolat
Rabot Estate, T758-572 9600, www. hotelchocolat.com/uk/boucan.
On the cocoa estate owned by the British chocolatier, **Hotel Chocolat** (see page 58), up in the hills south of Soufrière, the restaurant and some of the 14 modern, chic suites have amazing views of Petit Piton, complimentary treats include home-made cookies and slabs of chocolate, every dish in the restaurant is cocoa themed (see page 73), as are the treatments in the spa. There's a bar, swimming pool and shuttle/speed boat to the beaches. No children under 12. B&B.

$$$$ La Dauphine Estate
Off Sulphur Springs Access Rd, contact Villa Beach Cottages, T758-450 2884, www.villabeachcottages.com.
On a lush and peaceful 200-acre (80-ha) cocoa plantation with rainforest and fruit orchards, there are 2 magnificent houses to rent here; the 4-bedroom **Great House** (sleeps 10) and the 2-bedroom **Chateau Laffitte** (sleeps 4), built in 1890 with decorative gingerbread fretwork, jalousie windows and wooden shutters. Each has a kitchen and a housekeeper/cook is provided, the estate manager can give a tour of the plantation, and you'll find garden hammocks and an infinity pool.

$$$$ Ladera
Rabot Estate, T758-459 6618, www.ladera.com.
On the edge of a cocoa plantation in a spectacular setting 300 m up with an uninterrupted view down between the 'cleavage' of Gros Piton and Petit Piton, 32 luxury suites with an open west wall with a plunge pool, excellent **Dasheene** restaurant (see page 73), wine cellar, main pool and deck and shuttle to Sugar Beach. Room-only or B&B available and they offer 2-centre holidays with Cap Maison north of Rodney Bay (see above). No TV, a/c (none are needed with that view) or children under 15 and this is one of the best honeymoon retreats on St Lucia.

$$$$ Stonefield Estate Resort
2.5 km south of Soufrière, T758-459 7037, www.stonefieldresort.com.
A hillside 26-acre (10-ha) former cocoa estate, romantic and very peaceful with stunning views of Petit Piton, 17 cottages sleeping 2-8 with outdoor showers, kitchens, hammocks on the veranda and many have plunge pools. Excellent restaurant, the **Mango Tree** (see page 73), and you can pre-order a grocery pack if you want to self-cater, spa and a shuttle runs to Sugar Beach.

$$$$ Sugar Beach (Viceroy Resort)
Anse des Pitons, T758-456 8000, www.viceroyhotelsandresorts.com.
This former 100-acre (40-ha) sugar plantation runs down to the beach of blinding white sand at Anse des Pitons, and the near-sheer wall of Petit Piton rises dramatically on one side of the property. Built in colonial-style with a faux Great House as the central reception and 79 luxury rooms and villas in gingerbread cottages with gorgeous white-on-white interiors and Victorian bath tubs, extraordinary spa with tree house treatment rooms perched above the forest floor, restaurants and bars behind the beach and on the hillside. Rates range from room-only to all-inclusive.

$$$$-$$$ Crystals St Lucia
Colombette, 3 km before Soufrière, T758-384 8995, www.stluciacrystals.com.
Rustic spot with plenty of charm set in lush hillside gardens with ocean and Pitons views, 6 1- to 3-bedroom cottages with kitchen, sun deck and plunge pool, ethnic decor with wind chimes, tent-effect ceilings, draped 4-poster beds, a treehouse bar and dining area, sociable owners. No children under 12. B&B, other meals on request.

$$$ Fond Doux Plantation & Resort
Château Belair, T758-459 7545, www.fonddouxestate.com.
On a 135-acre (55-ha) historic plantation dating to 1745, 15 1- and 2-bedroom gingerbread cottages dotted around between fruit and palm trees, with wooden floors, 4-poster beds, verandas, some have their own garden, plunge pool and kitchen, the largest is a 19th-century French colonial house from Castries and rebuilt here, no a/c or TVs, 2 good restaurant/bars, tucked-away pool area, hiking trails, and free shuttle to Anse des Pitons beach and Soufrière. B&B. They also offers cocoa tours (see page 58).

$ The Downtown Hotel
Bridge St, Soufrière, T758-457 1485, www.thedowntownhotel.net.
One of the very few budget-friendly options around Soufrière, right in the main square (as the name suggests) above some shops and offices (3 flights of stairs), 18 fairly spacious rooms with fridge, microwave and kettle, the front ones have balconies, no breakfast but close to supermarket and plenty of bars and places to eat, and a short walk to water taxis for the beaches.

Towards Vieux Fort

$$$ Têt Rouge
La Point, T758-487-5054, www.tetrouge.com.
In an isolated spot on the south side of Gros Piton, 6 delightful individually decorated wooden studios with kitchen, each on 2 levels with balcony, outdoor showers, no TV or a/c but good flow of air, great attention to detail and good service, sweeping ocean views and there's no light pollution so the stars are clear at night, infinity pool and excellent food. A car is essential and it's a 15-min drive on an unsurfaced track to get to/from the main road and Choiseul. Room-only, no under 18s, minimum 4-night stay.

$$$-$$ Balenbouche Estate
Piaye, 6 km southeast of Choiseul, T758-455 1244, www.balenbouche.com.
On a former sugar plantation halfway between Soufrière and Vieux Fort, this is a beautiful 19th-century great house set in gardens with magnificent old trees and the ruins of a sugar mill and a historic aqueduct. 5 self-catering cottages sleeping 2-6, furnished with antiques, 2 small beaches within a short walk through the gardens. B&B and dinner by reservation, minimum 3-night stay.

Restaurants

In the peak winter months, make reservations at the smart restaurants a long way in advance, especially for a waterfront or sunset-facing table. Most (though not all) restaurants quote prices on menus that include 10% VAT and many automatically add a 10% service charge to the bill – beware of tipping twice.

Castries

$$$ The Coal Pot
Vigie Marina, T758-452 5566, www.coal potrestaurant.com. Tue-Sat 1200-1500, daily 1830-2130.
Established in 1968, this is the place to eat. It's an outstanding restaurant with a very romantic, candlelit interior and beautiful artwork or terrace dining overlooking the marina. The cuisine is sophisticated, mostly French and the local fresh fish (often dorado, barracuda and kingfish) is delicious, with tasty sauces and all the trimmings, accompanied by a good wine list.

$$$-$$ Brown Sugar
Vigie Cove, T758-458 1931, www.brownsugar restaurantandbar.com. Tue-Sat 1200-1500, daily 1800-2200.
Open-air waterfront restaurant in a lovely garden with a view of the harbour and all the boats coming and going, family-run with attention to detail and excellent service, international menu with local touches, good, hearty food such as lamb shanks or chicken curry and reasonably priced.

$$$-$ Auberge Seraphine
See Where to stay, page 62.
At the hotel of the same name, the partially open-sided restaurant with whitewashed arches, ceilings and banisters has a lovely garden setting next to a lily pond – in the evening white egrets nest in the trees above. Well known for its fish and seafood, including shrimps, scallops and lobster platters, plus there are pizzas, several pasta choices, sandwiches at lunchtime and some gooey desserts.

$$ The Pink Plantation House
Chef Harry Drive, The Morne, T758-452 5422, see Facebook. Mon-Fri 1130-1500, Fri 1830-2100, Sun 0900-1200.
Owned by ceramicist Michelle Elliot, you can pop in to the workshop and buy her pottery and combine it with a delicious lunch, Fri dinner or Sun brunch at tables on the veranda of this traditional wooden colonial house with pretty fretwork and shuttered windows and enjoy a lovely view through a beautiful garden on the hillside overlooking Castries harbour. Tasty food, anything from a goat's cheese salad to mahi mahi in ginger sauce and guava cheesecake. A very pleasant experience.

$$-$ Pink Papaya
Point Seraphine. T758-453 6862, www.pink papayarestaurant.com. Daily 1100-1700.
A friendly daytime café/pub offering burgers, wraps, salads, fresh seafood, wood-fired pizza and local dishes, popular with cruise ship passengers and a great place to see the ships close up. They run a water taxi service across the harbour from the Vendor's Market.

$ The Balcony
Corner of Laborie and Brazil streets, T758-458 3663, see Facebook. Mon-Sat 0800-1900.
Upstairs café and bar with veranda overlooking Derek Walcott Square and serving tasty and cheap Caribbean food, especially good for fish dishes, or a chicken and potato roti washed down with a local juice or beer overlooking. A good place for people watching and to renew your energy for sightseeing.

Rodney Bay Village

$$$ Big Chef Steakhouse
Reduit Drive, T758-450 0210, www.bigchef steakhouse.com. Daily 1800-2400.
Although not cheap, this classy restaurant offers tender, tasty Angus steaks, local fish and seafood, including lobster in season, and rich puddings, very popular and with good reason, the food is delicious with friendly, efficient service and a great cocktail and wine list. Behind the restaurant, on the waterfront with a dinghy dock, is the sister restaurant **Tapas on the Bay** (T758-451 2433, daily 1000-2200), with a good range of tapas accompanied by a short but appropriate selection of sherry, Spanish or world wines available by the glass.

$$$ Blue Olive Restaurant & Wine Bar
Baywalk Shopping Mall, T758-458 2433, www.blueolivestlucia.com. Thu-Tue 1800-2200.
The sister restaurant to The **Coal Pot** in Castries with a similar menu of Mediterranean cuisine such as bouillabaisse, moussaka and paella, plus seafood and a good choice of inventive pasta sauces, and an exceptionally long wine and champagne list by the glass or bottle, nice for a treat with a very chic atmosphere.

$$$ Buzz Seafood & Grill
Reduit Beach Av, T758-458 0450, www. buzzstlucia.com. Tue-Sat 1700-2300.

Seafood and grill serving steaks, lobster, lamb shanks, shepherd's pie, pepperpot and a few vegetarian options. Open and airy indoor tables with shutters raised in a blue and lemon West Indian-style building, or outdoor tables under a huge tree in the pretty garden. Good live music from 1900 in high season. Reservations recommended unless you are prepared to wait an hour or more with a cocktail.

$$$ Jacques Waterfront Dining
Reduit Beach Av, T758-458 1900, www.jacquesrestaurant.com. Daily 1200-1430, 1830-2200.
Upmarket bistro at the end of Reduit Beach overlooking the entrance to the marina, lovely atmosphere in the open-air dining room on the waterfront, French and Caribbean cuisine, all beautifully presented, one of the best restaurants in Rodney Bay Village, run by French chef, Jacques Rioux. Reservations recommended.

$$$ La Terrasse French Restaurant
Seagrape Av, T758-572 0389, www.la terrasse stlucia.com. Daily except Tue for dinner from 1800.
Nice and cosy with a lovely terrace in a beautiful tropical garden cooled by breezes from the lagoon, this offers very tasty French cuisine including duck, frogs' legs, rack of lamb and escargot, plus there's excellent local fish like mahi mahi and some delicious desserts. The staff are warm, friendly and attentive and there's an excellent choice of wine.

$$$ Memories of Hong Kong
Reduit Beach Av, T758-452 8218. Mon-Sat 1700-2200.
A breezy location with fairy lights and lanterns around the veranda and tables, the menu is extensive and is well known for its tasty Cantonese dishes including char siu (roast pork), stuffed duck in crab meat sauce and roast duck in plum sauce, good service but on the pricey side.

$$$ Spice of India
Baywalk Shopping Mall, T758-458 4243, www.spiceofindiastlucia.com. Tue-Sun 1200-1545, 1800-2200.
Considered by both St Lucians and tourists as the best Indian restaurant on the island, expensive but consistently good food and dishes are put in the middle of the table so you can share, service is excellent and Chef Adil and his 2 chefs from India love to explain the style of cooking and more often than not will take diners back to the open kitchen. See Facebook for tasting lunch menus. Reservations recommended.

$$$-$$ Fire Grill & Lounge Bar
Reduit Beach Av, T758-451 4745, see Facebook, Thu-Tue 1800-2400.
Casual spot where all the food, whether it's Angus steak, burgers, fish or seafood, is cooked over the barbecue, family friendly, weekly live jazz and blues, comfy leather sofas in the lounge bar, and well known for its huge selection of rums.

$$$-$$ Spinnakers
On Reduit Beach, T758-452 8491, www.spinnakersbeachbar.com. Daily 0900-2200.
Long-established, unpretentious beach bar, excellent location with a broad deck under thatch, though food and service suffer when it is busy. Lots of variety on the menu, from salads, jerk chicken sandwiches and burgers for lunch, to more sophisticated grilled fish, lobster and meat dishes for dinner, and plenty of cold beers and cocktails.

$$ Razmataz
Reduit Beach Av, T758-452 9800, www.razmatazrestaurant.com. Wed-Mon 1700-2300.
Serves traditional Tandoori cuisine with a wide range of dishes, particularly good for vegetarians, tables are set along a covered veranda and the Indian decor gives it an authentic atmosphere, very popular with British clientele, also does takeaway.

$$-$ Elena's Café, Pizzeria and Gelato
Rodney Bay Marina, T758-723 8800 (daily 0700-2200), and Baywalk Shopping Mall, T758-451 0043 (Mon-Fri 1000-2200, Sat 0900-2300), www.elenascafestlucia.com.
Elena's uses fresh fruits and natural ingredients in their delicious *gelato*, and also offer coffees, great breakfasts with lots of choice, pizza baked in wood-fired oven for lunch and supper or takeaway, and good salads, burgers, daily Italian specials, beers, wines and cocktails.

$$-$ Il Pappa Trattoria Pizzeria Gelateria
Castries–Gros Islet Hwy, Rodney Heights, T758-452 0282. Daily 1100-2200.
Family-run and family-friendly Italian trattoria offering creative wood oven-baked pizzas with good thin crusts, plus pasta dishes, salads, cold beer, and delicious and authentic *gelato* for dessert. It takes about 10 mins to walk here from Reduit Beach.

$ Café Olé
Rodney Bay Marina, T758-452 8726, see Facebook. Mon-Sat 0700-2200, Sun 0800-2200.
One of several side-by-side cafés with seating on wooden decking overlooking the smart yachts, which do good, inexpensive lunches and light dinners, Café Olé offers excellent smoothies, a big choice of made-to-order baguettes, wraps, paninis, salads and Italian ice cream.

Pigeon Island

$$$-$$ Jambe de Bois
T758-450 8166. Mon 0900-1700, Tue-Sun 0900-2200.
Named after the infamous pirate, this rustic, waterfront spot has stone walls and a thatched roof and it's very pleasant to sit at the tables on the deck at the water's edge. Offers reasonably priced drinks and sandwiches, rotis and salads for lunch with a view of Rodney Bay. The more sophisticated evening menu has the likes of grilled fish, calamari and lamb curry, and there's often live jazz on weekend nights. It's popular with

those on yachts moored in the bay, and you can go for dinner even when the Pigeon Island main gate is closed – just tell security you're going for a meal – or get a water taxi from Reduit Beach.

Gros Islet and Cap Estate

$$$ The Cliff at Cap
At Cap Maison (page 64), Smugglers Cove Drive, Cap Estate, T758-457 8681, www.the cliffatcap.com. Daily 1200-1430, 1800-2200.
Lots of non-residents eat at the stylish open-air restaurant at Cap Maison near St Lucia's northern tip thanks to its sensational clifftop location and panoramic views that extend to Martinique, but the creative French/Caribbean fusion cuisine is also a big draw. At the very least, go for a drink – the bar has an impressive selection of rums. Reservations recommended.

$$-$ Elegance Café
Castries–Gros Islet Hwy, T758-450 9864, see Facebook. Mon-Sat 1100-2100.
Charming roadside restaurant serving excellent Indian cuisine, plus sandwiches and salads, chocolate mousse cake and home-made ice cream for dessert, wine and beer, coffees and vegetable juices. Reasonably priced and a good option for lunch, an early supper or takeaway on the way to/from Pigeon Island, with parking right outside.

$$-$ Flavours of the Grill
Marie Therese St, T758-284 7906, see Facebook. Mon-Thu and Sat 1200-2200, Fri 1200-0100.
Just off the main drag, this friendly, modest and colourful little restaurant is in a brightly painted wooden house and is good place to sample authentic, inexpensive Caribbean cooking. Dishes include fried strips of blue marlin, shrimp in a Creole sauce, and banana bread with home-made ice cream. At lunchtime there's a buffet if it's busy and it stays open late on Fri for the fish fry (see page 42).

East coast to Vieux Fort

$$$-$$ The Fox Grove Inn
See Where to stay, page 65, www.foxgroveinn. com. Daily 1200-1500, dinner by reservation.
A useful stop if you're touring the east coast and going to Mamiku Botanical Gardens. From the balcony there's a spectacular view over Praslin Bay and the Atlantic. Very good food, try the smoked fish or smoked duck salad for a delicious lunch, washed down with a local juice such as guava or passion fruit. Other main dishes include fish, steak or pasta.

Vieux Fort

$$-$ Reef Beach Café
Anse de Sables beach, T758-454 3418, www.slucia.com/reef. Tue-Sun 0800-2200, Mon 0800-1800.
Pleasant bar with glorious view over bay to Maria Islands with kitesurfers for added interest, local drinks and delicacies, milk shakes and cocktails, seafood, fish and chips, roti, pizza, burgers and baguettes, reasonable prices, tables out by the beach under sea grape trees as well as inside the building. A good place to eat before going to the airport and there's Wi-Fi.

$ The Orbit Restaurant & Bar
Commercial St, T758-454 3061. Daily 0700-2200.
A popular local place in a wooden house with tin roof in the older part of Vieux Fort, laid-back atmosphere, good Creole food and local drinks including lime juice and rum punch. Limited menu options but all fresh and well cooked; a typical special of the day might be lentil soup followed by mahi mahi with plantains, rice and beans. A little hard to find, but most people know the friendly owner CeeCee.

Marigot Bay

$$$ Rainforest Hideaway
North side of the bay, T758-451 4485, see Facebook. Mon, Wed, Thu-Sat, bar from 1600, dinner 1800-2130.

Beautiful decor and setting – you dine on a wooden deck that extends right out over the water – a good fusion of European and Caribbean food, examples might be coconut-crusted lionfish or jerk chicken breast, à la carte or fixed-price menu and there's often live jazz. To get there it's a 2-min ride by the free ferry across from the jetty by the police/customs building. Opens 7 days a week in high season – mid-Nov to mid-May – when a shuttle from Rodney Bay can also be organized. Reservations essential.

$$$-$$ Doolittle's
At Marigot Beach Club, north side of the bay, T758-451 4974, www.marigotbeachclub.com. Daily 1100-2400.
Casual pub-style spot with a large terrace on the water and lovely views. The food – sandwiches, salads and noodle dishes for lunch and a more formal dinner menu of steaks, curries, pastas and seafood – can be a bit hit or miss, but is reasonably priced. You can use the private beach area at lunchtime and there's a lively bar scene in the evening. Again reached by ferry or water taxi.

$$$-$$ Marsala Bay
Marina Village, T758-451 4500, see Facebook. Tue-Sun1200-1530, 1730-2200.
Under the same ownership and chef as **Spice of India** in Rodney Bay, and on the 1st floor of the Marina Village with great views of the yachts and water taxis in the bay, serves delicious Indian and Indo-Chinese (*hakka*) cuisine, good choice for vegetarians and takeaways also available if you are on a yacht or self-catering.

$$-$ Chateau Mygo House of Seafood
1 Mama Sheila Drive, T758-458 3947, www.chateaumygo.com. Daily 0700-2300.
A very casual waterfront bar and grill with a wooden deck, serves traditional hot bakes and cocoa tea for breakfast, and sandwiches, burgers, rotis, chicken and chips, salads and grilled fish later in the day – the fish tacos and thin-crust pizzas are especially good. A separate bar called the **Hurricane Hole** is

popular with yachties (as you can imagine) and there's live music on Tue and Thu.

Soufrière and the Pitons

$$$ Boucan by Hotel Chocolat
See Where to stay, page 67.
Daily 1200-1500, 1800-2130.
The open-plan restaurant of Boucan by Hotel Chocolat is modern and chic with a glorious view of the Pitons. The food is innovative, with a chocolate theme for savoury and sweet dishes, using local cocoa and other local ingredients; for example, chocolate-infused vinaigrette for salads, Angus steak marinated with cocoa nibs, pork with a cocoa and herb crust. And, naturally, the desserts are divine. Reservations recommended.

$$$ Dasheene
See Where to stay, page 67.
Daily 1130-1430, 1830-2130.
Up on a hillside with views right down between the 2 Pitons, this marvellous terrace restaurant simply takes your breath away, especially at lunchtime or sunset. You can come here just for drinks but there is a cover charge of US$25 (still worth it), redeemable against a meal bill. The superb Caribbean Creole food mostly uses produce from local farmers and fishermen as well as some international delicacies. You're expected to dress up for dinner and reservations are recommended.

$$$ Orlando's
Bridge St, Soufrière, T758-459 5955, www.orlandosrestaurantstl.com. Daily for breakfast 0730-1000, lunch (except Tue) 1200-1400, dinner 1800-2100.
Set in a courtyard garden on the main road before the bridge coming into town, chef Orlando Sachell is at the helm of this Caribbean gourmet restaurant. Choose from either a 5-course prix-fixe tasting menu or a normal menu. Examples might be pumpkin and calalloo soup, blue marlin served on roasted breadfruit or mahi mahi with sweet potato chips. Service is attentive and it

makes a good lunch stop on an island tour. Reservations recommended.

$$$-$$ The Hummingbird
On the beach, north end of Soufrière, T758-459 7232, www.hummingbirdbeach resort.com. Daily 0700-2100.
A nice place to eat, have a beer and go for a swim, with good views of the town and Petit Piton. There's a varied menu of seafood, steak, vegetarian options, great fishcakes and pumpkin soup, lunchtime salads and sandwiches. Creole night on Wed has live music and dancing. Also a hotel ($$) but the rooms are a little faded and need refurbishment.

$$$-$$ Mango Tree
Stonefield Estate Resort, see Where to stay, page 67. Daily 0730-2200.
Gorgeous setting overlooking Petit Piton and Malgretout beach and great for sunset watching. Open for breakfast, lunch and dinner, the menu is wide ranging, with some vegetarian dishes as well as the usual seafood, meat and pasta. The barbecue on Thu evening with limbo dancing, fire eating and DJ music is very popular – you'll need to make a reservation.

$ La Haut Resort
Palmiste, 2.5 km north of Soufrière, T758-459 7008, www.lahaut.com. Daily 0800-1530.
Local Creole fare is available at this casual spot on a former cocoa estate, from cocoa tea at breakfast, to pumpkin chips and roti or salted cod fishcakes for lunch but it's not open for dinner, which is a bit awkward if you are staying in the 17 simple rooms here ($$). However, it's worth dropping in just for a beer on the terrace for what is the first stunning view of the Pitons if arriving in Soufrière from the north.

$ Martha's Tables
Malgretout, Jalousie Rd, T758-459 7270, www.marthastables.com. Mon-Fri 1130-1500.
This modest little lunchtime restaurant by the road to Sugar Beach, a Viceroy Resort, offers big portions of home-style cooking

such as Creole fish, chicken, vegetarian dishes, rice and peas, ground provisions, lots of choice of local food eaten at mismatched tables and chairs under a lean-to roof, or meals to go.

The southwest

$$-$ Debbie's Homemade Food
Sapphire Estate, Laborie, T758-455 1625. Tue-Sun 1100-2100.
A roadside local restaurant on the outskirts of the village of Laborie with a wide, shady veranda decorated with potted plants, Debbie's menu offers sizeable portions of tasty Creole food with lots of trimmings and side dishes, to eat in or takeaway, buffet lunch on Sun. Lots of car parking space.

Bars and clubs

The place to head for live music and dance is Rodney Bay. Elsewhere on the island, life after dark is low key, but hotels often lay on entertainment and are a frequent venue for steel pan music, folk dancing, limbo dancing and mock carnival singing and dancing. Most welcome guests from outside if you are drinking at the bar or eating at the restaurant. Jazz is popular and the big annual event is the Jazz Festival in May (see page 75). But St Lucians also love US-style country and western music, and you'll often hear bands play Kenny Rogers or Jim Reeves covers.

Castries

Antillia Brewing Company
Pointe Seraphine, T758-458 0844, see Facebook. Mon-Sat 1100-1700.
For an alternative to Piton beer, this brewer produces several craft ales with no chemicals or preservatives added. They have a beer garden at Pointe Seraphine, just north of the duty free shopping area, where you can try pale ales stouts or alternatively wine and rum drinks; there's a nice view of the marina and it's a popular spot for cruise passengers

waiting for their ship to depart. Contact them to arrange a tour of the brewery, which is in an industrial area of Castries.

Rodney Bay

Delirius
Reduit Drive, T758-451 3354, www.deliriusstlucia.com. Mon-Wed and Sun 1100-2400, Fri-Sat 1100-0200.
One of the most popular spots in Rodney Bay, a lively, contemporary bar and restaurant on the main street, the cocktail bar is shaped like a horseshoe and serves a selection of original martinis, caipirinhas and mojitos, all made using fresh fruits and herbs by bartenders who take their creations seriously. There's live music in the garden some nights, DJs Wed, Fri, Sat, see Facebook for what's on. There are plenty of other bars on this strip.

Entertainment

St Lucia Megaplex 8, *Allan Bousquet Hwy, T437 0480, www.caribbeancinemas.com.* An 8-screen multiplex cinema with snack bar. To get here turn off the Castries–Gros Islet Hwy at the roundabout just north of Choc Bay. Movie details are on the website.
Treasure Bay Casino, *Baywalk Shopping Mall, T758-459 2901, www.treasurebay stlucia.com. Daily 1100-0100.* St Lucia's 1st, and so far only, casino, located upstairs in the mall, has slot machines, and roulette, blackjack and poker tables. It's all very casual and there's no dress code, and no passport or ID is needed for entry.

Festivals

Last week in Jan Nobel Laureate Week, T758-485 3060, see Facebook. Lectures and events celebrating the island's 2 Nobel prize winners (Sir Arthur Lewis and Sir Derek Walcott). They were both born on 23 Jan.
22 Feb Independence Day. Celebrated extensively, including a large exhibition lasting several days from the various ministries, business and industry, and NGOs,

such as the National Trust. There are also sporting events, serious discussions and musical programmes.

May St Lucia Jazz & Arts Festival, T758-451 8566, www.stlucia.org/jazzfestival. Now an internationally recognized event drawing large crowds every year, most concerts are open-air and take place in the evening, although fringe events are held anywhere, anytime, with local bands playing in Castries at lunchtime. As well as jazz, played by international stars, you can hear Latin, salsa, soca and zouk, steel drums or reggae.

29 Jun St Peter's Day is celebrated as the **Fisherman's Feast**, a thanksgiving celebration by the islands Fishermen. An early morning Mass is followed by the ceremonial blessing of the elabotately decorated boats.

Jul Carnival, www.stluciancarnival.com. A weekend in mid-Jul is the high point of several weeks of Carnival celebrations. There are street processions of colourful bands and costumed revellers as well as lots of music, dancing and drinking. Everything goes on for hours, great stamina is required to keep going. On the Sat are the calypso finals, on Sun the King and Queen of the band followed by J'ouvert at 0400 until 0800 or 0900. On Mon and Tue the official parades of the bands take place. Most official activities take place at the Darren Sammy National Cricket Stadium but warming-up parties and concerts are held all over the place.

End Aug St Lucia Food and Rum Festival, www.stlucia.org/summerfestival/food-rum-festival. A week-long event show-casing top-notch gourmet food, wine and rum from around the Caribbean, with tastings and full meals at the best restaurants accompanied by musical and other artistic performances.

30 Aug Feast of the Rose of Lima (Fét La Wòz). Members of the Flower Society gather in various public places around the island to dance and sing in costume.

17 Oct La Marguerite, a festival to rival the Rose with a church service, parade with participants dressed as kings and queens,

officers and members of the court, then lots of music, food and drink. Both festivals have their origins in the secret 'flower' societies formed by slaves under French and British colonial rule. **Jounen Kwéyòl Entenasyonnal** (International Creole Day), on the last Sun of Oct, although activities are held throughout the month. 4 or 5 rural communities are selected for the celebration. There is local food, craft, music and different cultural shows. Expect traffic jams everywhere as people visit venues across the island. A lot is in Kwéyòl/patois, but you will still have a good time and a chance to sample mouth-watering local food.

22 Nov St Cecilia's Day, the patron saint of musicians and church music is celebrated in Roman Catholic churches.

End Nov Atlantic Rally for Cruisers, www.worldcruising.com/arc. An annual transatlantic competition for cruising yachts, starting in Las Palmas, Gran Canaria in November and ending before Christmas in Rodney Bay. Covering 2700 nautical miles, over 200 boats of different shapes and sizes take part, culminating in parties in St Lucia.

Dec 13 St Lucy's Day used to be called **Discovery Day**, but as Columbus' log shows he was not in the area at that time, it was renamed. It is now known as **National Day** and is celebrated by the **Festival of Lights** in Castries, which marks the start of Christmas. There is the Parade of Lanterns in Castries, accompanied by Christmas songs and dance, followed by the turning on of the lights at the Derek Walcott Square and finally a fireworks display.

Shopping

Art and crafts

Bagshaw's, *La Toc Rd, just before La Toc Beach, T758-451 9249. Mon-Fri 0830-1700, Sat 0830-1600, Sun 1000-1300.* Sells clothing and table linens in colourful tropical patterns and the fabrics are silk-screened by hand in an adjacent workroom; phone ahead if you want to see a demonstration. There are also

Bagshaw boutiques at Pointe Seraphine and La Place Carenage.

Eudovic's Art Studio, *La Toc Rd, Goodlands, follow the road down from the military complex at Morne Fortuné heading south, T758-452 2747, www.eudovicart.com. Mon-Fri 0730-1630, Sat-Sun 0730-1500.* Studio and gallery selling local handicrafts and beautiful large wood carvings made from local hardwoods such as mahogany, teak and red and white cedar, as well as the roots from various trees. The founder Vincent Joseph Eudovic established the gallery in 1975 and studied woodcarving in both Trinidad and Nigeria. Drinks, including rum punch, are available.

Vendor's Arcade, *John Compton Hwy, Castries. Daily 0700-1800.* Catering for cruise ship passengers, this arcade sells T-shirts, crafts, spices, basketwork and St Lucia's famous hot pepper sauce.

Zaka, *26 Bay St, Soufrière, T 758-457 1504, www.zaka-art.com. Mon-Sat 0830-1700, Sun 0900-1300.* Brightly coloured shop where the walls are covered with artist Zaka's beautiful hand-painted 'totems and masks' made from driftwood, branches, and other environmentally friendly wood sources. There's also a café selling coffee grown on the family's farm, smoothies made from local fruits and light meals, including omelettes for breakfast and fishcakes for lunch.

Food

There are plenty of supermarkets and small convenience stores but as nearly all food is imported, it is generally expensive.

Castries Central Market, *John Compton Hwy. Mon-Sat 0700-1800.* The best place to buy your fruit and veg if you are self-catering and is a colourful place to visit (see page 34). Also look out for roadside stalls around the island, which are good places to pick up bananas, coconuts and plantains, etc, and there are several village fish markets where you can get fish cleaned and filleted by the vendors.

Massy Stores Supermarket, *www.massy storeslu.com.* The biggest of the chain supermarkets (they are Caribbean-wide), always well stocked and have bakeries, deli counters and pharmacies. The larger branches are in Castries, off the Castries–Gros Islet Hwy near Choc Beach and at Baywalk Shopping Mall in Rodney Bay. Mon-Thu 0800-2000, Fri-Sat 0800-2100, Sun 0900-1400.

Shopping malls

Baywalk Shopping Mall, *Rodney Bay village, T758-452 6666, www.baywalkslu.com. Mon-Thu 0900-1900, Fri-Sat 0900-2000, Sun 0900-1400.* The biggest mall on the island with over 60 shops (many of them duty-free), several restaurants, banks and ATMs, a branch of **Massy Stores Supermarket** and a multi-storey car park.

Gablewoods Shopping Mall, *Castries–Gros Islet Hwy at Choc, T758-453 7752. Mon-Fri 0900-1800, Sat-Sun 0900-1400.* Has a selection of boutiques, gift shops, book shop, post office, pharmacy, deli, and open-air eating places.

JQ Rodney Bay Mall, *Rodney Bay village, T758-458 0700, www.shopjqmall.com. Mon-Thu 0900-2100, Fri-Sat 0900-2000, Sun 1000-1400.* Less glitzy than Baywalk opposite, with clothing shops, souvenir and craft shops, pharmacy, bank, post office, and fast-food outlets.

La Place Carenage, *Jeremie St, Castries, T758-453 2451, www.carenagemall.com. Daily 0900-2000.* Duty-free shopping mall right by the cruise ships at Queen Elizabeth II Dock with jewellers, arts and crafts, clothing, places to eat, tour desk, taxi service, tourist information and car rental desks.

Pointe Seraphine Shopping Centre, *at the St Lucia Cruise Ship Terminal, T758-457 3425, www.pointeseraphine.lc. Mon-Fri 0900-1630, Sat 0900-1400, Sun 0900-1400 if there's a cruise ship in port.* Another duty-free shopping centre with similar shops and services across the harbour from La Place Carenage and the two are linked by ferry every 10 mins when there are cruise ships in port; otherwise there are water taxis. Remember even if you haven't arrived in St Lucia on a cruise ship, you can still buy at duty-free shops if you have your passport and airline ticket.

What to do

Don't forget to add 10% VAT to prices.

Cricket

Darren Sammy National Cricket Stadium, *Beausejour, 2.5 km east of Gros Islet, T758-457 8834*. The island's main cricket venue was formerly called the Beausejour Stadium but was renamed in 2016 after St Lucian Darren Sammy who captained the West Indies side when it won the 2016 ICC World Twenty20 in India. Since its opening in 2002, it has hosted several Test and international matches including the 2007 World Cup. Benefiting from state-of-the-art technology, the 15,000-seater stadium has hospitality suites, a media centre and players' pavilion, and was the first ground in the West Indies to install floodlighting. For information on fixtures, check the website of the **West Indies Cricket Board** (www.windiescricket.com).

Cycling

Adventure Tours St Lucia, *T758-458 0908, www.adventuretoursstlucia.com. Mon-Sat 0800-1600.* Offers mountain biking and hiking (among other activities) at the Treetop Adventure Park and Errard Falls on the east coast near Dennery (see page 46 for more details).
Bike St Lucia, *on Anse Mamin beach accessible by foot or boat from Anse Chastanet Resort (see page 53), T758-459 7755, www.bikestlucia.com. Mon-Sat 0800-1530.* On the steep hill behind the beach here, 13 km of trails have been laid out for mountain biking in the forest. The trails are guided and are from novice level to the advanced and very steep **Tinker's Trail**, which has numerous switchbacks, ledges and drop-offs along the way; the view from the top at over 300 m is worth the effort. For day visitors (not staying in the resort), there are mesh bags secured at the bike facility on the beach to store items

such as towels or a change of clothes. Prices start from US$65 for 2½ hrs but there are other packages that include transport and lunch; book in advance.

Diving

For dive locations, see Planning, page 16. The best snorkelling and diving in St Lucia is in the protected marine reserve around Soufrière and the Pitons between Anse Jambon, north of Anse Chastanet, and Anse L'Ivrogne to the south. This area is administered by the **Sourfrière Marine Management Area** (SMMA; www.smma. org.lc) and there is an extra fee of US$5 daily for diving and US$1 for snorkelling – payable to the operators or at **Scuba St Lucia** (see below). Expect to pay in the region of US$90 for a single dive, US$120 for 2 dives in the same day, US$100 for a night dive, US$120 for a PADI Discover Scuba course, and US$500 for a PADI Open Water course. Dive companies charge 10% VAT on top of their quoted rates and often 10% service.

In the event of a diving emergency, there is a hyperbaric chamber at Tapion Private Hospital in Castries.
Dive Fair Helen, *Castries, T758-451 7716, www.divefairhelen.com.*
Dive St Lucia, *Rodney Bay Marina, T758-451 3483, www.divesaintlucia.com.*
Scuba St Lucia, *Anse Chastanet Resort, Soufrière, T758-459 7755, www.scuba stlucia.com.*
Scuba Steve's Diving, *Rodney Bay Marina, T758-450 9433, www.scubastevesdiving.com.*

Fishing

The waters off the coast of St Lucia offer ideal fishing for barracuda, blue marlin, yellowfin tuna, white marlin, sailfish, wahoo and dolphin fish (mahi mahi). Fishing is particularly good Feb-May when most of these game fish are in season (Aug-Dec for blue marlin). Charter boats for tag-and-release game fishing can be organized and trips include all tackle and bait, drinks and snacks, lunch on the full-day trips, and some will make a stop on a beach for a swim. Costs vary from around US$450 for a 4-hr charter for 4 people to US$2000 for an 8-hr charter for 8 people.

Captain Mike's, *Castries, T758-452 7044, www.captmikes.com.*

Exodus Boat Charters, *Rodney Bay Marina, T758-714 7940, www.exodusstlucia.com.*

Hackshaw's Boat Charters, *Castries, T758-453 0553, www.hackshaws.com.*

Mystic Man Tours, *Soufrière T758-459 7783, www.mysticmantours.com.*

St Lucia Fishing, *Rodney Bay Marina, T758-724 7922, www.stluciafishing.com.*

Golf

St Lucia Golf Club, *Cap Estate, T758-450 8523, www.stluciagolf.com.* A 6685-yd, par-71, 18-hole golf course and driving range, green fees US$95-105 for 9 holes, US$120-145 for 18 holes, depending on the time of year, golf carts mandatory. Club rental, Pro Shop, restaurant and group packages.

Kayaking

DFH Kayaking, *on the beach at Marigot Bay, T758-451 7716, www.dfhkayaking.com.* Offers guided kayaking tours Mon-Sat, half or full day, novice to advanced level. Tour examples are **Marigot Bay to Roseau River** (US$75), a combination of coastal, mangrove and river kayaking with snorkelling afterwards; **Marigot Bay to Pigeon Island** (US$155), which includes snorkelling and beach stops at Rodney Bay and Rat Island; **Marigot Bay to Anse Cochon** (US$132); and **Marigot Bay to Soufrière** (US$165), which includes a bit of everything (river, coastal, sea and mangrove kayaking, snorkelling, beach and lunch).

Kayak St Lucia, *Anse Chastenet Resort, Soufrière, T758-459 0000, www.kayakstlucia. com.* They can organize a number of options, from a beginner's course to kayak tours to Soufrière and the Pitons or along Anse Mamin with a beach picnic, sunset kayaking or a birdwatching kayak tour early in the morning to see nesting seabirds. If you're not staying at the resort, you'll need to book ahead.

Sailing

See also Planning your trip, page 19. The standard cruise ship excursion is a boat ride from Castries down the west coast; first sailing into Marigot Bay and then on to Soufrière to see the Pitons from the sea, before alighting at the town's jetty to go to the Sulphur Springs, Diamond Falls Botanical Gardens and Mineral Baths or one of the other sites; or go to Anse Chastanet for snorkelling and beach time, before the afternoon cruise back up the coast. A variety of craft is used depending on group size, from speedboats and catamarans to yachts and even a replica pirate ship. If you are already on the island, this excursion can be organized independently and expect to pay from US$95-140, children (under 12) half price, depending on what vessel is used, how many people, and whether you are departing from Castries, Rodney Bay or even Soufrière itself and going in the opposite direction. Usually this includes lunch, drinks and snorkelling gear. Groups can organize a charter with any of the boat charter companies already mentioned (see Fishing, above), or your hotel will be able to recommend an operator (each tends to go on certain days of the week). Alternatively, you can explore the company websites below for the options. Sailing time from Castries to Soufrière is about 2 hrs and from Rodney Bay to Soufrière about 2½-3 hrs. Other possibilities include 2- to 3-hr sunset cruises from the point where the boats are based with snacks and drinks from US$75, children (under 12) US$37.50; and day trips to Martinique with a barbecue lunch from US$165, children (under 12) US$135.

Adventure Tours St Lucia, *Rodney Bay village, T758-452 0808, www.adventure toursstlucia.com.*

Carnival Sailing, *Castries, T758-452 5586, www.carnivalsailing.com.*

Discover Soufrière, *St Lucia, Soufrière, T758-458 0123, www.discoversoufriere.com.*

Endless Summer Cruises, *at the jetty at the Landings Resort & Spa on Pigeon*

*Island Causeway, T758-450 8651, www.
stluciaboattours.com.*
Mystic Man Tours, *Soufrière, T758-459 7783,
www.mysticmantours.com.*
Sea Spray Cruises, *Rodney Bay Marina,
T758-458 0123, www.seaspraycruises.com.*

Segway tours
St Lucia Segway Tours, *Reduit Beach Av,
Rodney Bay village, T758-724 8300, www.
lucianstyle.com.* Offers very popular
adventures for all the family from 2-7 hrs
around Rodney Bay and Pigeon Island from
US$94; explore the website for the options.
You get a bit of training and practice to make
sure you can handle your Segway and then
you set off on trails with a guide who points
out plants and wildlife and explains and a bit
of the history of the area.

Tour operators
An example of a full-day road tour from
Rodney Bay or Castries (for cruise ship
passengers) would perhaps include Castries
and Morne Fortuné, Marigot Bay, a stop
in Anse La Raye, Soufrière and a couple
of sights around there, maybe a bit of
snorkelling, before the journey back. This
might appeal if you do not want to hire a
car or haven't got the time or inclination to
use public transport, and the convenience is
that you will be picked up at your hotel; but
bear in mind sometimes these types of tours
will feel rushed. For a 5- to 6-hr tour expect
to pay in the region of US$75-100, children
(under 12) half price. Other options are
rainforest hiking or across to the east coast.
Hotels will recommend a tour operator or
explore the websites below. Another option
is that most tours are by small 8- to 12-seater
minibus, so a group/family can charter a
vehicle and guide and make up their own
itinerary. Finally, you could find a taxi driver
you like, or get a hotel to recommend one
and set off on your own; the rate for 6-7 hrs
is from about US$200 split by 4 passengers.
Joe Knows St Lucia, *T758-450 3847,
www.joeknowsstlucia.com.*

Real St Lucia Tours, *T758-717 8604,
www.realsaintluciatours.com.*
Simon Say's Tours, *T758-716 2583,
www.simonsaystoursaintlucia.com.*
Smarty St Lucia Tours, *T758-722 7620,
www.smartystluciatours.com.*
St Lucia Reps/Sunlink Tours, *T758-
452 8232, www.stluciareps.com.*
St Lucia Taxi & Tours, *T758-715 1881,
www.taxiandtoursstlucia.com.*

Whale and dolphin watching
Whales generally visit the waters around
St Lucia between Dec and Apr. Sperm and
short-finned pilot whales are the most
commonly seen, but humpbacks, Bryde's
whales and orcas are also occasionally
sighted. Bottlenose, spinner, and spotted
dolphins are present year-round. In
season, boat trips for whale and dolphin
watching are operated by the same charter
companies that operate fishing trips (see
above); expect to pay around US$60, children
(under 10) US$30, for a 3-hr trip.

Windsurfing and kitesurfing
Aquaholics, *Cas-en-Bas Beach, T758-726
0600, www.aquaholicsstlucia.com.* Offers
kitesurfing beginners' lessons from US$60
per hr plus multi-day courses.
Kitesurfing St Lucia, *Cas-en-Bas Beach,
T758-714 9589, www.kitesurfingstlucia.com.*
Beginners' lessons from US$60 per hr and
board and kite rental from US$35 per hr.
The Reef Kite & Surf, *next to The Reef Beach
Café, Anse de Sables Beach, Vieux Fort, T758-
454 3418, www.slucia.com/reef.* Windsurfing:
beginners' lessons from US$40 per hr and
equipment rental from US$60 for 4 hrs.
Kitesurfing: beginners' lessons from US$75
per hr and equipment rental from US$70
for 4 hrs. Multi-day and weekly options are
available too. The **Reef Beach Huts ($)** are
4 en suite double or twin rooms with fans
and mosquito nets in rustic wooden cabins
behind the café under the sea grape trees
that cater for wind- and kitesurfers that want
to stay a few days.

Transport

Air

See Finding your feet, page 31, for details of airports, and Getting there, for how to get to St Lucia by air. **St Lucia Helicopters**, T758-453 6950, www.stluciahelicopters. com, provides an air shuttle between the 2 airports – Hewanorra International Airport and George F Charles Airport – by helicopter, which takes about 10 mins, US$165 per person, or 15 mins, US$180 for a more scenic route around the Pitons and Soufrière. The helicopters can take a maximum of 6, but children under 2 can sit on parents' laps and fly for free, while children (2-12) get a 10% discount. They also operate 2 sightseeing tours: the **North Island Tour**, 10 mins, US$108, over Castries, Rodney Bay, Pigeon Island and Cap Estate; and the **South Island Tour**, 20 mins, US$176, over Castries, Marigot Bay, Soufrière and the Pitons; the latter being a highly recommended way of seeing the Pitons if you can afford it.

Bus

Buses are the most affordable local way of getting around and a great way to experience island life. Privately owned and operated 14-seater minivans with green M licence plates run individual routes between major communities, and this is the way many islanders get to town, school and work. There is no schedule, simply wave them down along the road and pay the fare directly to the driver. Within larger communities, there are specific bus stops, where buses will not depart until they are full and you may have to wait up to 30 mins. In most places, they stop running at around 1800, although around Castries, Rodney Bay and Gros Islet they run until about 2200. There are more buses in the morning than later on in the day, so don't leave it too late to make your return trip, and very few buses run on Sun. Fares range from US$0.80 for very short distances to US$5 to get from one end of the island to the other. The 4 major

bus routes are: **Vieux Fort–Soufrière (4F), Soufrière–Castries (3D); Castries–Vieux Fort (2H)** and **Castries– Rodney Bay/Gros Islet (1A)**. There are then of course many more sub-routes across the interior of the island. There isn't a central bus terminal in Castries. If you are travelling from Castries to Rodney Bay/Gros Islet, most buses (including Route 1A) are located on the eastern side of the Castries Central Market at the bottom of Darling Rd. For Soufrière and the southwest (including 3D), they depart from Hospital Rd on the south side of the river.

Car hire

See also Getting around, page 31. Drivers must be over 25 and those over 65 may require a medical certificate that shows that they are fit to drive. You must have a valid (photo) driving licence from your own country of residence and a credit card. A local driver's permit is required, US$22 valid for 3 months; the car hire companies will arrange this. Rates range from US$65 for a small car to US$110 for a minivan or SUV, with discounts for 3 days or more. Basic hire generally only includes statutory 3rd-party insurance; you are advised to take out the optional collision damage waiver premium at US$12-15 per day, as even the smallest accident can be very expensive. A 4WD is only necessary for access roads to certain hiking trails, otherwise a normal car is sufficient to get around the island. All companies will arrange pick-up/drop-off at the airports and hotels, and can arrange a drop-off at a different location for no extra fee. They will also provide a free road map of the island. Many offer GPS/Sat-Nav systems as well as baby and child booster seats for an extra fee.

There are dozens of car hire companies on St Lucia; recommended for more than 30 years' experience, good service and island-wide fleet of more than 100 vehicles is **Drive-A-Matic Car Rentals**, T758-458 0156, www.drivestlucia.com. They have desks at both Hewanorra International

Airport (1000-2300) and George F L Charles Airport (0630-2300).

Ferry

L'Express des Iles ferries (www.express-des-iles.com; see Getting there, page 132) operate from the ferry terminal on the south side of Castries' harbour, a short taxi ride from any of the hotels in and around the capital. Check timetables before planning a trip. L'Express des Iles agency in Castries is **Cox & Company Ltd**, Castries-Gros Islet Hwy, just north of the roundabout at Vigie, T758-456 5022/23/24, www.coxcoltd.com. Mon-Fri 0800-1800, Sat 0800-1300.

Taxi

Taxis are readily available and regulated and vehicle licence plates are designated by a blue TX. There are plenty of taxis at both airports, and any hotel and restaurant can phone for one. Rates, fixed and set by the government and taxi associations, are fairly high, although drivers will sometimes cut you a deal if you use them more than once. Most are knowledgeable and they make excellent guides for an island tour, so it's always handy to get their card and/or phone number if you find a driver you like. Sample taxi fares from Hewanorra International Airport are: to **George F L Charles Airport**, US$75; to **Soufrière**, US$75; and to **Rodney Bay**, US$85. From George F L Charles Airport: to **Rodney Bay** US$25; to **Soufrière**, US$90; to **Marigot Bay**, US$30, and from Rodney Bay to **Soufrière**, US$100.

Water taxi

There are some water taxi services along the west coast: in **Castries** they scoot across the harbour linking the 2 cruise ship berths and duty-free shopping centres; in **Rodney Bay**, they shuttle between Reduit Beach, the Rodney Bay Marina and Pigeon Island; at Marigot Bay, they link the main town with the resorts, restaurants and beach on the north side of the bay; and in **Soufrière** they go to **Anse Chastenet** (much easier than driving the awful road there). Rides are arranged directly with boat operators and can cost anything from US$3-15 per person depending on distance.

Martinique
Fort-de-France

Ferries leave Castries usually daily for Roseau with a stop in Fort-de-France. It is well worth spending a day or two here: the bars, restaurants and shops give a French atmosphere quite unlike that of other Caribbean cities.

Fort-de-France was originally built in the 17th century around Fort St-Louis. The settlement's first name was Fort-Royal and its inhabitants are still called Foyalais. The city of today consists of a crowded centre bordered by the waterfront and sprawling suburbs extending into the surrounding hills and plateaux. Traffic is very dense. Most people live in the suburbs and even the clubs are away from the old town centre, which is deserted at weekends after Saturday midday.

The port is to the east of the town centre, where the Baie du Carenage houses the naval base, yacht club, cargo ships and luxury cruise liners.

La Savane

Adjacent to Fort St-Louis (see below), La Savane (or La Savane des Esclaves), the old parade ground, is a 5-ha park planted with lawn, palms, tamarinds and other tropical trees and shrubs. The park contains statues of two famous figures: Pierre Belain d'Esnambuc, the leader of the first French settlers on Martinique, and Empress Joséphine (now beheaded by *Indépendentistes*), first wife of Napoléon Bonaparte, who was born on the island. Martiniquais vendors sell snacks, crafts and souvenirs, and there's a long strip of cafés, restaurants and bars along the park's western side.

Fort-de-France

Where to stay 🛏
Bayfront 1
Carib 2
Fort Savane 3
Hotel L'Impératrice 4

Karibea Le Squash 5

Restaurants 🍴
Chez Geneviève 2
La Cave à Vins 1

Le Foyaal 3
The Yellow 4

Bars & clubs 🎵
Garage Popular 5

Fort St-Louis

Open for 1-hr guided tours Tue-Sat 0900-1600, visitors must first check in at the Office de Tourisme on the corner of the La Savane at the junction of rue de la Liberté and blvd Alfassa, €8, children (at least 6 years old) €4. At least 2 tours per day are conducted in English.

The impressive 17th-century solid stone stronghold of Fort St-Louis towers over Fort-de-France and the city's namesake bay. Built in Vauban style by Jacques Dyel du Parquet, then lieutenant-general of Martinique during the Anglo-French rivalry for possession of the island, it dominates the waterfront; the ferry terminal is just east of the massive walls. It is still an active military base for the French Navy. Tours take in some of the underground rooms and tunnels and climb to the ramparts for a view over town.

Bibliothèque Schoelcher

Corner of rue Victor Sévère and rue de la Liberté, across the road from La Savane, T596-596-702667, Mon 1300-1730, Tue-Fri 0830-1730, Sat 0830-1200.

Schoelcher (1804-1893), who devoted his life to the abolition of slavery, gave much of his library to Martinique, but most was burned in a fire of the town centre in 1890. The building to house the collection was commissioned, but not built, before the fire. It was designed by Henry Picq, a French architect married to a woman from Martinique. The Eiffel engineering company constructed it in iron, shipped it to the island and it opened in 1893. On the outside you can see the names of freedom campaigners, including John Brown, of the USA, William Wilberforce, of the UK, and Toussaint Louverture, of Haiti. Today it still functions as a library and regularly holds exhibitions.

Cathedral of St-Louis

In the centre of town, in the Square of Seigneur Romero, rue Schoelcher, there is a second chance to see the architecture of Henri Picq with the cathedral, which towers above the Fort-de-France skyline. This is the seventh to have been erected on the site after fires and hurricanes destroyed previous structures. This one was completed in 1895 and the reason for its longevity is an iron frame and reinforced concrete, and it is in romanesque-byzantine style with 19 stained-glass windows, a fine organ and a wrought-iron balustrade.

Musée Régional d'Histoire et d'Ethnographie de la Martinique

10 blvd Générale de Gaulle, opposite Atrium Theatre, T596-596-728187, Mon, Wed-Fri 0830-1700, Tue 1400-1700, Sat 0830-1230, €3, children €1.

In a beautiful Creole villa dating back to 1887 with balconies and fretwork, which was fortunate to escape the great fire that ravaged the capital in 1890, this museum is strong on the customs and traditions of the people of Martinique during the 19th century. On display are furniture, paintings, jewellery and costumes including typical West Indian dresses made with satin and madras cotton, known as *douillettes*. The ground floor puts on temporary exhibitions, and has some cases displaying local stone carvings and ceramics.

Parc Floral et Culturel

Place José Marti, T596-596-713396, Mon-Thu 0900-1600, Fri 0900-1200, €2, children €1.

The Parc Floral et Culturel, which includes the **Galerie de Géologie et de Botanique** and the **Exotarium** (aquarium) is a shady park containing two galleries, one of which concentrates on the geology of the island, the other on the flora, and mid-19th-century wooden barracks now housing workshops for local artisans. Almost 2800 species of plant have been identified in Martinique and the Parc Floral has a very good selection.

Markets

The **fish market** is by the Madame River, facing the Place José Martí, where fishermen unload from their small boats or *gommiers*. Close by, on rue Isambert, is **Le Grand Marché Couvert**, or Covered Market, the third of Henri Picq's metal creations (1901) and one of several markets selling fruit, vegetables and flowers as well as exotic spices and handicrafts. At the restaurants upstairs, you can sample some of the local Creole cuisine. The markets hum with activity from 0500 to sunset, but are best on Friday and Saturday.

Listings Fort-de-France *map page 83.*

Where to stay

It is difficult to find anywhere to stay for less than about €75 in the city. Cheaper rooms can be found in the suburbs or further afield, but astronomical taxi fares from the ferry terminal make them uneconomical. If you are only staying a night or 2 it is best to get a room within walking distance of the ferry and of all the sights, restaurants, shops and bars.

$$$-$$ Fort Savane
5 rue de la Liberté, T596-596-807575, www.fortsavane.fr.
Smart, modern and comfortable, designed for business and leisure travellers with the perfect location in walking distance of the ferry terminal and all other transport and places of interest. Staff are friendly and helpful, some speak English. 20 rooms with minibar fridge and coffee machine and 8 studios with kitchenettes, all with Wi-Fi and TV and there's a pleasant courtyard garden. Right in the centre of things but double windows overlooking La Savane keep out any noise.

$$$-$$ Karibea Le Squash
3 blvd de la Marne, T596-596-728080, www.karibea.com.
105 modern rooms in 2 buildings with sea view, a little impersonal with a concrete ambience and bathrooms a bit shabby but breakfast is good and there's an outdoor pool, gardens and sea views. A 20-min walk uphill from town centre, so best to get a taxi on arrival.

$$ Bayfront
3 rue de la Liberté, T596-596-555555.
Overlooking La Savane and the waterfront and within walking distance of the ferry, the 13 simply furnished rooms are a good size, some are triples and quads. It can be noisy at night in that area, there's tight security and you have to ring the bell to leave or enter. Café/bar/patisserie on the ground floor.

$$ Hotel L'Impératrice
15 rue de la Liberté, T596-596-630682, www.limperatricehotel.fr.
Overlooking La Savane and convenient for the ferry, shops and restaurants, this is one of the best options and is very well priced. Some of the decor and furnishings are apparently unchanged since it was built in 1957 which leads to a charming quirkiness. The largest rooms have balconies with a view over the harbour, the smallest and cheapest rooms look on to an inner courtyard. There's a restaurant and terrace café.

$$-$ Carib
9 rue Redoute du Matouba, T596-596-601985, www.carib-hotel.com.
In the heart of the older part of town, a 3-min walk from the ferry terminal, 16 simple, but neat, spotless and economical rooms with fridge, Wi-Fi and a/c, the larger ones have balconies with views of the La Savane, no breakfast/restaurant, but several bistros, cafés and restaurants close by and a supermarket with late opening hours 20 m away, friendly, English-speaking staff.

Restaurants

During the daytime, there are good snack bars and cafés in the centre of Fort-de-France. In the evening head for **blvd Chevalier de Ste-Marthe** next to La Savane. Here, vans and caravans serve delicious meals to take away, or to eat at tables under canvas awnings accompanied by loud zouk music. The scene is bustling and lively, in contrast to the rest of the city at night-time, and the air is filled with wonderful aromas. Try lambis (conch) in a sandwich or on a *brochette* (like a kebab) with rice and salad, paella and *Colombo* are good buys and the crêpes whether sweet or savoury are delicious.

$$$ La Cave à Vins
124 rue Victor Hugo, T596-596-703302.
Tue-Sat 1200-1400, 1930-2130.
Smart with white table linen, offering traditional French (duck, lamb, terrines, rillettes) with a local twist, combining ingredients such as foie gras with fried banana. Extensive wine list as the name suggests, but also malt whiskies. The 2 dining rooms are behind a small shop selling French food items, chocolates and fine wine.

$$$-$$ The Yellow
51 rue Victor Hugo, 1st floor, T596-596-750359, see Facebook. Mon-Fri 1200-1500, Mon-Sat 1900-2300.
The decor is yellow, as you'd expect, and this modern restaurant is a good place to try typical Martinique cuisine, consisting largely of fish, rice, vegetables and mashed plantains, as well as seafood specialities such as fish chowder, and French options such as duck or steak. There is a set lunch menu, monthly special theme nights and tasty cocktails too.

$$-$ Chez Geneviève
Le Grand Marché Couvert, T596-596-719309. Mon-Sat 0700-1500.
Upstairs, above the market, overlooking shoppers, are small kiosks selling Créole *menu du jour* (set menu), and Chez Geneviève is considered the best – always heaving; get there early to get a seat at lunchtime. For about €17 you get rum punch (bottle on the table, self-service), starter, main course, wine or beer, dessert or coffee. Food is very tasty and for the main course you can expect the likes of fish, octopus or chicken, accompanied by rice, red beans, yams and green bananas.

$$-$ Le Foyaal
On the corner of rues Desproges and Schoelcher, T596-596-630038, see Facebook. Daily 0700-0130.
On the waterfront, downstairs, separated from the sea by a car park, a busy and popular brasserie with indoor and outdoor tables, lime green, modern decor, always full at lunchtime, serving salads, savoury crêpes and sandwiches as well as full meals such as grilled seafood and burgers. Some waiting staff speak English.

Bars and clubs

Check the local newspaper, *France-Antilles*, for what's on. There are several bars (piano bar or café théâtre) where you can listen to various types of music, some have karaoke or cabaret certain nights. In Fort-de-France, the best place to find nightlife is the **blvd Allègre** on the bank of the Madame River, where there are lots of places to choose for late-night music and dancing.

Garage Popular
121 rue Lamartine, T596-596-798676, see Facebook. Mon 1200-2300, Tue-Thu 1200-2400, Fri 1200-0200, Sat1800-0200.
Simple fare like pizzas and sandwiches and affordable drinks are the norm at Garage Popular, an often-crowded car-themed restaurant and pub, that hosts karaoke nights, themed parties, big-screen sports (mainly football), etc.

Dominica

With a towering interior covered in dense rainforest, volcanic hills, high-drop waterfalls, thermal springs and a boiling lake, Dominica (pronounced Domineeca) is known as the 'Nature Island' of the Caribbean. It's an exciting island for hikers, whether intent on gentle rambles or arduous treks along sections of the Waitukubuli National Trail, which curls for 115 miles (185 km) over the island. It is also a highly regarded diving destination, with a good marine reserve system, and for much of the year you can see whales and dolphins offshore. It's the only place in the Caribbean where Caribs have survived and they still retain many of their traditions, such as canoe carving. The island's culture and language are an amalgam of the native and immigrant peoples: Carib, French, English and African.

The island is mountainous with very little flat terrain; most settlements hug the coast, usually where the many rivers – 365 in total – reach the sea. It is almost twice the size of Barbados, but has very few beaches and, because of this, hotels around the island are small, intimate and low key. Further development is deterred by the lack of a big international airport and direct long-haul flights, and Dominica only gets modest attention from the cruise-ship circuit. But sandwiched between Guadeloupe and Martinique, it is accessible by ferry and is just a 30-minute flight south of Antigua.

Essential Dominica

Finding your feet

Douglas-Charles Airport (DOM; T767-445 7109), formerly known as Melville Hall Airport, is located on the northeast coast of Dominica just northwest of Marigot. It is very small with a check-in hall on one side with a snack bar, and a lounge with duty-free kiosk airside; there is no ATM or bank. Taxis (minivans) meet the flights, and on arrival it is usual to share a vehicle with other people on the plane – there are after all only two directions to go – so expect to pay in the region of US$35 per person to get to Roseau (two hours), and US$28 to Portsmouth (one hour); otherwise it will cost nearer US$200 to hire a vehicle for exclusive use. Note: the roads are very twisty and the drivers can drive fast, so anti-sickness remedies are advised. It is possible to walk along the airport access road on to the main road and hail down a public minivan which will be cheaper, but they are infrequent and you may have to wait on the side of the

road for a long time. If you are arriving on L'Express des Iles ferry, the terminal is on Dame Eugenia Charles Blvd in central Roseau and an easy walk into town.

Getting around

Minivans and taxis will take you from Roseau all over the island, but bear in mind few vehicles run on a Saturday afternoon and none run on a Sunday. If hiring a car you need to have a bit of confidence about driving and, at the very least, a high-clearance vehicle is required as the around-the-island roads are twisty and steep in places and many of the access roads to the hiking trails require a 4WD. All companies will arrange pick-up/drop-off at the airport, L'Express des Iles ferry terminal and hotels, and can arrange a drop-off at a different location for no extra fee. If you don't want to drive yourself, there are tours to anywhere you might want to go and guides can always be arranged.

Weather Roseau

January	February	March	April	May	June
29°C 22°C 95mm	29°C 22°C 69mm	30°C 22°C 60mm	30°C 23°C 74mm	31°C 24°C 88mm	31°C 25°C 131mm

July	August	September	October	November	December
31°C 24°C 171mm	31°C 24°C 219mm	32°C 24°C 200mm	31°C 23°C 250mm	30°C 23°C 222mm	30°C 22°C 138mm

Roseau, pronounced 'roze-o', St Lucia's capital and main town (population 16,000), is squeezed onto a small area of flat land between the Caribbean Sea and the mountains, and is small, ramshackle and friendly, with a surprising number of pretty old buildings still intact. The houses look a bit tatty with rusting tin roofs and a general lack of paint through weather damage, but there is still some attractive gingerbread fretwork in the traditional style on Castle Street and others. The centre of Roseau is compact enough to walk around, but to get to outlying attractions in the Roseau Valley you can drive, catch a bus (minivan) or a taxi.

Old Market area and waterfront

Off King George V Street, the **Old Market** (daily 1000-1600), also known as **Old Market Plaza** and **Dawbiney Market Square**, has been a thriving hub of activity and trade in Roseau since the French and British colonial times; it was also the site of the slave market. The old, red market cross has been retained, with 'keep the pavement dry' picked out in white paint. Today it's a cobblestoned pedestrian area, with vendors selling tropical fruit, spices, handicrafts and souvenirs for the benefit of cruise passengers (the Roseau Cruise Ship Berth is just a short walk away).

Between the market and the waterfront is the old post office dating to 1810, which now houses the **Dominica Museum** ⓘ *Dame Mary Eugenia Charles Blvd, T767-448 2401, Mon-Fri 0900-1600, Sat 0900-1200, US$3*, which is well worth a visit and takes about 40-60 minutes to look around, although some of the exhibits are in need of a little TLC. There is a tourist information desk for Discover Dominica on the ground floor and the museum is on the second floor where there are good views from the balcony. The museum contains a small display on the geological origins of the island, the first inhabitants, colonization, slavery and emancipation. It includes old photographs and portraits of past rulers, specimens of birds and fish, colonial agricultural items and indigenous cultural articles including the *pwi pwi*, a miniature form of raft, a replica of a Carib hut and Arawak pottery and tools.

The sea wall was completed in 1993 and has greatly improved the waterfront area between L'Express des Iles ferry jetty and Victoria Street. It was once (and usually still is) called Bay Front, but its official name is Dame Eugenia Charles Blvd after the former Prime Minister (1980-1995). A promenade with trees and benches, parking bays and the T-shaped Roseau Cruise Ship Berth take up most of the space; in the winter season from about October to mid-April ships tower above the town and tourists pour forth. One of the historic buildings to look out for is the Caribbean's last-standing Barracoon just north of the General Post Office and opposite L'Express des Iles ferry. From the mid-18th century it was a holding centre for recently arrived slaves waiting to be auctioned until the abolition of the trade in 1807. Today with its baby-blue enclosed balcony on the second floor, it is the home of the Roseau City Council and a court house.

Roseau Market or the **New Market** ⓘ *at the north end of Dame Mary Eugenia*

> **Tip...**
> Roseau (New) Market is especially lively and colourful on Saturday mornings from about 0600-1000, and to a lesser extent Friday afternoons from 1500-1800, when it is full of Roseau residents doing their weekly shop.

Dominica

Guadeloupe Channel

Cape Melville
Capuchin
Carib Point
Pennville
Northern Link Road
Cold Soufrière ▲
Autrou Bay
Toucari Bay
Toucari ⑬
Morne aux Diables (861m)
Vieille Case
Anse de Mai
⑩ Thibaud
Hampstead Beach
Hodges Bay Beach
Pointe Baptiste Beach
Douglas Bay
Fort Shirley
Cabrits National Park
Hampstead ⑨
⑰ ㉒ Turtle Beach
Point Dubique
Calibishie ④
Purple Beach ⑦
Portsmouth ⑪
Dos D'Âne
Woodford Hill
Larieu
Crompton Point
Picard Beach
Glanvillia
⑲
Indian River
Wesley
Londonderry Bay
Prince Rupert Bay
Secret Beach
Edward Oliver Leblanc Hwy
Melville Hall
Mango Hole Bay
Pte Augustine
Anse Mulâtre
Northern Forest Reserve ♦
Douglas-Charles Airport ✈
Marigot
⑮
Pagua Bay
Dublanc
Syndicate Nature Trail
Morne Diablotin National Park
Morne Diablotin (1447m) ▲
Hatton Garden
Colihaut
Salybia
Isulukati Waterfall
Kalinago Barana Autê
Crayfish River
Coulibistrie
Carib Territory ♦
Horse Back Ridge
Jenny Point
Sineku
L'Escalier Tête-Chien
Salisbury
⑳
Jacko Flats ④
Penrice Falls ⧩
Bells
Central Forest Reserve ♦
Castle Bruce
㉗ ①
Mero ⑤
Mero Beach ②
St Joseph
Layou River
Dr Nicholas Liverpool (Transinsular) Highway ⑲
Emerald Pool
Grand Marigot Bay
Layou
Mourne Couronne ▲
Waitukubuli National Trail Headquarters ■
Petite Soufrière
Tarou Pt or Rodney's Rock
Layou Valley
Salton Waterfalls ⧩
Mahaut ⑧
Pont Cassé
Morne Trois Pitons (1424m) ▲
Rosalie
② ⑱
Rosalie Bay
Massacre
Canefield Airport ✈
Canefield
Sylvania
Cochrane
Middleham Boeri Falls ⧩
Freshwater Lake
Morne Trois Pitons National Park
Morne Macaque (1479m) ▲
La Plaine ③
Papillote Tropical Gardens ■
Laudat ⑯
Titou Gorge
Boiling Lake
Sari-Sari Waterfall
Goodwill
Woodbridge Bay ⛵
⑨
Trafalgar ③ ⑥
Trafalgar Falls ⧩
Screw's Sulphur Spa ■
Roseau
①
Wotten Waven
Valley of Desolation
Victoria Falls ⧩
Delices
Pointe Daniel
Castle Comfort
Giraudel
Morne Anglais ▲
Savane Mahaut ⑫
Pointe Mulâtre Bay
Pointe Michel
Anse Bateaux
Bellevue Chopin
Geneva Estate
Petite Savane
Loubiere
Pointe Guignard
Soufrière-Scotts Head Marine Reserve ♦
Tête Morne
Berekua
Grand Bay
Caribbean Sea
Scotts Head
Soufrière Bay
Soufrière Bubble Spa
Morne Rouge Estate
Petit Coulibri Estate
Pointe des Fous
Martinique Channel

N

2 km
2 miles

Where to stay
3 Rivers & Rosalie Forest
  Eco Lodge **2**
Anchorage Hotel
  & Dive Centre **1**
Beau Rive **27**
Calibishie Cove **22**
Castle Comfort Lodge **1**
The Champs **11**
Chez Ophelia Cottage
  Apartments **6**
Citrus Creek Plantation **3**
Cocoa Cottages **6**
Comfort Cottages **10**
Crescent Moon Cabins **8**
Escape **17**
Jacoway Inn **4**
Jungle Bay **12**
Manicou River Eco Resort **13**
Mango Island Lodges **5**
Pagua Bay House **15**
Papillote Wilderness
  Retreat **16**
Picard Beach Cottages **7**
Pointe Baptiste **17**
Rosalie Bay **18**
Sea Cliff Cottages **9**
Secret Bay **19**
Sisters Sea Lodge **7**
Sunset Bay Club
  Beach Hotel **20**
Sunrise Farm Cottages **14**
Tamarind Tree **21**
Veranda View **9**
Zen Gardens **19**

Restaurants 🔧
Islet View **1**
Karib Bay Beach Bar **2**
River Rock Café & Bar **3**
Riverstone Bar & Grill **4**

Waitukubuli National Trail ┈┈┈┈

Best places to stay
Cocoa Cottages, page 108
Secret Bay, page 109
Beau Rive, page 111
Pagua Bay House, page 112
Rosalie Bay Resort, page 112
Jungle Bay, page 112

Fact file
Location The most northerly of the
Windward Islands chain lying between
the Atlantic Ocean and the Caribbean
Sea, with Guadeloupe to the north and
Martinique to the south
Capital Roseau, 15° 25′ 0″ N,
60° 59′ 0″ W
Time zone Atlantic standard time
GMT -4 hrs, EST +1 hr
Telephone country code +767
Currency East Caribbean dollar, EC$

Charles Blvd and along the river, Mon-Sat 0600-1800, the largest on the island, sells fruit, vegetables, herbs, spices, meat and fish, and you can see wonderful displays of freshly cut flowers including white anthuriums, bird-of paradise and red ginger lilies. A fairly recent addition to the riverfront near the Roseau Market is the Chinese-built **Friendship Bridge** that opened in 2012. The four end points of the bridge are adorned with statues of Chinese guardian lions or 'Foo Dogs'. This is now the fourth bridge across the Roseau River, which has aided traffic congestion tremendously.

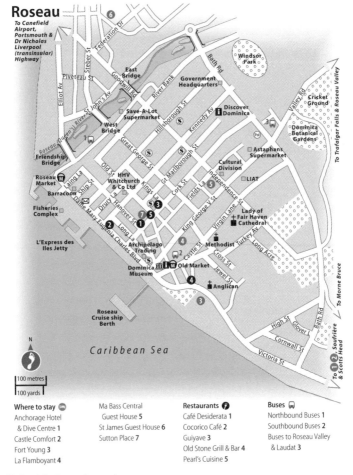

Where to stay 🛏
Anchorage Hotel
& Dive Centre **1**
Castle Comfort **2**
Fort Young **3**
La Flamboyant **4**

Ma Bass Central
Guest House **5**
St James Guest House **6**
Sutton Place **7**

Restaurants 🍴
Café Desiderata **1**
Cocorico Café **2**
Guiyave **3**
Old Stone Grill & Bar **4**
Pearl's Cuisine **5**

Buses 🚌
Northbound Buses **1**
Southbound Buses **2**
Buses to Roseau Valley
& Laudat **3**

BACKGROUND

Roseau

Built on the site of the ancient Carib village of Sairi, a small French settlement was established here in the 1690s, when French woodcutters from Martinique and Guadeloupe set up timber camps to supply the Caribbean French islands with wood and gradually they become permanent settlers. They named it from the French for river reeds, *roseaux*. After the island was ceded to Britain in 1763, the British initially chose Portsmouth in the north as their capital in the natural harbour of Prince Rupert Bay. But the area was surrounded by swamp and many settlers became sick from diseases such as malaria and yellow fever. Most of the settlers had moved south to Roseau by 1771, and the town was laid out and divided into neat, small blocks and fortifications and government structures were built. In the early years natural disasters and battles between the French and the British had their impact on the town's development: in 1781, French troops were blamed for a fire which almost destroyed the entire town; then in 1806, there was a devastating hurricane causing the Roseau River to burst its banks, destroying many homes and killing more than 130 people; and in 1880, a phreatic (steam) eruption in the Boiling Lake area covered Roseau in ash. In spite of all this, examples of French and the British architecture can still be seen, with verandas, porticos and fretwork, the roofs steeply pitched and the ends hipped, giving additional bracing against hurricanes. Today Roseau remains the main commercial hub of Dominica and is home to government offices, shops and the port and ferry terminal. A redevelopment programme over the last few years has improved access and made the waterfront area more attractive.

Our Lady of Fair Haven Cathedral
Virgin Lane, T767-448 2766.

This imposing Roman Catholic cathedral is a couple of blocks back from the waterfront and dates to 1916. The first church here was constructed in 1730 and was made of wood; over time it was enlarged and replaced with stones from the Roseau River, and was known as Église de Notre-Dame du Bon Port du Mouillage de Roseau. This survived until 1816 when it was destroyed by a hurricane. Today's cathedral is an impressive Gothic-Romanesque structure built of black volcanic stone with a stubby bell and clock tower and some fine stained-glass windows, one of which depicts the journeys of Christopher Columbus, and there are ornate Victorian murals behind the side altars. At the time of writing it was closed for roof repairs.

Dominica Botanical Gardens
Bath Rd, daily 0600-1900, free.

The main open space and recreational area for Roseau, these 40-acre (16-ha) botanical gardens are nestled below Morne Bruce Hill and are accessed from the waterfront area via King George V Street. They were established in 1891 as an offshoot for Kew Gardens in London as a way of encouraging the supply of properly propagated seedlings to the island farmers. Today they have a collection of plant species, including an orchid house, and several Jaco/Jacquot (*Amazona arausiaca*) and Sisserou (*Amazona imperialis*) parrots

ON THE ROAD

To beach or not to beach

The Caribbean side of Dominica gains or loses sand according to swells and storms but the black coral sandy areas are few and far between. A small one exists just off Scotts Head (favoured as a teaching ground for divers, snorkellers and canoeists, so sometimes crowded), but further north you must travel to Mero Beach or Castaways Beach. Macoucheri Bay and Coconut Beach near Portsmouth are probably the best areas for Caribbean bathing. For some really beautiful, unspoilt white sandy beaches, hire a 4WD and investigate the bays of the northeast coast. Turtle Beach, Pointe Baptiste (impressive red cliffs), Hampstead and Woodford Hill are all beautiful but the Atlantic coast is dangerous. Look at the sea and swim in the rivers is the safest advice. Very strong swimmers may be exhilarated by Titou Gorge, near Laudat, where the water flows powerfully through a narrow canyon and emerges by a hot mineral cascade. Several beaches, coves and rivers were used as locations for the filming of *Pirates of the Caribbean 2* and *3*; tours are available to some sites (see page 101).

can be seen in an aviary. Storms and hurricanes over the last 100 years have taken their toll on the gardens and wiped out the ornamental garden area. You can still see the old bus crushed by a baobab tree during Hurricane David in 1979. If you climb the 35 steps of **Jack's Walk** up Morne Bruce Hill you will get a panoramic view over Roseau, the harbour and the sea. The manicured, rolling lawns are popular for picnics and casual cricket matches, while just to the northwest of the gardens and also on Bath Road is the formal cricket ground and national sports stadium, Windsor Park, which opened in 2007 (see page 117).

★ South of Roseau to Soufrière and Scotts Head

In the far south of the island are the villages of Soufrière and Scotts Head, with a wonderful marine reserve offshore. Both are worth visiting for their stunning setting, backed by mountains and with brightly painted fishing boats on the shore. To get there follow Victoria Street (which becomes Loubiere Road) south out of Roseau and it's 11 km to Soufrière, where the bay of the same name lies within the rim of a sunken volcanic crater. In front of St Mark's Church sits **Bubble Beach Spa** ⓘ *T767-317 2526, daily 0900-1700, free but donation/tip expected*, which is an enterprise created by Dale Mitchell, a local man who has built a low makeshift wall of rocks forming a small shallow pool just on the shoreline. Here you can immerse yourself in the hot bubbly water from the geothermal springs(see below); it is very soothing, especially for any aches and pains you might have after hiking. Drinks are also for sale from a little hut, there are a few sun loungers on the beach, and on some days a local girl does massages. Do leave a good tip as he has put a lot of effort into the creation.

From Soufrière it's another 3.5 km to Scotts Head at the south of Soufrière Bay. It's a tiny village of about 700 people that shares its name with the Caribbean's only tied island (connected to land by a spit); the small peninsula with a rising

Tip...

There are not many facilities in these two villages, but if you need food and drink, Soufrière has a small grocery shop and Scotts Head a couple of snackettes.

headland extends westward as Dominica's southwest tip or 'toe'. There's a path across the narrow strip of rocks and sand and you can climb to the top of the little hill for outstanding views over the bay to Roseau, and across the channel to Martinique. It effectively divides two seas: the Atlantic lies to the south while the Caribbean is to the northwest. Scotts Head was named after Colonel George Scott who served in the British invasion force that captured Dominica from the French in 1761, and then became Lieutenant Governor of Dominica from 1764 to 1767. Scott oversaw the construction of a fort on Scotts Head, but the bulk of this fortification has collapsed down the cliff into the water, though some ruins remain, including a small cannon.

Tip...

Buses (minivans) to Soufrière and on to Scotts Head depart from behind the Old Market and cost US$2. Scotts Head is the end of the road where minivans turn around and head back to Roseau.

Offshore in the bay, the **Soufrière-Scotts Head Marine Reserve (SSMR)** ① *www. ssmrdominica.org, the nominal entry fee of US$2 is included in the price of excursions,* was ratified in 1998 to protect the spectacular features of the underwater Soufrière crater, which plummets to indeterminate depths as a lava chute. There are dramatic drop-offs and walls, huge pinnacles rising from the sea bed, and expansive coral reefs, all full of life. The sites include **Craters Edge**, **Scotts Head Pinnacles**, **L'Abym** and **Dangleben's**, but perhaps the most unusual is **Champagne Reef**, which gets its name from the millions of tiny bubbles that continuously emerge from the sea floor, giving the effect of diving, swimming or snorkelling through a glass of champagne. The bubbles are a product of the active fumaroles beneath the sea bed. Most dive companies operate in this area, including the dive shops at **Anchorage Hotel** and **Castle Comfort Lodge** just to the south of Roseau and **Nature Island Dive** in Soufrière (see page 118 for details). The current is quite light and the water generally very calm, so at some sites you can snorkel too.

Roseau Valley and Morne Trois Pitons National Park
Dominica's volcanic interior; great scenery and views across the island

The Morne Trois Pitons National Park covers 69 sq km in the south-central interior of the island above the 500-m contour line; it was established in 1975 and designated as a UNESCO World Heritage Site in 1997. It is named after its highest mountain, Morne Trois Pitons (1424 m), meaning mountain of three peaks, referring to the basaltic spike-like remains of the volcano. Evidence of volcanic activity is manifested in hot springs, sulphur emissions and the occasional small eruption. The main access to the park is from Laudat in the Roseau Valley for the challenging hike to the Boiling Lake. But if that's too much to undertake, there are other attractions in the Roseau Valley and alternative hikes into the park can be accessed from other parts of the island including Pont Cassé in the interior and Delices and La Plaine on the southeast coast.

★ Trafalgar Falls

Paillotte Rd, Trafalgar, daily 0800-1800, US$5 per person. To get there, drive out of town on Valley Rd alongside the Dominica Botanical Gardens to the village of Trafalgar and continue straight until you reach the end of the road (it is well signposted). You can also get there by bus (minivan) from the corner of Bath Rd and Valley Rd in Roseau.

On the edge of Morne Trois Pitons National Park, the Trafalgar Falls in the Roseau Valley, 8 km or a 20-minute drive from the capital, have been the island's most popular tourist site for many years and most cruise ship passengers get whisked straight here. Hot and cold water flow in two spectacular twin waterfalls which cascade over huge volcanic boulders in the pretty tract of forest. From the large parking area which has some vendor stalls and a visitor centre with toilets and a snack bar, it is a pleasant, 10- to 15-minute walk to a platform with views of both falls; 'Father', to the left, is about 85 m high, and 'Mother', to the right, is about 40 m high. The more intrepid can continue on to swim in the refreshing waters of the pool beneath Mother or hike up to the top of Father. But beyond the viewing platform a guide is recommended as there is a lot of scrambling over rocks and it can be difficult at times; agree the price before setting out.

Papillote Tropical Gardens

Paillotte Rd, Trafalgar, T767-448 2287, www.papillotegardens.com, see also Papillote Wilderness Retreat, page 108, day visit US$65 per person, maximum 6, advance booking essential.

There used to be some hot water pools for a dip along the trail to Trafalgar Falls, but unfortunately they were covered by a landslide during Tropical Storm Erika in 2015. However, there are a few hot sulphur pools and cold waterfall-fed pools for bathing at the **Papillote Wilderness Retreat** about 500 m before the entrance to Trafalgar Falls. They lie in 4 acres (1.6 ha) of tremendous tropical gardens full of indigenous flowering plants with more than 600 individual species and several dozen varieties of orchid, both native and imported (better than the Dominica Botanical Gardens in Roseau). There are hummingbirds and butterflies and trails criss-cross between the pools. This is all part of the experience for overnight guests, but the hotel also offers a daytime package which includes a guided garden walk, lunch at the **Papillote Rainforest Restaurant**, and time in the pools and at the small waterfall on the property. Alternatively, you can just go for a meal at the restaurant (see page 114, advance booking required).

Screw's Sulphur Spa

Wotten Waven Rd, T767-440 4478, www.screwsspa.com, Tue-Sun 1000-2200, U$10 per person for 1 hr.

Another attraction in this area east of Roseau is Screw's Sulphur Spa at Wotten Waven – and again it's often on cruise ship excursions. On the way towards Trafalgar Falls take the road that forks right and crosses the Roseau River and then follow it 3-4 km through forest and banana plantations. Each of the five pools here is a different temperature starting with the hottest at the top near the entrance (muscles relax instantly) and then you can gradually cool off in the warm and cold pools. It's a rustic locally owned spot (Screw is a friendly and charismatic Rasta) with no facilities other than a rudimentary changing area and toilets, but sometimes reggae music plays in the background and the bar is open with enough people around and you will be offered a plate of fruit afterwards; it's a relaxing spot and an hour here is easily combined with Trafalgar Falls and lunch at Papillote.

★ Boiling Lake

For a description of the hike, see www.avirtualdominica.com/the-boiling-lake.

One of the Morne Trois Pitons National Park's main attractions is the Boiling Lake (92°C), which, at about 60 m across, may be the largest of its kind in the world (the other contender is in New Zealand). It is actually a flooded fumarole. Rainwater and a couple of streams flow through the clay and pumice around the lake to hot lava below, where the grey-blue water is heated to boiling point and is enveloped in a cloud of vapour as though in a massive cauldron.

> **Tip...**
> Guides for the Boiling Lake can be found in Laudat or you can ask around in Roseau in the days before you go. Alternatively, you can organize it through your hotel. Expect to pay US$50-60 per person, although this can be negotiated down depending on the size of the group.

The lake is reached on a 13-km trek that takes about six hours from the village of Laudat, returning on the same path. This is probably Dominica's most challenging trail, but also one of the most rewarding and spectacular as you progress through different ecosystems, rising ever higher above the rest of the island with tremendous views. An experienced guide is essential as, although easy to follow, the trail is wet and slippery in places and can be treacherous, particularly when mist descends. Make sure you wear clothes you don't mind getting wet and muddy and wear good hiking boots or trainers. Hiking poles can be helpful to reduce stress on your knees. Bring drinks and snacks for energy.

Hikers usually start early in the morning from Laudat, stop for a break at **Breakfast River** (where water bottles can also be refilled) and then continue up **Morne Nicholls** (996 m) before descending into the **Valley of Desolation**, a volcanic area of steam vents, fumaroles, and boiling mud supported by the sharp, acrid smell of sulphur. There is usually another rest stop and time for a look around here, and then it's about another hour past sulphur springs and hot pools, until you finally reaching a peak overlooking the Boiling Lake for a lunch stop. On the return, a drink and a bathe in the **Titou Gorge** (where hot and cold streams mingle) is a soothing and relaxing way to end the hike.

Freshwater Lake and Boeri

One of the main sources of the Titou Gorge, Trafalgar Falls and Roseau River, volcanic Freshwater Lake lies within the Morne Trois Pitons National Park. It was dammed in the 1990s for a hydroelectric scheme, and as a result has a drivable road up from Laudat (about 3 km) and a car park. Several hiking trails begin in the area including the **Freshwater Lake Loop Trail**, a one- to two-hour circular trail around the lake, and the 45-minute trail to the island's highest lake, **Boeri**, which sits at an elevation of 854 m. Boeri is located in the crater of an old volcano between Morne Macaque (1170 m) to the south, the highest mountain in the Roseau Valley, and **Morne Trois Pitons** (1424 m) to the north. Note that the weather around these lakes is not usually great and there is often a a bracing breeze and a chilly and penetrating mist obscuring the mountains in the background (although some visitors like the surreal other-worldly character).

Middleham Falls

This tall 76-m waterfall in the rainforest on the northwest border of the Morne Tois Pitons National Park is accessible from a trail that turns north off the road just before Laudat. There is another trail from the Cochrane side, although the signs are not clear and the one from Laudat is the easier of the two to drive to. It takes about one hour to reach the falls and, after an initially steep climb up, it is mostly easy going through the lush rainforest. Some rock clambering is required towards the end if you want to swim in the very cold but beautiful blue pool.

Portsmouth and the north
a harbour town, historical fort and some of Dominica's beast beaches

The second largest town in Dominica, Portsmouth is situated on the Indian River in the northwest of the island, while Fort Shirley and Cabrits National Park are located on a peninsula to the north of town. There are many sheltered sandy coves and inlets in this area, some are suitable for snorkelling, and the northern tip of the island is covered by segments of the Waitukubuli National Trail. The sea is a bit rougher on the Atlantic, or windward side, but the Calibishie coast features impressive beaches of black sand.

North of Roseau
To the north of Roseau on the leeward coast, Goodwill Road first goes past Woodbridge Bay Deep Water Harbour and then to **Canefield** (5 km from Roseau), where there is a turning for the twisting Imperial Road to the centre of the island and the Pont Cassé roundabout (see page 103). After the small Canefield Airport, the coast road becomes Edward Oliver Leblanc Highway and passes through **Massacre**, reputed to be the settlement where 80 Caribs were killed by British troops in 1674. Among those who died was Indian Warner, Deputy Governor of Dominica, illegitimate son of Sir Thomas Warner (Governor of St Kitts) and half-brother of the commander of the British troops, Colonel Philip Warner. From the bright pink-painted St Paul and St Ann Catholic Church perched above the village there are good views of the coast. The next village is **Mahaut** (4 km from Massacre), and just north of here Warner Road climbs steeply up towards **Morne Couroune** (370 m). It then levels out, joins the main Layou Valley road and goes southeast to the Pont Cassé roundabout. After another 6 km, Edward Oliver Leblanc Highway crosses the Layou River, Dominica's longest and deepest river. If you turn right immediately after the bridge, another road heads uphill in the Layou River Valley and joins Imperial Road (from Mahaut; see above). To the left, the road re-joins the coast at the fishing village of **Layou**, then immediately goes through St Joseph, which has a couple of small grocery shops and restaurants, a post office and petrol station, and the handsome white-painted Saint Joseph Catholic Church (1891) perched on a hill.

Just north of St Joseph is **Mero Beach**, one of the very few beaches along this rocky coastline and a popular weekend picnic spot for people from Roseau. It has warm and calm waters for swimming (although don't go very far out as there's an undertow) and a nice long stretch of dark grey sand shaded by palms. Facilities include parking, toilets and cold outdoor showers; at weekends vendors sell snacks and drinks and it's the location of **Karib Bay Beach Bar** (see page 114) which rents out sun loungers. From here the Edward Oliver Leblanc Highway continues for 19 km through several villages and dry tropical forest typical of this side of the island to the fishing village of Dublanc on the western flanks of Morne Diablotin.

Morne Diablotin National Park
Covering 33.3 sq km of the mountainous northern interior, Morne Diablotin National Park was established in 2000, primarily to protect the habitat of the endangered Sisserou parrot

BACKGROUND

Postsmouth

Prince Rupert Bay has a long history. The Caribs were attracted by the sheltered bay, fresh water, reefs and fishing banks, land for cultivation and abundant forests for wood. Christopher Columbus first saw Dominica from a distance in 1493, but it was not until June 18, 1502 that he landed at "the Bay on the Northwest Shore". It became a refreshment stop for ships of all nations after they had crossed the Atlantic and reached the bay via the Guadeloupe Channel. Its name is derived from Prince Rupert of the Rhine (nephew of Charles I) who captained one such ship in the 1650s. By the mid-1700s the French had made permanent settlements, but when the Treaty of Paris in 1763 transferred Dominica to the British, surveyors and engineers were quickly sent out to the island to lay plans for the town of Portsmouth as the capital of Dominica. But it only served in that capacity for a short time from 1765; it was a swampy area and malaria and yellow fever forced the first inhabitants to abandon it, the capital was moved to Roseau, and by 1771 Portsmouth looked like a deserted village. The threat of disease was only eradicated in the 1950s, after which Portsmouth flourished again.

(*Amazona imperialis*), an endemic bird that is a national symbol of Dominica, as well as the more common red-necked Amazon parrot (*Amazona arausiaca,* also known as Jacquot or 'Jaco'). Other birds include the blue-headed hummingbird, purple-throated carib and Lesser Antillean bullfinch. Within the park is 1447-m-high Morne Diablotin, the tallest mountain on the island and the second highest in the Lesser Antilles after La Grande Soufrière in Guadeloupe. It is a beautiful peak, but almost perpetually shrouded in mist.

> **Tip...**
> You have a good chance of seeing the parrots on this trail and the best times are early morning or late afternoon; the Sisserou has a modulated call that rises and falls, while the Jaco has a high-pitched squawk.

From just north of Dublanc on the coast, turn inland for 6 km along a minor road through banana and citrus farmland and up to an elevation of about 530 m and you'll reach the old visitor centre for the **Syndicate Nature Trail** ① *T767-245 0959/295 1323, www.syndicatefalls.com, US$5, children (12-16) US$2.50, under 12s free, daily 0700-1700,* if there's no one there put your money into the drop box, you can also phone ahead to arrange a bird guide. The centre itself has been closed for a number of years, but these days members of the local community maintain the trail and the toilets, and therefore collect an entry fee. It's a fairly easy walk along the 1.8-km loop trail on the edge of Morne Diablotin National Park; it takes about 1½ hours and is suitable for families with smaller children. It has a dense canopy of rainforest overhead, spreading buttresses on the forest floor and part of the trail meanders along the rim of the Picard River Gorge to a waterfall.

Portsmouth

Portsmouth in Prince Rupert Bay is 45 km north of Roseau. It's the second largest town on the island, even though it has only about 3000 permanent inhabitants. Nonetheless, it is a vibrant place, enlivened by the students from the Ross University School of Medicine, which swells the town's population by another 1000 or so in term time. Mainly from the US and Canada, the students keep the bars and restaurants humming and there is a plentiful supply of good-value accommodation for when their families come to visit. Supermarkets and other food shops are well stocked and there is a farmers' market for local produce on Tuesday, Friday and Saturday mornings.

Tip...
L'Express des Iles ferry stops in Portsmouth at the Cabrits Cruise Ship Jetty en route to/from Pointe-à-Pitre in Guadeloupe.

Beaches South of town, adjacent to Ross University Medical School, **Picard Beach** is not one of Dominica's most secluded beaches but the narrow strip of dark sand is lined with palms and it's the location of the **Picard Beach Cottage Resort**, see page 109. On the edge of Prince Rupert Bay as you approach Portsmouth from the south is **Secret Beach**. With its caves and rock arches, it is small, quiet and quite beautiful, the ocean is clear and warm, and there are great spots for snorkelling and diving offshore. Access is a tricky scramble down a steep, rocky path, so it is a better reached by boat. One of Dominica's top places to stay, **Secret Bay** (see page 109), is perched on top of the cliffs above it. Just north of Portsmouth on the way to Fort Shirley, **Purple Beach**, protected by a reef, is calm, good for swimming and snorkelling and has soft grey sand shaded by almond trees. **Purple Turtle Beach Club** is here (see page 114).

Indian River

Boat trips are organized by the Portsmouth Indian River Tour Guides Association, T767-613 6332, but the boat guides hang out on the river near the bridge, trips last 1-3 hrs, US$20-40 per person, but the price depends on duration and number of people.

The Indian River, which flows into the Caribbean Sea between Portsmouth and the village of Glanvillia, is the widest river in Dominica; the river mouth was once a Carib 'Indian' settlement; hence the name. From the bridge just south of Portsmouth, large rowing boats make regular trips up the river, first through marshland where migrating birds come in the winter, and then through a tunnel of vegetation. Used as a film location in 2005 for the movie *Pirates of the Caribbean: Dead Man's Chest*, the river is tidal and brackish through the Glanvilla Swamp, with 50 acres (20 ha) of swamp to the south side. It is a productive fish nursery and you will see lots of crabs eating the algae on the roots of swamp fern and maybe an iguana on a tree overhanging the water. After about 30-45 minutes you get off the boat for a short walk in the forest, and a drink at the wooden forest café/bar (which serves a very potent spiced rum, aptly named **Dynamite** or alternatively there are local juices and herbal teas) before heading back to the starting point. This excursion is popular with cruise ship passengers but if you are not accompanied by boatloads of other tourists, it's a very peaceful trip, especially in the early mornings.

★ Fort Shirley and Cabrits National Park

Off Bay St, 4 km northwest of central Portsmouth and 600 m west of Purple Beach, daily 0800-1800, US$5 per person, US$5 parking.

Although Portsmouth had been virtually abandoned as a town by 1771, the Royal Engineers who came out to establish forts to defend the island against the French had noted the strategic importance of the Cabrits headland. Construction of Fort Shirley began in 1774 under the direction Sir Thomas Shirley, Governor of Dominica (1774-1776). The fort had a polygon layout marked by two batteries for guns overlooking the bay, plus barracks for more than 600 soldiers, officers' quarters, kitchens and mess, guardroom, powder magazines, three cisterns, and artillery and ordnance stores. The main action

ON THE ROAD
Pirates of the Caribbean

Whether you've seen the movies or not, the image of Johnny Depp as Captain Jack Sparrow has become synonymous with pirates, and the now five *Pirates of the Caribbean* films have been a worldwide runaway success. Number two and three in the series – *Dead Man's Chest* (2006) and *At World's End* (2007) – were shot partly on location in Dominica and the coast, cliffs and forests formed the backdrop to many key scenes. In *Dead Man's Chest*, the Valley of Desolation became 'Cannibal Island', and the Indian River became the 'Pantano River', which had to be navigated to reach the treehouse of voodoo mystic Tia Dalma. A 'cannibal village' was built across the steep rocky cliffs between Point Michel and Soufrière and linked by a rope bridge, and another set was built at Vieille Case for the ruined church, graveyard and mill on 'Isla Cruces'. A giant water wheel breaks free from the mill here and rolls to Hampstead Beach where a swordfight between Sparrow, Will Turner (Orlando Bloom) and James Norrington (Jack Davenport) was staged. Other film locations included Pagua Bay and Titou Gorge, where Will Turner and his shipmates were suspended in cages made of bones. In *At World's End* (2007) the ominous approach in the *Black Pearl* to 'Shipwreck Island' was filmed at Capuchin Point on the northwesterly tip of the island, while Londonderry Bay over on the northeast coast provided the black-sand beach where Jack's crew lands and finds the remains of the dead Kraken. Inhabitants still tell tales of the bountiful time when the island was dazzled by the filming and movie stars dined in local restaurants. Taxi drivers are full of stories of who they had in the back of their cab and hotels are proud to show you the rooms where Kiera Knightley and Geoffrey Rush slept. Johnny Depp lived on his private yacht offshore, but he was said to be generous with his time and many a home can boast a photograph of Depp shoulder to shoulder with a Dominican extra.

witnessed here was a revolt of the Eighth West India Regiment in 1802 and an attempted attack by the French in 1805. But with the end of hostilities between Britain and France, the garrison became obsolete and was finally abandoned in 1854. In the 1920s it was used as a quarantine station and hospital, abandoned again, and initial restoration began in 1982.

Today the remains of Fort Shirley can be visited in the 1313-acre (531 ha) Cabrits National Park, which encompasses the peninsula, the surrounding coast and coral reefs, and the island's largest swamp. The name 'cabrits' comes from the French for the goats which roamed wild on the island before it was joined to the mainland by a causeway. Unlike Pigeon Island on St Lucia, Fort Shirley has been beautifully restored and the location is scenic enough for weddings to be held in the former officers' quarters. There are washrooms at the entrance, and then it's a steep 10-minute walk up a paved road to the fort. From there clearly marked paths lead to Douglas Battery and other outlying areas.

North of Portsmouth

From Portsmouth, Bay Street carries on past the Cabrits National Park to **Douglas Bay** where the beach has a few spots of soft sand on the rocky shore and a very gradual slope with no waves or current so is good for swimming. Snorkelling is good too, as coral grows on the top of volcanic rocks just underwater and the bay floor is covered with sea grass that is home to shoals of tiny fish. There is parking but no other facilities. Just north, turn left off the main road as it heads inland at Tanetane as the Northern Link Road to **Toucari Bay**, overlooked by the village of the same name; it's a twisty narrow road so drive slowly. There's a dark-sand beach here and if you are hiking the Waitukubuli National Trail (see box, page 118) you'll walk right through **Toucari**, which is only a small village of about 40 dwellings and a couple of rum shops. The best reasons to come here is for the snorkelling and the great little beach bar. Like Champagne Reef in the south (see page 95), volcanic gases vent from the sea floor and create a wall of bubbles, and close to the cliffs on the north end in shallow water is an old wreck of a wooden ship, believed to be a First World War German vessel; the hull is no longer there, but you can swim around the ship's ribs that rest on the bottom and you'll see plenty of colourful fish. **Keepin'It Real** ① *T767-225 7657, see Toucari Bay on Facebook, daily 0900-2300,* is run by affable Derrick Augustine who rents out beach chairs, inflatable kayaks, stand-up paddle boards and snorkelling gear and there are toilets and cold showers. Advance reservations are recommended for lunch or dinner (phone ahead) and Derrick prepares a delicious meal of grilled fish, octopus or lobster with salads and vegetables. He also caters to yachts mooring in the bay.

From Toucari the coast road continues and ends at the most northerly village of **Capuchin** and **Cape Melville**, the northern tip of the island where there are paths on the clifftops for hiking and great views north to Guadeloupe. Meanwhile from Tanetane the inland road (Northern Link Road) cuts across the north of the island to **Penville** on the northeast coast (a distance of about 7.5 km), where you can pick up the road heading south. It's a precarious stretch so drive very slowly (see box, page 135). It is a beautiful journey over the **Morne aux Diables** (861 m), and through a valley with sulphur springs known as **Cold Soufrière**. While you can still see bubbling water and smell the sulphur, these ones are cold and there are no fumaroles belching out steam or hot gases. You can park on the road (there's a sign) and the several small pools and ponds can be reached on a trail that takes about 10 minutes and goes through plots of dasheen and downhill via some wooden steps.

Calibishie coast

Another road from Portsmouth heads east, following the Indian River for much of the way, winding up and down to the bays and extensive coconut palm plantations of the north coast; it goes through Anse De Mai, Hampstead, Calibishie and Larieu to the Douglas-Charles Airport at Melville Hall and on to Marigot. Much of this route on the east coast faces due north, which means many of the beaches are sheltered from the Atlantic winds. However, while some beaches are protected by rocks and reefs, take advice locally about where to swim as the Atlantic currents can be strong. A particularly beautiful dark black stretch of sand is **Hampstead Beach** (where *Pirates of the Caribbean: Dead Man's Chest* was filmed), which is fringed by coconut palms, sea grape trees and white mangroves and has a formidable stone arch pounded by waves at the eastern end. The 1.5-km access track is off the main road just west of Calibishie, but requires a 4WD so it's better to walk there; go prepared as there are no facilities. The reward is complete solitude and the memory of Jack Sparrow being chased across the beach by enraged cannibals.

Calibishie itself is a charming fishing village looking north to Guadeloupe. The name is thought to be a Carib term meaning 'net of reefs' and refers to the island's longest barrier reef that lies offshore. It is well served with small shops, post office, petrol station, an

ATM, grocery stores and restaurants, and the good choice of accommodation is mostly self-catering and characterful cottages. It also has a tourist information office on the main road operated by the **Calibishie Tourism Development Committee** ① *T767-445 8344, www.calibishiecoast.com, Mon-Fri 0900-1600*, a community-based tourism initiative that promotes the northern region of the island and can also organize local guides to take you on hikes to beaches, waterfalls and forests in this area.

Located on the western outskirts of Calibishie, **Hodges Bay Beach** is one of the nicest. It is protected by a series of small islands and a little reef where you can snorkel. Hodges River comes out to the sea here, a great playground for children and somewhere to wash off salt and sand. **Pointe Baptiste Beach** is within walking distance of Calibishie, and on the Pointe Baptiste and Point Dubique headlands above is some of Calibishie's best accommodation. It is an arc of golden sand surrounded by beautiful red-coloured cliffs and boulders, and is the location of the very pleasant and secluded **Escape Beach Bar** (see page 115). Just beyond Pointe Baptiste, Turtle Beach is, as the name suggests, visited by turtles which lay their eggs in the sand in March-May; the leatherbacks come first, followed by the hawksbills, all of them protected by local volunteers.

Roseau to the east coast
Dominica's mountainous interior and rugged, windswept Atlantic coastline

The shortest route from Roseau to Marigot and Douglas-Charles Airport at Melville Hall is via the road that cuts through the central interior of Dominica. First, as Imperial Road, it climbs steeply with many bends from Canefield, 5 km north of Roseau. You will then see coconut palms, cocoa groves and banana plants all along the gorge, together with dasheen, tannia, oranges and grapefruit. At Pont Cassé, the road divides three ways at one of the island's few roundabouts. Dr Nicholas Liverpool Highway, or the transinsular road, goes northeast towards the airport, while another road heads southeast to the rugged, windswept Atlantic coastline with its scalloped bays and dramatic cliffs.

West from Pont Cassé
Heading north and then west from Pont Cassé, there are some spectacular views down the Layou River Valley towards the Caribbean Sea. About midway the road splits and goes to Mahaut (13 km) and Layou (14 km) back on the coast (see page 98). About 1.5 km after the roundabout are the **Salton Waterfalls** ① *T767-277-8645, daily 0800-1700, US$5*. Also known as **Soltoun Waterfalls**, they have one main fall that drops into a pool where you can splash around, and some other cascades on the surrounding rocks with fine spray like a natural shower. It's a pretty spot with vines and leaves growing up the cliff behind the waterfall. It is about a 20 minutes' walk from the road, although the trail is steep in places.

Northeast from Pont Cassé
Dr Nicholas Liverpool (transinsular) Highway heads north from Pont Cassé, and it's 27 km to Marigot and 29 km to Douglas-Charles Airport on the east coast. Between Pont Cassé and Belles, there are two beautiful waterfalls known as **Penrice Falls**, but also sometimes known as **Spanny's Falls** after Spanny's Bar on the main road where the trail starts (the owners here maintain the trail so it's only polite to make a small donation or buy drinks). The trail, which has wooden bridges and stairs with handrails goes first through a banana

plantation, and then into the forest. It takes about five minutes to the first waterfall and 20 minutes to the second larger one with a rope-assisted scramble down to the pool where you can swim (although it's very cold).

At **Bells** there is a fascinating and beautiful walk to **Jacko Flats**, where a group of maroons (escaped slaves) led by Jacko had their encampment in the late 17th and early 18th centuries. Carved into the cliffs of the Layou River gorge is a flight of 135 giant steps (built by the maroons) to the plateau where they camped. They are very narrow, extremely steep and excessively high, which would have made it very difficult for British troops to quickly and easily attack them. It's only a short hike – about 45 minutes each way – but do not attempt it without a knowledgeable guide; the river crossings are not obvious and the Layou River is well known for its flash floods (it is inadvisable to go there on a rainy day). Ask in Bells village for a guide; **Riverstone Bar & Grill** (see page 115) is as good a place as any to ask.

> **Tip...**
> Dress appropriately for the walk to Jacko Flats, and take a change of clothes/shoes, since much of the trail involves wading in the river.

East from Pont Cassé

Heading east from Pont Cassé, the **Morne Trois Pitons Trail** is signposted on the right just after the roundabout. Within the Morne Trois Pitons National Park this is a challenging two- to three-hour hike to the summit (1424 m) and, while the beginning – passing through secondary rainforest – is moderate, it gets steep and tricky once in the elfin woodland. It requires both good physical condition and a sense of balance due to slippery log steps (which are getting more rotten as time goes on) and some rocky scrambles. It is advisable to wear long trousers because of the razor grass. It is often misty but if the weather is clear there are some fine views over the island from the summit.

About 5.5 km east of Pont Cassé, turn off north to Castle Bruce and, after 800 m, you'll come to the **Emerald Pool** ⓘ *daily 0800-1800, US$5 per person*, a small, but pretty waterfall in a grotto in the forest on the northern edge of the Morne Trois Pitons National Park and a popular cruise ship excursion. The walk takes about 15 minutes from the Pont Cassé–Castle Bruce road, where there is a visitor centre, with a snack bar, souvenir stalls and toilets. The easy gravel path takes you through magnificent overhanging trees and lush vegetation to the shimmering pool, which appears green in the tree-filtered sunlight (hence the name). You can go for a dip and swim right up to the waterfall, but it is a little chilly. On your way back there are two viewpoints where you can see the Atlantic coast to your left. Buses between Roseau and Castle Bruce pass by. From the Emerald Pool it's another 10 km northeast to Castle Bruce on the east coast and the road travels along the southern edge of the Central Forest Reserve.

Castle Bruce and the Carib Territory

Castle Bruce is a small fishing village in a lovely bay with good views all around. North of here the road enters the Carib Territory, also known as the **Carib Reserve** or **Kalinago Territory**, a 15-sq-km 'reservation' established by the British in 1903 for the Carib people, also known as the Kalinago, who inhabited Dominica prior to European colonization and settlement. Back then it was a remote and mountainous area and the Caribs remained largely isolated from the rest of the island throughout most of the 20th century. There were no roads until the 1970s and telephone lines and electricity were only established in the 1980s. Today it is one of the most productive areas on the island and the Carib farmers produce bananas, coconuts, copra and passion fruit. The present population is estimated to be around 3000, descendants of the original 400 inhabitants, but overall the Carib people are integrated into mainstream Dominican life.

From Castle Bruce, the coast road winds its way into the Carib Territory. L'Escalier Tête-Chien at Jenny Point is a short walk from the village of Sineku, 6.5 km from Castle Bruce. It is a finger of volcanic rock climbing out of the sea and up the headland. Its name translates as Staircase of the Snake, and on each rock are circles or lines, like the markings of scales on a snake, and it is said that the Caribs used to follow the snake staircase up to its head in the mountains, thus gaining special powers. From the wooden deck there are dramatic views of the windswept Atlantic.

At the hamlet of Crayfish River, 3 km further on, is the **Kalinago Village by the Sea**, or **Kalinago Barana Autê** ① *T767-445 7979, www.kalinagobaranaaute.com, daily 0900-1700, US$10 per person*, where there is a reception centre, snack bar and gift shop and an easy circular trail round the huts (*ajoupas*) in the village. Each hut exhibits a feature of traditional Kalinago life, such as canoe building, cassava processing, calabash decorating and the use of herbs and plants in medicine and cooking. There are skilful demonstrations of basket weaving and sometimes cassava breadmaking (you can try the bread and buy pottery, woven goods, coconut products and other crafts. There are also craft stalls along the road. A short walk from the village at the mouth of the Crayfish River, the **Isulukati Waterfall** tumbles into a pool where you can splash around, and then drops over rocks into the sea by a beach of large stones. Overall, it's an interesting excursion and the guides are informative; allow about an hour.

About 2 km north in the next village, the **Salybia Catholic Church of the Immaculate Conception** was built in 1991 and is based on the traditional A-frame *karbet* (the nucleus of the extended Carib family group); it has a canoe for its altar, murals about Carib history both inside and out including one on the front that shows Christopher Columbus' fleet passing through on his second voyage in 1493. Outside is a cemetery and a three-stone monument to the first three Carib chiefs after colonization: Jolly John, Auguiste and Corriette.

About 6 km north of Salybia the road crosses the Pagua River and joins the Dr Nicholas Liverpool Highway from the Pont Cassé roundabout. The river itself flows out on to the beach at Pagua Bay, where the stylish **Pagua Bay House** is located (see page 112). The hotel's restaurant, **Pagua Bay Bar & Grill**, with its outdoor deck and Atlantic views, is a fine place to have lunch (see page 116). From here it's another 5.5 km to Douglas-Charles Airport via Marigot.

South of Castle Bruce
If, instead of taking the road past the Emerald Falls to Castle Bruce, you take the right fork, you get to the Atlantic coast at **Rosalie Bay** after 8.5 km. A black-sand beach extends south from the mouth of the river and is a favoured nesting site for turtles: leatherbacks (March-July) and greens and hawksbills (July-September). There is a turtle-watch programme on the beach in front of the **Rosalie Bay Resort** (see page 112). Working with the **Wider Caribbean Sea Turtle Network** (WIDECAST; www.widecast.org), owners of the resort, Beverly Deikel and Patris Oscar, founded the first turtle conservation program on Dominica, and it has since become the island-wide **Dominica Sea Turtle Conservation Organization** (DomSeTCO). The resort organizes turtle watching for their guests, and non-guests can arrange a night time trip on Rosalie Beach in season through a conservation group that is part of DomSeTCO. The **Nature Enhancement Team** (NET)

ⓘ *T767-277 1608, see NET Rosalie on Facebook, US$10 per person*, patrol the beach from dusk to dawn throughout the nesting season to protect and monitor the nesting turtles, safeguard vulnerable eggs and rescue baby hatchlings trapped by beach debris or disoriented by lights. Visitors can join them with a NET guide; contact them in advance to make arrangements.

At **La Plaine**, 10 km south of Rosalie, you can follow a trail to the **Sari-Sari Waterfall** which is a single and powerful drop of about 45 m. The hike is moderately difficult and starts with a steep incline to the Sari-Sari River and then goes along the riverbed, crossing the water several times; there's a certain amount of scrambling over boulders, expect to get wet and muddy but it's an adventure. Allow two to three hours for the return hike with time to enjoy the waterfall and swim in the pool at its base. Local boys in the village will offer to guide you but it's not essential.

At **Delices**, 8.5 km south of La Plaine, you can see the **Victoria Falls** from the road but you can also hike to them along the White River. The source is the Boiling Lake which makes the water a whitish-blue from the sulphur (hence the name of the river). It can be a slippery walk, and you need to take a guide as there is a real possibility of getting lost (ask around in the village, but they will probably find you). It takes about 30 minutes each way, and again you can swim in the pool at its base. The White River falls into the Atlantic at **Pointe Mulâtre Bay**, reached by a steep road from Delices. At the weekend local families picnic and wash their cars here and you can swim in the river, but be wary of flash floods and do not cross the river after heavy rainfall. The **Jungle Bay** resort is just south of the river mouth (see page 112).

The road continues from Delices and after 7.5 km reaches the village of **Petite Savanne**. It is extremely steep but offers spectacular views of both the Victoria Falls and the steam rising from the Boiling Lake. Tragically, on August 27, 2015, Tropical Storm Erika devastated Dominica, and torrential rain, flooding and mudslides completely eliminated the village of Petite Savanne. Several people were killed, a total of 217 homes were destroyed and 823 people were evacuated. Since then, the road has been repaired and has reopened, and the government is currently planning to rebuild housing so residents can move back.

Tourist information

See the website www.dominica.dm
for useful information.

Discover Dominica Authority
*Roseau on 1st Floor, Financial Centre, Kennedy
Av, T767-448 2045, www.dominica.dm.
Mon-Fri 0800-1800.*
There is also an information office on the
ground floor of the Dominica Museum on
Dame Mary Eugenia Charles Blvd near the
Roseau Cruise Ship Berth, Mon-Fri 0900-
1600, Sat 0900-1200.

Where to stay

Unless otherwise stated, all hotel rooms
have a/c, TV and Wi-Fi. Hotel VAT (10%)
and service charge (10%) is charged across
the board, usually as a single charge of
20%. Check if this has been included in
quoted rates.

Roseau and around

$$ Fort Young Hotel
*Within the old fort, Victoria St, T767-448 5000,
www.fortyoung hotel.com.*
Set in the ramparts of an old military fort
with bronze cannons at the entrance and
close to the ferry and centre of town. There
are 53 rooms, some of the standard ones
in the original fort buildings are small and
slightly dated, the newer ones are more
spacious and have balconies with sea views.
Facilities include a tour desk that organizes
island tours, dive shop linked to **Dive
Dominica**, small spa, waterfront restaurant
and **Warner's Bar**, which is popular during
the day with cruise ship passengers. Rates
are B&B.

$$-$ Anchorage Hotel & Dive Centre
*Victoria St, Castle Comfort, 1.7 km south
of Fort Young Hotel, T767-448 2638,
www.anchoragehotel.dm.*

Long-established PADI dive resort with 32
poolside or oceanfront rooms, nothing fancy
and a bit spartan, but friendly service and can
arrange lots of activities including diving and
snorkelling to Champagne Reef and other
sites in the Soufrière-Scotts Head Marine
Reserve, catamaran trips and whale watching,
waterfront restaurant and bar by the pool.
B&B with a basic continental breakfast.

$$-$ Sutton Place Hotel
*25 Old St, T767-449 8700, www.
suttonplacehoteldominica.com.*
Only steps away from L'Express des Iles ferry,
super-friendly option in a 3-storey block
with 5 rooms and 3 suites with kitchenettes
and balconies, 1st-floor lounge with coffee
machine, microwave and fridge, simple
decor but comfortable and quiet, small
restaurant/breakfast room, **Cellar Bar** with
stone-vaulted ceiling, rear courtyard with
pot plants and seating area. Room-only.

$ Castle Comfort Lodge
*Victoria St, Castle Comfort, next door to
Anchorage Hotel & Dive Centre, T767-448
2188, www.castle comfortdivelodge.com.*
Another dive-focused lodge and home to
Dive Dominica, with 12 simple rooms with
ceiling fan or a/c, excellent local food at the
restaurant/bar with wooden deck and good
sunset views, occasional live music at the
weekends, diving, snorkelling and boat trips
can be arranged. B&B or room-only.

$ La Flamboyant
*22 King George V St, T767-440 7190,
www.laflamboyanthotel.dm.*
Convenient for the town centre and
ferry, La Flamboyant is a tall block with
multicoloured exterior. It has 16 rooms on
4 floors opening out to communal balconies,
well priced, bright and clean, some have a
fridge and a/c, but avoid street-side rooms
overlooking the noisy bar opposite. B&B
with continental breakfast, can provide
dinner if you book by 1500.

$ Ma Bass Central Guest House
44 Fields Lane, T767-448 2999.
Simple budget lodging, clean and friendly, 11 rooms on 4-floor house with, fans or a/c, en suite or shared bathrooms, some have balconies and views over town, no TV but there is Wi-Fi. Ma Bass will cook or give you use of the kitchen, is full of useful information and can recommended hiking guides. Room-only.

$ St James Guesthouse
Federation Drive, Goodwill, T767-448 7170, see Facebook.
A 5-min walk north of Roseau centre in a quiet neighbourhood, this smart, modern, 2-storey yellow guesthouse has 16 simple but neat rooms with ceiling fans, either en suite or spotless shared bathrooms and some with balconies and TV, fresh fruit and toast for breakfast, small but attractive garden, owners Carol and Phil are very friendly and give advice on buses, restaurants and can book tours. B&B.

Roseau Valley and Morne Trois Pitons National Park

$$ Papillote Wilderness Retreat
Paillotte Rd, just before Trafalgar Falls, T767-448 2287, www.papillote.dm.
Set in the beautiful Papillote Tropical Gardens (see page 96), landscaped by owner Anne Jno Baptiste, with hot mineral pools, a birdwatching house and interesting garden tours available, the retreat has 5 charming rooms, each different, with tiled floors and wood-shuttered windows, the cottage has 2 bedrooms and a kitchen, rates are room-only but all meals are available with good Creole-style cooking in the restaurant, which is a popular venue for cruise ship excursions at lunchtime. There's also an arts and crafts boutique.

$$-$ Cocoa Cottages
Paillotte Rd, 5 km from Roseau, 2.6 km before Trafalgar Falls, T767-295 7272, www.cocoacottages.com.

Deep in the Roseau Valley with a rustic charm and comfort, 6 large rooms decorated with local art and with mosaic-tiled bathrooms, the treehouse can accommodate up to 6, set in lush tropical gardens with hammocks, verandas and a back-to-nature feel, very laid back and relaxing. Breakfast (US$15) and dinner (US$35) are served communal style around a large table, friendly and sociable. A short drive to the start of hiking trails and home to **Extreme Dominica** for canyoning, abseiling and other adventure tours (see page 117).

$ Chez Ophelia Cottage Apartments
Wotten Waven Rd, 4.3 km from Roseau, T767-448 3438, www.chezophelia.com.
Country retreat nestled on the mountainside in the Roseau Valley with 5 simple cottages in traditional style with kitchenettes, 1 sleeps 4 in a small bedroom and living room with twin beds, continental breakfast (US$10), dinner (US$23). Close to the hiking trails, Screw's Sulphur Spa and Trafalgar Falls. You can swim in the the Roseau River which runs through the property, and hostess Ophelia can advise on tours.

North of Roseau

$$ Crescent Moon Cabins
Rivière La Croix, high above Mahaut but reached from the Pont Cassé roundabout, about 30 mins from Roseau, T767-449 3449, www.crescentmooncabins.com.
In a delightful secluded setting with magnificent views down to the Caribbean Sea, 4 well-furnished wooden cabins, no a/c or TV but a peaceful rural retreat run by Americans Ron (chef) and Jean Viveralli (teacher), good home cooking, fresh organic fruit and vegetables from on-site greenhouse and gardens, own roasted coffee and cocoa, goats and chickens, fresh spring water for drinking, breakfast included, packed lunch U$10, dinner US$40, car hire recommended or packages available including meals and tours.

$$ Sunset Bay Club Beach Hotel
Edward Oliver Leblanc Hwy, Batalie Beach,
7.3 km north of St Joseph, T767-446 6522,
www.sunsetbayclub.com.
Run by a French-speaking Belgian family,
12 rooms in concrete bungalows (the ones
in the front row have sea views), no TV or
a/c but fans, simple furnishings, some can
sleep 4, pool, black-sand beach with sun
loungers, restaurant/bar famous for its
lobster and dive shop on site. Nothing
fancy but a peaceful beach resort with
good service. B&B or full board.

$$-$ Tamarind Tree Hotel
Edward Oliver Leblanc Hwy,
near Salisbury, T767-449 7395,
www.tamarindtreedominica.com.
On cliff between Macoucherie and
Salisbury beaches, halfway between
Roseau and Portsmouth, 15 rooms with
ceiling fan and fridge, superior rooms have
a/c, no TVs but Wi-Fi, very quiet with a big
terrace over the Caribbean Sea and sunset,
swimming pool with sun loungers, good
Creole-style and European food, bar with
Kubuli beer on tap, Swiss/German-run.
B&B and meal plans available.

$ Mango Island Lodges
Syers Estate, Mero, turn east and uphill
from Edward Oliver Leblanc Hwy about
2.3 km north of St Joseph, 767-617 7963,
www.mangoislandlodges.com.
Up in the hills, 2 delightful wooden and
stone cottages with tea and coffee maker
and fridge, 1 can accommodate extra beds
for children, the other has TV, no a/c but
ceiling fans and mosquito nets. The lovely
stone swimming pool has a littleseating
area and sea views; snorkelling gear and
stand-up paddle boards can be rented and
they'll run you down to Mero Beach, about
a 5-min drive. There's a restaurant/bar, rates
are room-only but all meals are available by
arrangement. Minimum stay 2 nights, great
spot for a family/group.

Portsmouth

$$$$ Secret Bay
Ross Blvd, 2.5 km south of the centre
of Portsmouth, T767-445 4444,
www.secretbay.dm.
Tucked away on a 4-acre (1.6 ha) private
headland and high on a cliff with fabulous
views of the Caribbean, this is Dominica's
most luxurious hideaway. 6 contemporary 1-
and 2-bedroom villas with plunge pools set
on stilts, plus 2 hardwood treehouse-style
bungalows, fully equipped state-of-the-art
kitchens, great sunset watching from the
verandas, extras like iPod docking stations
and Netflix, fruit and herbs in the garden are
for your own use if you want to self-cater
or have a cook to do so, or excellent meals
are served on your deck. Access to 2 sandy
beaches, Tibay and Secret Bay, and the
resort provides mountain bikes, kayaks,
stand-up paddleboards and snorkelling gear
and can arrange yoga and cooking classes.
Minimum stay 3 nights, no children under 16
(under 7 in the 2-bed villa), rates are room-
only, B&B or full-board.

$$$-$$ Picard Beach Cottages
Picard Beach, Ross Blvd, T767-445 5131,
www.picardbeachcottages.dm.
Set in lovely gardens with fruit trees and
coconut palms on the long sandy Picard
Beach with good swimming and snorkelling,
the 18 wooden cottages have verandas
and kitchenettes, those closest to the sea
are bigger and more expensive, with larger
kitchens and can sleep a family of 4, but
those furthest away are the quietest. There's
also **Le Flambeau Restaurant & Beach Bar**
(see page 114), a small spa, and kayaking and
boat trips to Secret Bay can be arranged. B&B
or room-only. The **Portsmouth Beach Hotel**
is on the same property, but the multi-storey
block is mostly used by students at Ross
University School of Medicine.

$ The Champs
Banana Trail, turn east and uphill off Ross Blvd opposite the university, T767-445 4452, www.thechampsdm.com.
On the hillside above the bay with views across Portsmouth and Cabrits National Park, there are 5 rooms with fairly basic furnishings but they open up to pretty balconies and terraces full of flowering pot plants, friendly and helpful service, rates are room-only but there are good Dominican breakfasts, and the restaurant, pizzeria and lively bar are also frequented by Ross University School of Medicine students.

$ Sisters Sea Lodge
Lizard Trail, turn west off Ross Blvd just south of the Picard River, T767-445 4501.
Set in gardens of banana, mango and coconut trees with lawns running down to the sea, the 5 spacious, self-contained studios have kitchenettes, no TV or a/c but fans and mosquito nets, 2 double beds for families and outdoor stone showers. Within walking distance of buses and a supermarket for self-catering or there's a sandy outside beach bar/restaurant offering tasty food including plenty of fresh seafood. Room-only.

North of Portsmouth

$$$ Manicou River
Everton Hall Estate, Tanetane, 6.6 km north of Portsmouth, T767-616 8903, www.manicouriver.com.
On a former lime and bay oil producing estate, up a steep access road (4WD needed), this peaceful and idyllic timber villa and 3 hexagonal treehouses on a hillside use local furniture and, with no windows except for the bathroom, the front is completely open with lovely views down to Douglas Bay, gentle breezes mean no a/c needed and beds are draped with mosquito nets. There are kitchens, verandas, hammocks, solar power (no TV) and restaurant/bar area for good pre-booked breakfasts and dinners. Room-only.

$$ Comfort Cottages
Terre Platte, Blenheim Estate, T767-445 3245, www.comfortcottagesdominica.com.
On a hillside overlooking the Atlantic coast about a 15-min drive northeast of Portsmouth towards Pennville, the 4 1- and 2-bedroom well-furnished, comfortable and brightly painted wooden cottages (Lime, Pink, Orange and Lilac) have plunge pools on the veranda, all very private set in flowering gardens, barbecue pit and gazebo for communal use. Rates include breakfast supplies in your kitchen which are replenished daily and other meals are on request in the bar/restaurant. They will pick up/drop off at hiking trails if you don't have a car.

Calibishie coast

$$$ Pointe Baptiste
North of the main road in Calibishie, T767-445 7368, www.pointebaptiste.com.
Pointe Baptiste Estate covers 25 acres (10 ha) of gardens, orchards and forest looking out north across Guadeloupe Channel with access to 2 coves below the headland and close to Hodges Bay Beach. The main house dates from the 1930s and has high ceilings and wooden floors, a sitting room decorated with antiques, kitchen, spectacular views from the airy veranda and sleeps 6-8. A smaller garden cottage sleeps 2 ($). Self-catering, although rates includes a cook and maid, weekly discounts apply.

$$$-$$ Calibishie Cove
Point Dubique, Calibishie, T767-265 1993, www.calibishiecove.com.
On a hilltop with expansive views over the ocean to Marie Galante, 4 spacious and breezy suites, all with patios and louvred windows and sea view on both sides, good kitchens, 1 has a plunge pool, solar power. There's no restaurant but rates are B&B and breakfast is delivered to your room; packed lunches and dinner on request, minimum 3-night stay, and the whole house can be rented for groups/families.

$$$-$ Escape
Pointe Baptiste, Calibishie, T767-225 7813,
www.escapedominica.com.
Small resort on the beach at Pointe Baptiste
at the beach bar of the same name with a
choice of a 2-bedroom villa up the hill with
great sea views, sofa beds for children and
its own swimming pool and kitchen, or
2 cheaper wooden thatched cabanas above
the bar (which closes at 2000; see page 115)
without kitchen but with tea/coffee facilities.
Peaceful, no TVs, good service from the
Dutch/Canadian owners, all meals available
at the beach bar. Room-only.

$ Jacoway Inn
*John Baptiste Ridge Rd, Calibishie, T767-613
2908, www.jacowayinn.com.*
Small pretty yellow house on the inland side
of the road in Calibishie, a 450-m walk from
buses The 2 studios have full kitchens, ceiling
fans, screened windows, solar hot water,
upstairs has a balcony with ocean view and
the garden unit has a patio; there's also
1 double budget room with basic cooking
facilities, lovely garden with a gazebo and
hammock. Rates are room-only, excellent
hot breakfasts are US$12, and host Carol Ann
also bakes pies and cakes.

$ Sea Cliff Cottages
Point Dubique, Calibishie, T767-445 8998,
www.dominica-cottages.com.
Spread over several acres of grounds with
fruit trees and flowers above Hodges Bay
Beach, 5 spacious cottages from a studio
to 2-bedrooms, kitchens, verandas with
views, a steep path to the beach, no meals
but you can pick bananas and mangoes in
the garden, fresh bread is delivered and it's
a 20-minute walk to Calibishie for grocery
shops and restaurants as well as buses.

$ Veranda View
*On the main road in Calibishie, T767-445
8900, www.lodgingdominica.com.*
Run by multilingual Hermien Kuis, on the
beach opposite the tourist information office
with a beautiful view north to Guadeloupe,

Wi-Fi but no TV or a/c. The 2 rooms upstairs
share a large breezy veranda and sun deck,
while the downstairs room has another
private patio. Light cooking facilities and
fridge, rates are room-only or B&B, other
meals are available by reservation and
Hermien is a great cook.

Northeast from Pont Cassé

$ Zen Gardens
*Dr Nicholas Liverpool (transinsular)
Hwy, Belles, T767-449 3737,
www.zengardensdominica.com.*
On the way to the east coast in the lush
valley around the village of Bells alongside
the Central Rainforest Reserve, 3 delightful
wooden and tin-roofed double bungalows
with kitchens in the middle of a luxuriant
garden: **Faith Cottage**, **Love Shack** and
Peace Place are simple, peaceful and rustic
(toilets and showers are outside) and there's
a river on the property where you can swim.
By arrangement, friendly owners Kirk and
Rita Bruce can prepare excellent meals using
fresh local produce.

Castle Bruce and the Carib Territory

$$ Beau Rive
*Between Castle Bruce and Sineku,
T767-445 8992, www.beaurive.com.*
Set in 3 acres (1.2 ha) of tropical gardens
and forest looking down to the Atlantic, and
built in the style of a colonial manor house
by owner, Mark Steele, you are made to feel
like house guests at quiet and elegant Beau
Rive. The 10 bright and airy rooms have
balcony/terrace, wooden floors and simple,
uncluttered decor, no TV or a/c but ceiling
fans, pool, library and bar. Buffet breakfast on
the terrace is included; dinner is a 3-course
set menu (US$40). No children under 16,
minimum 2-night stay.

$ Sunrise Farm Cottages
*Between Castle Bruce and Sineku, about
500 m north of Beau River, T767-446 0000,
www.sunrisefarmcottages.com.*

Scattered around a grassy patch in the forest, the 10 wooden chalets are set on concrete stilts with kitchen and veranda, nothing fancy but well equipped and most have Atlantic views and can sleep up to 3 if an extra bed is requested. The **Zaboka Restaurant and Bar** is available for breakfast and lunch but dinner must be pre-booed before 1630, decent-sized swimming pool with sundeck, quiet, and walking distance to a small grocery store for supplies.

South of Castle Bruce

$$$$-$$$ Pagua Bay House
Pagua Bay, Marigot, T767-445 8888, www.paguabayhouse.com.
Stylish and modern, built to look like tin banana-processing sheds, 6 ocean-view cabanas with wooden floors and vaulted ceilings, huge beds, verandas and coffee-makers, 2 have extra living areas and 1 has a plunge pool. Rates are room-only but all meals are available at the **Pagua Bay Bar & Grill** (see page 116) with its stunning swimming pool overlooking the ocean. Also offers massages, yoga classes, kayaks and boogie boards and can arrange car hire. 3-night minimum stay.

$$$$-$$$ Rosalie Bay Resort
Rosalie Beach, T767-446 1010, www.rosaliebay.com.
Set in 22 acres (9 ha) of flowering gardens and forests, this resort is located on a black-sand beach where the Rosalie River meets the Atlantic, with 28 huge, luxury rooms in cottages with cathedral ceilings, large bathrooms, and wraparound decks with swing chairs. Rates depend on size and views. Facilities include the **Gló Spa**, saltwater pool, gym, yoga, kayaks for hire, and **Zamaan's** restaurant with bar and outdoor terrace at the river mouth. Garden walks and sea turtle conservation are part of a stay; there's even a night-time 'turtle alarm' for guests during the Mar-Oct nesting/hatching season. B&B, or packages that include spa treatments and local tours.

$$$ Jungle Bay
Just south of the White River mouth, Delices, T767-446 1789, www.junglebaydominica.com.
The 35 wooden cabins here are accessed by a series of footpaths and stone staircases and are built on stilts in the forest. Rustic elegance with no a/c or TV but very comfortable and characterful with tea/coffee facilities, balconies, hammocks and locally made furniture. The **Pavilion Restaurant** serves excellent organic food and has a deck with ocean views, pool and a yoga studio. This is a good choice for an active, one-stop holiday with a daily programme that includes excursions, hikes, cookery classes and spa treatments. Rates are B&B or all-inclusive.

$$$-$ Citrus Creek Plantation
Felicite Hwy, La Plaine, T767-446 1234, www.citruscreekplantation.com.
This historical estate close to Sable Beach used to grow sugar and still has old buildings and ruins dotted around the 20 acres (8 ha) alongside the Taberi River and its pools. The French owners offer 5 very comfortable self-catering 1- and 2-bedroom cottages, plus a huge 'glamping' safari tent that sleeps 4 with an outdoor shower, no TV or a/c, but peaceful and breezy, lovely forested grounds to explore and swimming in the river. The excellent **Riverside Café** (see page 115) is available for meals, or guests can have their own cook or get their fridge filled with produce from the restaurant's kitchen.

$ 3 Rivers & Rosalie Forest Eco Lodge
Newfoundland Estate, Rosalie, T767-446 1886, www.3riversdominica.com.
Delightful spot on the Rosalie River in 12 acres (4.8 ha) of lush grounds of palm, banana and fruit trees and natural forest offering a variety of accommodation from self-contained cottages with private gardens to rustic bamboo treehouses and cabins, a dormitory and a campsite with tents and bedding for rent or hammocks to sleep in. Good bathrooms with warm water in the evenings, communal kitchen, restaurant/bar, and loads of things to do, from hiking

trails and river swimming on the property to day tours around the island and community-based activities such as cooking classes or farm visits. A great spot for budget travellers and families to stay and owner Jem Winston will go out of his way to help you to explore Dominica. Rates are room-only or there's a variety of meal/activity packages.

Restaurants

Most (though not all) restaurants quote prices on menus that include 15% VAT; many automatically add a 10% service charge to the bill – beware of tipping twice.

Roseau

$$$-$$ Palisades Restaurant
At Fort Young Hotel, see Where to stay, page 107. Daily 0700-1000, Mon-Fri 1200-1430, Tue-Sun 1830-2200.
Upstairs with a long terrace, good ocean views, a comfortable a/c interior and a relaxing ambience, Palisades Restaurant offers a long menu of well-prepared local favourites like callaloo soup with dasheen, conch fritters, coconut chicken and catch-of-the-day, plus steaks and rack of lamb and a couple of vegetarian options. Also in the hotel, the waterfront **Warner's Bar** (daily 1600-2300) downstairs is a popular sunset spot and has live music on Fri, and **Bala's Bar** (daily 1000-2200) in the lobby serves drinks, bar food, lighter meals such as burgers and pastas, coffees and cakes.

$$$-$ Café Desiderata
5 Old St, T767-448 6522, see Facebook. Mon-Thu 0930-1730, Fri 0930-2230, Sat 0930-1500.
A stylish café in a stone-walled house with a great breakfast menu with the like of muesli or avocado on toast, plus delicious tapas, wraps, salads, and sandwiches, and daily special hot meals such as grilled tuna or skewered chicken. Also serves wine, cocktails and coffees, there's Wi-Fi, and owner Portia always greets everyone warmly. Open on Fri for dinner.

$$ Old Stone Grill & Bar
15 Castle St, T767-440 7549. Mon-Sat 1700-2100.
A small place close to the Fort Young Hotel with ocean views from the deck, fresh and tasty chicken, pork and seafood dishes, the fish sampler appetizer is good, friendly if not speedy service, exceptionally well-stocked bar with cocktails using locals ingredients; try the coconut daiquiri.

$$-$ Cocorico Café
Dame Mary Eugenia Charles Blvd, T767-449 8686, www.cocoricocafe.com. Mon-Fri 0830-1600, Sat 0830-1400.
Sidewalk café with seating under umbrellas, excellent range of food from full Creole meals to sandwiches and crêpes, plus espresso coffee and fresh local juices, good service, convenient place to have breakfast while waiting for the inter-island ferry to arrive after you've booked in.

$$-$ Guiyave
15 Cork St, T767-448 2930, see Facebook. Mon-Fri 0830-1600, Sat 0830-1400.
Colourful restaurant with a few tables on the 1st-floor plant-lined balcony offering a lunchtime buffet from 1130 of local dishes from goat stew to fried fish – it's a good place to try a lot of different dishes – or opt for the sandwiches and pastries from the patisserie downstairs. It can get crowded after 1300 with Roseau people coming for lunch, but the atmosphere is bustling and chatty.

$ Pearl's Cuisine
At Sutton Place Hotel, 25 Old St, T767-449 8700, www.suttonplacehoteldominica.com. Mon-Sat 0900-1630.
Simple dining area within the typical stone walls of a historical Roseau building, a good cool retreat from the heat outside, very tasty Creole food such as fish with rice, peas and salad, breadfruit cakes and yam pie, and coconut ice cream and rum cake for dessert, also inexpensive takeaway rotis, all delicious and filling; no alcohol but you can have cocoa tea and fresh juice.

Roseau Valley and Morne Trois Pitons National Park

$$$-$ Papillote Rainforest Restaurant
At Papillote Wilderness Retreat, Paillotte Rd, just before Trafalgar Falls, T767-448 2287, www.papillote.dm. Lunch and dinner by reservation only.

Surrounded by beautiful gardens with a sweeping view from the roof terrace down the Roseau Valley and across to the mountains, Papillote serves excellent Caribbean fare, from flying fish sandwiches to mahi mahi steamed in banana leaves and fruit cake with rum for dessert. It gets busy at lunchtimes on cruise ship days; packages include garden tours and swimming in the hot pools on the property (see Papillote Tropical Gardens, page 96).

$ River Rock Café and Bar
Paillotte Rd, just before Trafalgar Falls, T767-225 0815, see Facebook. Daily 1000-1800.

A simple place in a wooden hut just a short distance before Trafalgar Falls, book and order in advance on your way up to the falls and lunch will be ready on your return, the bar faces the road, the restaurant's open deck faces the river at the back with great views down the valley, Creole lunches like goat and chicken stew or lighter sandwiches, cold beer and rum punch.

North of Roseau

$$-$ Karib Bay Beach Bar
Mero Beach, T767-449 7922, see Facebook under Romance Café. Daily 1000-2200, later for events.

Until recently called the **Romance Café**, this is a colourful blue and pink building on the beach where Frederica is a welcoming host. There's a varied menu of food French and Creole dishes: the mahi mahi with coconut sauce is delicious and there are lighter dishes such as burgers or sandwiches, as well as papaya smoothies and plenty of rum. This is a popular venue for people from Roseau at the weekends (it's the closest beach to town) so there are often DJs or live bands playing from 1500 on Sat-Sun and sometimes bonfires and reggae parties late into the night. You can hire sun loungers, use the outdoor showers and spend the day on the beach.

Portsmouth

$$$-$ Le Flambeau Restaurant & Beach Bar
At Picard Beach Cottages, Picard Beach, Ross Blvd, T 767-445 5142. See Facebook. Daily 0700-2300.

With a lovely terrace over Picard Beach, Le Flambeau offers good and friendly service, and a varied tasty menu with generous portions, including excellent breakfasts – Dominican with bakes and saltfish, full English, or American with pancakes, bacon and syrup. Later you can take your pick between international and Creole seafood, pork and chicken dishes, good desserts and cocktails.

$$ Purple Turtle Beach Club
Purple Beach, Bay St, T767-445 5296. Daily 1100-2130.

This beach bar is in a great location overlooking the yachts moored in Prince Rupert Bay, and west-facing so good for sunsets, and you can swim and lounge on the beach. There are plenty of drinks but availability of food is a bit hit and miss; you can usually get snacks like rotis or burgers at lunchtime, but there tend to be a better choice in the evening after the fishermen have come in when you might get mahi mahi or tuna.

$$-$ Tomato Fresh Food Café & Deli
Banana Trail, Picard, T767-445-3334. Mon-Sat 0800-2100.

Another Ross University School of Medicine student hangout and Canadian-owned offering. The North American-style menu features breakfasts, burgers, wraps, wings, paninis, pizzas, pastas, brownies and cheesecake, there are vegetarian and gluten-free options, and Kubuli beer on tap served in frozen glasses. A little overpriced but some visitors may be craving such items

$ The Shacks
Ross Blvd. Daily 0800-2200.
This parallel strip of local vendors' stalls next to Ross University School of Medicine caters for students but is also a convenient place to grab a meal while touring the island. Food includes local-style meals of chicken/fish with beans and rice or rotis, plus there's pizza, nachos, pastries, smoothies, coffee, fresh fruit and other snacks. Not all the stalls are open all the time, but something always is.

Calibishie coast

$$$-$$ Rainbow Restaurant Beach Bar
Main Rd, Calibishie, T767-245 4838, see Facebook. Mon-Fri 1000-2130, Sun 0900-2130.
Friendly family-run spot on the main road but with tables on the upper deck overlooking a small beach with great sea views, generous portions of French/Creole food beautifully presented in banana leaves, the lion fish and curried chicken with pineapple are particular specialities, great rum punch, owner Michael is a reggae singer and often gets his guitar out; if you make a reservation they'll send a taxi to collect you.

$$ POZ Restaurant & Bar at Calibishie Gardens
Main St, Calibishie, T767-445 8327. Tue-Sun 1600-2400.
POZ is short for 'positive attitude' and there's always positive feedback about the food here, all freshly prepared, allergies and special diets can be accommodated. Local favourites such as goat curry, crayfish and mahi mahi are washed down with some excellent rum punch. There's a swimming pool, and you're welcome to go earlier before the restaurant/bar opens if you want to make a day of it or entertain the children.

$$-$ Escape
Pointe Baptiste Beach, Calibishie, T767-225 7813, www.escapedominica.com. Daily 1200-2000.
A charming and secluded spot on the small Pointe Baptiste Beach surrounded by dramatic red-coloured cliffs and with giant boulders in the sea that makes calm pools for swimming. Tables under shady palms and almond trees, thatched bar, sun loungers, and a menu of tasty grilled mahi mahi, fishcakes and curries. A good place to escape for a peaceful day on the beach.

$ Coral Reef Restaurant & Bar
Main Rd, Calibishie, T767-445 7432, see Facebook. Daily 0800-2230.
Open-air Creole restaurant/bar with a wooden deck over a strip of sand, tucked behind the **Coral Reef Supermarket** right in the middle of Calibishie, serving Caribbean favourites such as yam, fried plantains, ribs and goat curry, accompanied by a locally made hot sauce (which they also sell). The supermarket itself is well stocked with groceries, beers and wines in the event you are self-catering.

Northeast from Pont Cassé

$$ Riverstone Bar & Grill
Dr Nicholas Liverpool Hwy, Bells, T767-449 3713, see Facebook. Daily 1200-1900.
On the highway near the village of Bells, Riverstone offers an inexpensive menu of grilled fish/pork/chicken, pastas and rotis and has a lovely deck overlooking the Laurent River; there is also a pool where you can take a (cold) swim. Ask here for a guide for the walk to Jacko Flats.

South of Castle Bruce

$$$-$ Riverside Café
At Citrus Creek Plantation, see Where to stay, page 112. Daily 1000-1700, dinner by reservation only.
Located in the main stone building at Citrus Creek Plantation, with tables under an open

veranda overlooking the Taberi River where you can bathe while waiting for your food, which is French/Creole fusion using local, organic produce and lots of fish and seafood. Try the callaloo soup and smoked fish quiche, a good option for lunch or a snack while touring the island.

$$ Pagua Bay Bar & Grill

Pagua Bay, Marigot, T767-275 9699, www.paguabayhouse.com. Breakfast and dinner for hotel guests or by reservation only, lunch 1200-1600.
Indoor and outdoor seating overlooking Pagua Bay and the crashing Atlantic. The food is modern, innovative and beautifully presented, from tacos, burgers and sandwiches to mahi mahi ceviche and grilled calamari. It's a great place to stop for lunch when touring the island, or you could come here en route to the airport, which is only a 10-min drive away.

$ Islet View

On the main road, Castle Bruce, T767-446 0370. Daily 0800-2100.
This rustic and characterful hilltop roadside bar has a wonderful view over the bay and Castle Bruce and makes a lovely lunch stop with good local food such as callaloo soup, fried plantains and grilled chicken. There's an extensive selection of infused rums with hand-written labels listing the ingredients which range from hibiscus and pawpaw to more esoteric flavours such as olive and eggplant.

Bars and clubs

Nightlife on Dominica is not what you would describe as pumping.

The main centres are **Roseau**, where Fri is *the* night out, when people (both locals and tourists) move from **Fort Young Hotel**'s Happy Hour across to **Cellar's Bar** at Sutton Place Hotel; and **Portsmouth**, where the students at the Ross University School of Medicine ensure that restaurant and beach bars stay open a little longer than normal hours at the weekend during term time.

Other than that, all restaurants double up as bars, and most of the villages around the island have rum shops where local communities meet for a drink, although some often don't get any more rowdy than a heated game of alcohol-infused dominos.

Festivals

For information about any festivals and how to get tickets contact the **Dominica Festivals Committee** (T767-448 4833, www.dominicafestivals.com).
Feb/Mar Carnival. On the Mon and Tue before Ash Wed; it lacks the sponsorship of a carnival like Trinidad's, but it is one of the most spontaneous and friendly with 2 days of 'jump-ups' in Roseau and other villages as well as parades, Calypso and Carnival Queen contests.
Jun Jazz 'n Creole Festival. On a Sun at the beginning of Jun at Fort Shirley in the Cabrits National Park, this is a family event with music, food and drink, and picnics and dancing in front of the main stage.
Jul DiveFest, www.dominicawatersports. com. Held in the Soufrière-Scotts Head Marine Reserve, this week of activities includes scuba diving, snorkelling, underwater treasure hunts, whale-watching cruises, etc, with beach barbecues and parties in the evening.
Oct World Creole Music Festival. A 3-day day music festival held during the final weekend in Oct at Windsor Park in Roseau, with Cadence-lypso, Zouk, Compas, Bouyou and Soukous. Artists come from other islands such as Haiti, Martinique and Cuba, or further afield from Africa, the UK and Louisiana, as well as from Dominica.
Last Fri in Oct Creole Day. The vast majority of girls and women wear the national dress, 'la wobe douillete', to work and school and most shop assistants, bank clerks, etc, speak only Creole to the public.
3-4 Nov Independence Day. Celebrations feature local folk dances, competitions, storytelling, music and crafts.

Shopping

Arts and crafts

Dominica is not the best place for souvenir shopping, but vendors sell an assortment of locally made items including Carib straw baskets, natural coconut soaps, island spices, pepper sauce and herbal teas. Most of these can be found in the markets in Roseau and when a cruise ship pulls in, vendors set up stalls along Dame Mary Eugenia Charles Blvd near the Roseau Cruise Ship Berth. Many can also be bought at the Kalinago Barana Autê in the Carib Territory.

Duty-free

Dominica receives a lot less cruise ship traffic than St Lucia, but there are a couple of duty-free shops for wines and spirits, tobacco, leather goods, jewellery, watches, etc near the Roseau Cruise Ship Berth; the best of which is **Archipelago Trading** (Dame Eugenia Charles Blvd, T767-448 3394, www. archip.com. Mon-Fri 0800-1700, weekends when a ship is in port). Don't forget that to benefit from lower, duty-free prices, you'll need to show your passport and airline ticket (or travel documents for cruise ship passengers) when making a purchase.

Food

If you are self-catering, local farmers may visit your cottage offering fresh fruit and vegetables. In Roseau, the fresh produce markets are excellent and fish can be bought at the **Fisheries Complex** on Dame Mary Eugenia Charles Blvd next to L'Express des Iles ferry jetty or in the market on Fri and Sat. Around the island, Calibishie, Anse de Mai and Marigot are good sources of fresh fish and the boats usually come in around 1630, and there's another Fisheries Complex in Portsmouth. Vendors will clean and fillet the fish. There are a few reasonably stocked supermarkets in Roseau and Portsmouth; usually open Mon-Fri 0800-1700, Sat 0800-1300, but bear in mind hardly any shops at all are open on Sun. In Roseau, the best for fresh and frozen meat, frozen foods, fruit and vegetables, and a good selection of groceries are **Astaphans** (King George V St) and **Save-A-Lot** (River Bank near the market). In Portsmouth, the best is **Whitchurch IGA** (Ross Blvd just south of the university which is open all week – Sun 1000-1700 – which also has a deli counter and bakery and carries many US brands thanks to the student contingent in town.

What to do

Prices both here and on the activity company websites exclude the 10% VAT, so don't forget to factor that in.

Canyoning

Extreme Dominica, *Cocoa Cottages, Roseau Valley, T767-295 7272, www.extremedominica. com*. Runs exhilarating half-day canyoning excursions; wading, rock-hopping, floating in tubes and abseiling, usually in the Titou Gorge. Rates include transfers, all gear and a training session (from US$160 with discounts for groups).

Cricket

Built in 2007 and with a capacity for 12,000 spectators, **Windsor Park** is the national stadium in Roseau and is of International Cricket Council (ICC) standard for cricket. However, Dominica presently does not have a major presence in cricket, and local players generally play for the West Indies ('Windies'). Nevertheless, there are occasionally local friendly games played at the stadium.

Diving and snorkelling

For dive sites, see Planning your trip, page 17. The best diving and snorkelling in Dominica is in the **Soufrière-Scotts Head Marine Reserve** (SSMR; www.ssmrdominica.org) located on the southwestern tip of the island south of Roseau. Here there are dramatic drop-offs and walls, expansive coral reefs full of life and the famous Champagne Reef (see page 95). There is a fee of US$2

★ Waitukubuli National Trail

The Caribs, or Kalinago, who supplanted the Arawaks on Dominica, called the island Waitukubuli ('tall is her body'), and it is this name which has been adopted for the Caribbean's first long-distance walking trail which opened in 2011. Divided up into 14 manageable sections, the trail runs for 115 miles (185 km) from the far south at Scotts Head to the north at the Cabrits Peninsula, taking in most of Dominica's attractions. Along the way it will take you through coastal villages, up woodland hills, into lush rainforest, past waterfalls, down to rivers, back up to the mountains and then down again to the sea. Very much a community tourism project under the aegis of the Forestry Department, old roads have been rehabilitated, whether they were originally slave trails, smugglers' routes, Kalinago paths or donkey tracks, with each village clearing bush and undergrowth, building bridges, steps and handrails on their sections. You can tackle the whole trail over several days or walk just one or two segments, which vary in length from 4½ to 9 miles (7-14 km) and are graded from 'easy and family-friendly' to 'challenging and long'. On any segment, hikers should begin by 0930 at the latest and always be mindful of weather conditions before setting out.

Hikers should register with the **Waitukubuli National Trail Management Unit** (T767-266 3593/440 6125, www.waitukubulitrail.com) over the phone or online. There is ample advice on planning your hike on the website, including downloadable maps, GPS coordinates, lists of campsites and homestays along the segments if you don't want to stay in hotels, and also a list of certified guides (although the trails are well marked and the maps good if you want to do it without). You also need a **Trail Pass**: a day pass to hike one or more segments is US$12, while a 15-day pass to hike all 14 segments is US$40. These are available from the **Waitukubuli National Trail Headquarters** on Dr Nicholas Liverpool Highway near the Pont Cassé roundabout and from a number of other outlets including fuel stations, car rental companies and shops – again there's a list on the website.

to snorkel or dive in the SSMR; it's included in the price of the excursions, and all dive companies operate in this area. Expect to pay in the region of US$60 for a single dive, US$100 for 2 dives in the same day, US$70 for a night dive, US$190 for a PADI Discover Scuba course, and US$500 for a PADI Open Water course. **Snorkelling trips**, from around US$30-40, are particularly recommended for the Champagne Reef area.

In the event of a **diving emergency**, there is a hyperbaric chamber at the Princess Margaret Hospital in Roseau. **ALDive**, *Loubiere, T767-440 3483, www.aldive.com.*

Anchorage Dive Centre, *Anchorage Hotel, Victoria St, south of Roseau, T767-448 2638, www.anchoragehotel.dm.*
Cabrits Dive Centre, *Lizard Trail, Portsmouth, T767-445 3010, www.cabritsdive.wordpress.com.*
Dive Dominica, *Castle Comfort Lodge, Victoria St, south of Roseau, T767-448 2188, www.divedominica.com.*
East Carib Dive Centre, *Salisbury, T767-499 6575, www.dominicadiving.com.*
Nature Island Dive, *Gallion Rd, Soufrière, T767-449 8181, www.natureislanddive.com.*

Fishing

Most deep-sea fishing is done on the leeward side of the island and the Guadeloupe

Channel off the north coast. Popular catches include barracuda, bonito, dorado, mackerel, blue marlin, sailfish, tarpon, wahoo and yellowfin. Fishing is particularly good Dec-Jun when most of these game fish are in season (Aug-Dec for blue marlin).

Island Style, *T767-265 0518, www.island stylefishing.com*. Fishing charters from US$500 for half a day for 8 people.

Hiking
Hiking in the mountains is excellent all over Dominica and many of the trails are self-guided. In theory, site passes (US$5 per site or US$12 for a week pass and unlimited visits) are required for visits to the sites maintained by the **Division of Forestry, Wildlife and National Parks** (T767-266 5852/5856/5857, www.agriculture.gov.dm/index.php/division/division-of-forestry), although there may not always be someone there to take payment and give you a ticket. If you want a guide, some of the hotels will be able to organize one for you and many of the tour operators below can organize guided hiking with transport to the trailheads. For the Waitukubuli National Trail, there is a list of certified guides on the website of the **Waitukubuli National Trail Management Unit** (www.waitukubulitrail.com); also see box, opposite.

Tour operators
From Roseau, a 6- to 7-hr tour around the island (from US$65, children under 12 half price) would typically take in the west coast to Portsmouth for the Indian River and Cabrits National Park, before crossing over to the east coast for the Carib Territory, and returning across the middle via the Emerald Pool. Shorter trips go to any number of destinations, including sites in the Roseau Valley, the lakes in the Morne Trois Piton National Park or Titou Gorge, and the tour operators can also make arrangements for guided hiking, kayaking, whale watching and snorkelling at Champagne Reef. Hotels will recommend a tour operator or you can

explore the websites below. Most tours are by small 8- to 12-seater minibus, so a group/family can charter a vehicle and guide and make up their own itinerary. Alternatively, you could find a taxi driver you like, or get a hotel to recommend one (some of them make very good and entertaining tour guides) and set off on your own; the rate is around US$70-90 for up to 5 hrs or typically US$15 per hour divided by up to 4 people.

Bumpiing Tours, *T767-265 9128, www.bumpiingtours.com*.

Fredos Taxi & Tours, *T767-615 5200, www.fredostours.com*.

Ken's Hinterland Adventure Tours, *T767-448 4850, www.khattstours.com*.

Nature Island Destinations, *T767-449 6233, www.natureisland.com*.

Wacky Rollers, *T767-449 8276, see Facebook*.

Waitukubuli Adventure Tour Co, *T767-440 2628, www.waitukubulitours.com*.

Whale and dolphin watching
See Planning your trip, page 19. Whale-watching trips can be arranged by all the diving and fishing operators listed above; each operator usually goes out once or twice a week year-round, given that sperm whales are seen around Dominica throughout the year (although sightings are most common Nov-Mar). Dolphins too can be seen year-round. Costs are about US$60, children (under 10 or 12) US$30 for a 3-hr trip.

Transport

Air
See Finding your feet, page 88, for details of airports, and Getting there, page 132, for how to get to Dominica by air.

Bus
Buses are the most affordable local way of getting around and a great way to experience island life, but there is a relatively limited service. Privately owned and operated 14-seater minivans with green H licence plates run routes between Roseau

and major communities; each village, across the island, has its own buses, and each goes to Roseau and back again. There is no schedule, simply wave them down along the road and pay the fare directly to the driver. Buses are frequent towards Roseau in the morning from 0600-0900 then it goes quiet until about 1330, when return trips from Roseau begin. They mostly stop running at around 1700, and there are no buses on Sun and public holidays and very few on Sat afternoon. The most-frequented route is the main west coast road between Roseau and Portsmouth. Each community has a designated bus stop in Roseau and buses will not depart until they are full – you may have to wait up to 30 mins. To the north they leave from between the West Bridge and Roseau Market; to the Roseau Valley and Laudat from Bath Rd, near the Police HQ; and for the south from directly behind the Old Market. Fares range from US$0.60 for very short distances to US$4 to get from one side of the island to the other.

Car hire

See also Getting around, page 88. Drivers must be between 25 and 65 and have at least 2 years' driving experience. You must have a valid (photo) driving licence from your own country of residence and a credit card. A local driver's permit is required, US$12 valid for 1 month (the car hire companies will arrange this). Rates range from US$40 for a small car to US$80 for a minivan or SUV, with discounts for 3 days or more. Basic hire generally only includes statutory 3rd-party insurance; you are advised to take out the optional collision damage waiver premium at US$6-10 per day as even the smallest accident can be very expensive. At the very least, a high-clearance vehicle is required as the around-the-island roads are twisty and steep in places (see Driving in Dominica, page 135) and many of the access roads to the hiking trails require a 4WD. All companies will arrange pick-up/drop-off at the airport, L'Express des Iles

ferry terminal and hotels, and can arrange a drop-off at a different location for no extra fee. They will also provide a free road map of the island and many offer GPS/Sat-Nav systems as well as baby and child booster seats for an extra fee.

Courtesy Car Rental, T767-448 7763, Douglas-Charles Airport, T767-445 7677, www.dominicacarrentals.com.
Island Car Rentals, T767-255 6844, www.islandcar.dm.
Valley Rent-A-Car Dominica, T767-275 1310, www.valleyrent acar.com.

Ferry

L'**Express des Iles** ferries (www.express-des-iles.com) operate from the ferry terminal on Dame Eugenia Charles Blvd in Roseau to **Fort-de-France** (1½ hrs), **Pointe-à-Pitre** (1¾ hrs) and **Castries** (3-3¾ hrs), see Finding your feet, page 88, and Getting there, page 132. Check timetables before planning a trip. L'Express des Iles agency in Roseau is **HHV Whitchurch & Co Ltd**, which is upstairs in the Whitchurch Centre, Old St, T767-255 1125, www.whitchurch.com, Mon-Fri 0800-1600, Sat 0800-1300.

Taxi

Taxis are regulated and vehicle licence plates are designated by H, HA or HB. There are plenty of taxis at Douglas-Charles Airport and L'Express des Iles ferry terminal (when flights/ferries arrive) and any hotel and restaurant can phone for one. However, they can be difficult to find after around 1800 and on Sun, so book ahead if you can. Rates, fixed and set by the government and taxi associations, are fairly high, although drivers will sometimes cut you a deal if you use them more than once. Most are knowledgeable and they make excellent guides for an island tour, so it's always handy to get their card and/or phone number if you find a driver you like. Almost all taxis are minivans so on arrival at the airport it is usual to share a vehicle with other people on the plane – there are after all only 2 directions to go – so expect to pay in the region of US$35 per person to get from Douglas-Charles Airport to **Roseau**, and US$28 to **Portsmouth**; otherwise it will cost nearer US$200 to hire a vehicle for exclusive use.

Background

St Lucia

A sprint through history

Early history St Lucia was first settled by Arawaks in AD 200. By AD 800 their culture had been superseded by that of the Amerindian Caribs who called the island 'Iouanalao' and 'Hewanorra' meaning 'Island of the Iguanas'.

1502 It is believed that Christopher Columbus sailed past St Lucia on his fourth voyage to the West Indies but missed it completely.

1520 A Vatican globe marked the island as Santa Lucía, suggesting that it was claimed by Spain.

1550 François le Clerc, a French pirate known as Jambe de Bois because of his wooden leg, created his base on Pigeon Island where he could attack and raid passing Spanish ships.

1605 There is evidence of a Dutch expedition establishing a fortified base at Vieux Fort, and also the landing of 67 Englishmen after having been blown off course en route to Guyana.

1638 The first recorded settlement was made by English from Bermuda and St Kitts but the colonists were killed by the Caribs about three years later.

1642 The King of France, claiming sovereignty over the island, ceded it to the French West India Company.

1650 The French West India Company sold the island to M Houel and M Du Parquet. There were several attempts by the Caribs to expel the French and several governors were murdered.

1660 The British renewed their claim to the island and fighting for possession began in earnest.

1746 The French established the first official settlement of Soufrière.

1762 British forces under Admiral George Rodney took St Lucia, only to lose it again in 1763.

1765 The first sugar plantation was started by two Frenchmen in 1765, and more settlers arrived and developed a plantation economy based on slave labour.

1778 The English briefly recaptured St Lucia in the Battle of Cul de Sac and established a naval base at Gros Islet and fortified Pigeon Island. Admiral Rodney wrote that St Lucia was a far greater prize than neighbouring Martinique because of its excellent harbour; then called Carénage (now Castries).

1782 Admiral Rodney led the English fleet in an epic assault on the French navy, on its way to attack Jamaica. The Battle of Les Saintes took place around the French islands of Les Saintes and resulted in the death of some 14,000 French soldiers and sailors when Rodney broke the French formation. The battle marked a turning point in the political balance of power and recognized British supremacy in the West Indies. However, in the subsequent Treaty of Versailles, St Lucia was returned to France and intermittent fighting continued.

ST LUCIA BACKGROUND
The first visitors

The first Amerindians to make the migration from the Orinoco and the northern coast of the Guianas arrived in St Lucia around AD 200, somewhat later than in the other islands of the Lesser Antilles. It is not known whether they bypassed St Lucia during earlier migrations or whether indeed they landed and their settlements are yet to be discovered by archaeologists. Remnants of the first settlers to arrive by canoe have been found at Grand Anse on the east coast and at Anse Noir in the south near Vieux Fort. They are now referred to as Island Arawaks, although Arawak really refers to a language rather than a people. They stayed on St Lucia until around 1450, when they were replaced by the Caribs. No one yet knows what happened, whether they were killed or driven out, but the pottery made by the Island Arawaks ceased to be made after that date and when the first European settlers arrived at the beginning of the 16th century, there were only Caribs in residence. Caribs survived here until the late 17th century but were then sent off to St Vincent and later to Central America. Nowadays only a small community survives on Dominica. These early Amerindian cultures called the island *Iouanalao* and *Hewanorra*, meaning 'Island of the Iguanas'.

Even though some St Lucians have claimed that their island was discovered by Columbus on St Lucy's Day (13 December, the national holiday) in 1502, neither the date of discovery nor the discoverer are in fact known, for according to the evidence of Columbus' log, he appears to have missed the island and was not even in the area on St Lucy's Day. A Vatican globe of 1520 marks the island as Santa Lucía, suggesting that it was at least claimed by Spain. In any case, there was no European presence established on the island until its settlement in the 1550s by the notorious French buccaneer François le Clerc – known as Jambe de Bois because of his wooden leg – who created his base on Pigeon Island where he could attack and raid passing Spanish ships. Then a Dutch expedition may have briefly established a base at present-day Vieux Fort in 1605. In the same year, 1605, 67 Englishmen en route to Guiana made an unsuccessful effort to settle. After a month the party had been reduced to just 19, and those were soon forced to flee from the Caribs in a canoe. In 1638 the first recorded settlement was made by the English from Bermuda and St Kitts under Sir Thomas Warner, but the colonists were killed by the Caribs about three years later.

By the mid-1600s, the French had arrived and overwhelmed the Caribs and the island's first settlements and towns were all French, beginning with Soufrière in 1746. By 1780 there were 12 settlements and a large number of sugar plantations. Needless to say, the persevering British were less than enchanted with this idea, and Anglo-French rivalry for the island continued for more than a century and a half. By 1814, after a prolonged series of enormously destructive battles, the island was finally theirs.

1796 During the French Revolution, Victor Hugues used his base in St Lucia to support insurrections in nearby islands. The guillotine was erected in Castries and the island became known by the French as St Lucie La Fidèle. Britain invaded again and fought a protracted campaign against a guerrilla force of republicans known as L'Armée française dans les bois, until it was finally pacified by General John Moore.

1814 The Treaty of Paris awarded St Lucia to Britain and it became a British Crown Colony, having changed hands 14 times.

1834 Britain abolished slavery.

1838 The island was included in a Windward Islands Government, with a Governor resident first in Barbados and then in Grenada.

1842 English became the island's official language.

1882 Indentured Indian labourers arrived to work in the agricultural industry. They continued to arrive over the next 30 years and many decided to settle.

1885 St Lucia was chosen as one of Britain's two main coaling stations, selling Welsh coal to passing steam ships.

1897 947 ships entered Castries harbour, 620 of them steam powered, and Castries was the 14th most important port in the world in terms of tonnage handled.

1935 The rise of oil brought the decline of coal and the post at Castries fell into decline.

1939 After sugar workers went on strike demanding higher wages, St Lucia's first trade union was formed; it grew into the St Lucia Labour Party (SLP), led by George FL Charles (1916-2004).

1951 Universal adult suffrage was introduced. The SLP won the elections and retained power until 1964. George Charles was the first Chief Minister. He pushed through several constitutional reforms, enhancing labour legislation for the benefit of workers and introducing the system of ministerial government.

1958 St Lucia joined the short-lived West Indies Federation.

1960s The sugar industry, in decline for well over a century following the abolition of slavery, was gone by the mid-1960s when bananas became the island's major crop.

1964 The United Workers' Party (UWP), led by Mr John Compton, won the elections. Compton held power as Chief Minister from 1964-1979 and subsequently won elections in 1982, 1987, 1992 and 2006.

1967 St Lucia became fully self-governing in internal affairs, with Britain remaining in charge of external matters and defence. The first St Lucian Governor General was appointed, Sir Frederick Clarke (1912-1980), serving from 1967-1971.

1979 St Lucia gained full independence with John Compton, leader of the UWP, as Prime Minister.

1996 John Compton resigned and was succeeded by Vaughan Lewis as Prime Minister and leader of the UWP.

1997 The SLP triumphed in the elections, winning 16 of the 17 seats in the Assembly, and Dr Kenny Anthony became Prime Minister.

2006 The UWP, once again led by John Compton (now a Sir), defeated the SLP in general elections, winning 11 of the 17 seats.

2007 Prime Minister Compton became ill in May and the Minister for Health, Stephenson King, was appointed acting Prime Minister. After Compton passed away in September, King was sworn in as official Prime Minister.

2011 The SLP regained power in elections with an 11- to 6-seat victory bringing Dr Kenny Anthony back as the island's Prime Minister.

2016 The UWP won 11 of the 17 seats and returned to power with Allen Chastanet as Prime Minister. Previously he had served as St Lucia's Minister for Tourism and Civil Aviation.

Modern St Lucia

Despite becoming a British Crown Colony in 1814 and fully independent in 1979, there is still a good deal of French cultural influence on St Lucia. The style of architecture is French provincial; most place names are French; about 70% of the population is Roman Catholic; and, while the main language is English, about 75% of the population also speak a patois, Lesser Antillean Creole French, called Kwéyòl. It is spoken by St Lucians in all walks of life, including politicians, doctors, bankers, ministers and the Governor General of St Lucia (since 1997), Dame Pearlette Louisy, who has done a great deal to promote it as a written language. Kwéyòl evolved to enable African slaves to communicate with their French masters and it has survived. It is similar to the Creole spoken in Haiti, Guadeloupe, Martinique and other former French colonies. But it is closest to the Kwéyòl of Dominica, and it is said that Dominicans and St Lucians understand each other 98% of the time. A visit to the markets in Castries is one of the easiest ways to listen to Kwéyòl being spoken in the street.

Sugar was the main crop from the 17th century until the 1920s, but by the mid-1960s the cultivation of sugar cane had stopped altogether. Bananas, which were introduced in the 1950s, became the major crop and improved the economic situation of small farmers because bananas, unlike sugar, could be grown on small plots. They became the island's main export, benefiting from preferential access to the British market and, after independence from Britain in 1979, to the entire European market. The heyday of the banana industry was during the 1980s, when exports were consistently above 100,000 tons annually, representing as much as 70% of export income. But in the mid-1990s, the banana trade on St Lucia took a knock as the European Union and the World Trade Organization (WTO) announced that it would no longer offer preference to Windward Island bananas and export prices declined sharply. The government has since been encouraging farmers to diversify into crops such as cocoa, mangos and avocados. Tourism, which began in earnest in the mid-1970s when international flights and cruise ships arrived, is now the biggest earner for the island, accounting for 65% of GDP. Annual stayover visitors number more than 350,000, while cruise ship visitors can number between 500,000 and 700,000 every year between October and April, and there is a growing yacht market too.

Dominica

A sprint through history

Early history As on the other islands in the Windward chain, there were waves of migration from the Orinoco Delta area of South America up through the island arc to the Greater Antilles. The Caribs, who supplanted the Arawaks on Dominica, called the island Waitikubuli ('tall is her body').

1493 Christopher Columbus sailed past east coast on Sunday, 3 November, 1493, and named the island Dominica after Dominigo (meaning Sunday).

1660 The island was fought over by the French, British and Caribs. In 1660, the two European powers agreed to leave Dominica to the Caribs, but the arrangement lasted very few years.

1686 The island was declared neutral, again, with little success. As France and England renewed hostilities, the Caribs were divided between the opposed forces and suffered the heaviest losses in consequence.

1763 Dominica was ceded to Britain in accordance with the Treaty of Paris but France continued to challenge this until 1805.

1805 Possession was finally settled, and the British began to establish sugar and coffee plantations. Nevertheless, its position between the French colonies of Guadeloupe and Martinique, and the strong French presence over the years, ensured that despite English institutions and language the French influence was never eliminated.

1834-1838 The abolition of slavery enabled Dominica to become the only British Caribbean colony to have a Black-controlled legislature. Most Black legislators were smallholders or merchants and there was a small, wealthy British planter class.

1898 British Crown Colony rule was introduced, with first administrator Sir Henry Hesketh Bell, who made great improvements to infrastructure and the economy.

1930s The British government's Moyne Commission discovered a return to a high level of poverty on the island. Assistance to the island was increased with some emphasis put on road building to open up the interior. This, together with agricultural expansion, house building and use of the abundant hydro resources for power, contributed to development in the 1950s and 1960s.

1939 Dominica was transferred from the Leeward to the Windward Islands Federation.

1960 Dominica gained separate status and a new constitution. The Dominica Labour Party dominated island politics after 1961, ushering in all the constitutional changes.

1967 Dominica gained full internal autonomy.

1978 The Commonwealth of Dominica became an independent republic within the Commonwealth.

1979 Hurricane David struck the island with devastating force and 75% of the islanders' homes were destroyed or severely damaged.

1980 Following Independence, internal divisions and public dissatisfaction with the administration led to its defeat by the Dominica Freedom Party in the 1980 elections. The DFP Prime Minister, Eugenia Charles, adopted a pro-business, pro-United States line to lessen the island's dependence on limited crops and markets.

1985 and 1990 Charles was re-elected.

1995 Charles retired at the age of 76, having led her party since 1968. The general election was won by the United Workers Party (UWP) and Edison James was sworn in as Prime Minister.

2000 The general elections gave the Dominica Labour Party (DLP) 42.9%, the UWP 43.4% and the DFP 13.6% of the vote. The DLP and DFP formed a coalition and on 3 February Rosie Douglas was sworn in as Prime Minister. However, he died, aged 58, later that year and was replaced by his deputy, Pierre Charles.

2004 Pierre Charles died suddenly in January 2004. He was replaced by Roosevelt Skerrit, who became the world's youngest prime minister at the age of 31 and has remained in office ever since (winning the elections of 2009 and 2014). The next elections are due in 2018.

2007 Hurricane Dean wipes out 99% of Dominica's banana crop, putting further pressure on the island's struggling economy.

2015 In August, Tropical Storm Erika hit Dominica; it was the island's deadliest natural disaster since Hurricane David in 1979.

Modern Dominica

The French and British spent more than a century squabbling over Dominica, but the mountainous terrain deterred the European powers from developing the island; they preferred to build bigger ports and agricultural settlements on other islands. But the French settlers left behind a powerful reminder of their presence. Place names are still markedly French, Catholicism predominates and, although English is the official language, most of the inhabitants also speak Kwéyòl (French-based patois). Dominica is also the only Caribbean island with a remaining population of pre-Columbian Carib Indians, who had migrated in waves from South America and had settled on the island by 1000 AD. Today, over 2000 Carib descendants, properly known as the Kalinago, inhabit a 3700-acre (1500-ha) territory, established in 1903, on the northwestern side of the island.

Agriculture has always been the top economic pursuit on Dominica, and the rich, well-watered soil makes fertile planting grounds for many crops. Historically the island's mountainous terrain discouraged the creation of large estates and so traditionally there have always been many small farmers. Like St Lucia, the major crop since the 1950s has been bananas, and by the 1980s and early 1990s, these accounted for about 80% of Dominica's GDP. But again, like St Lucia, in the mid-1990s the European Union and the World Trade Organization (WTO) withdrew any preference for Windward Islands bananas in an attempt to open up the worldwide market. But bananas are still important, and production employs, directly or indirectly, more than one-third of the work force. But the economy has had to diversify, and the government has opened up the export of aloe vera, cut flowers and fruit, such as mango, guava and papaya. It is also exploring the possibilities of Dominica becoming an island for offshore finance.

Dominica's crops have suffered further from tropical storms – the latest being the disastrous Erika, which battered the island in 2015, causing numerous deaths and destroying villages, fields, roads, bridges, much of the electricity and telephone grids, and almost the entire piped water system. Dominica is still coming to terms with some of this damage although considerable progress and many repairs have been made; the next major project, funded by a £$30 million grant from the UK government, is a new road from Loubiere to Bagatelle in southeastern Dominica.

The biggest area for expansion in Dominica's economy is tourism, which is in its infancy compared to other Caribbean islands – it has been described as the one Caribbean island that Columbus would still recognize. The rugged terrain, lack of white-sand beaches, limited transport and other infrastructure and no international airport, has prevented large-scale development. Nevertheless, Dominica's mountains, rainforests, freshwater lakes, hot springs, waterfalls and diving spots make it an attractive destination – hence the tourist board presently promoting it as 'The Nature Island' of the Caribbean. Annual tourist arrivals are estimated at approximately 200,000, of whom about 75,000 are stayover visitors and the rest cruise passengers. Although the economy could certainly benefit from more visitors, an advantage of the slow growth in tourism is that Dominica's environment has not suffered from the over-development of hotels, etc, as many other islands have.

Practicalities

Getting there

Air

St Lucia

The island is well served by scheduled and charter flights from Europe and North America. You can often pick up quite cheap deals on package holidays; combining the flight with a hotel can often work out cheaper than booking each separately, and it can also save hassle – among other things, the tour operator can sort out airport-to-hotel transfers. Connections with other islands such as Antigua, Barbados or the French Antilles are good too and it is easy to arrange a multi-centre trip.

There are two airports in St Lucia; always check your ticket for the airport code. **Hewanorra International Airport (UVF)** ① *T758-454 6355, www.hewanorrainternationalairport.com*, is on the outskirts of Vieux Fort in the very south of the island and handles the long-haul flights. It has one bank with bureau de change (daily 1200-1600) and an ATM, plus a snack bar and duty-free shops airside. The smaller **George F L Charles Airport (SLU)** ① *T758-452 1156, www.georgeflcharlesairport.com*, is at Vigie just to the north of Castries and is mainly used for short-hop inter-island flights. It has an ATM, a small restaurant/bar, a tiny bookshop/stand and a duty-free shop airside. Across the road, Vigie Beach has a good assortment of local bars/food kiosks and is a good option for waiting (sitting under an almond tree) should your flight be delayed. For details of how to get from the airports see Finding your feet, page 31.

> **Tip...**
> There is a 10-minute helicopter shuttle between the two airports, US$165 per person, or 15 minutes, US$180, for a more scenic route around the Pitons and Soufrière, www.stluciahelicopters.com.

Flights from the UK The main scheduled carriers from the UK are **British Airways** ① *www.britishairways.com*, who fly daily from London Gatwick, and **Virgin Atlantic** ① *www.virgin-atlantic.com*, who fly four times a week in summer, and five times a week in winter, from London Gatwick. Both have connecting services to/from mainland Europe. In the winter months (November-April), **Thomas Cook Airlines** ① *www.thomascookairlines.com*, has a weekly Manchester–St Lucia flight, and **Thomson** ① *www.thomson.co.uk*, a weekly Gatwick–St Lucia flight. The flight time from the UK is just under nine hours.

Flights from the rest of Europe Most flights from mainland European cities to St Lucia connect through the UK. Others go via Miami or Atlanta and connect from there with a US airline flying to St Lucia. Europeans also have the option of flying with **KLM** or **Air France** to Saint Martin/Sint Maarten, connecting to St Lucia with the Caribbean regional airline **LIAT** ① *Leeward Islands Air Transport; www.liat.com*.

Flights from North America **American Airlines** ① *www.aa.com*, fly to St Lucia from Miami, **Delta** ① *www.delta.com*, from Atlanta, and **JetBlue** ① *www.jetblue.com*, from New York. Canadians have the option of flying via the US or from Toronto to Port of Spain in Trinidad from where **Caribbean Airlines** ① *www.caribbeanairlines.com*, or LIAT fly to St Lucia.

Dominica

Dominica's **Douglas-Charles Airport (DOM)** ① *T767-445 7109*, formerly known as Melville Hall Airport, is located on the northeast coast. It is very small with a check-in hall on one side with a snack bar, and a lounge with duty-free kiosk airside; there is no ATM or bank. For details of how to get from the airport see Finding your feet, page 88. Almost all flights arrive here, with the exception of some of the regional airlines that utilize small Twin Otters, which may also land at the short airstrip at **Canefield**

Tip...
Flights on the small airlines between the islands of the Caribbean are generally reliable, but schedules may change and they tend to run on 'island time' (some suggest that LIAT is an acronym for 'Leave Island Any Time'). But this has in fact got its advantages; they could wait for you if an international connection is delayed.

Airport, a 15-minute drive north of Roseau. There are no direct flights from Europe or North America to Dominica so there will be at least one change. If you are booking a through ticket to Dominica using a combination of a major carrier and smaller aircraft between the islands, it's important to check luggage weight restrictions for the full journey. When leaving, departure tax of EC$59/US$22 for all passengers over the age of 12 is payable at the kiosk at Douglas-Charles Airport (cash only).

Flights from the UK and mainland Europe The quickest option from the UK is to connect via Antigua or Barbados and both **British Airways** and **Virgin** sell through tickets combining **LIAT** flights from these destinations to Dominica. If you are coming from Europe, the quickest route is via the UK, but via the US is an option too. Another is flying with **KLM** or **Air France** to Saint Martin/Sint Maarten, and connecting to Dominica with the Caribbean regional airline Windward Islands Airways (WINAIR) ① *www.fly-winair. sx*, who fly to Dominica at least four times a week via Guadeloupe and have a ticketing arrangement with **KLM/Air France**. It is also worth investigating flights from France to Martinique (or Guadeloupe) and then catching the ferry (see below).

Flights from North America From the US, **Seaborne Airlines** ① *www.seaborneairlines. com*, provide a daily service to Dominica from Puerto Rico. The airline has code share agreements with **American Airlines**, **Delta** and **JetBlue**, allowing travellers to book their flights to Dominica via Puerto Rico directly through these carriers. **WINAIR**, another option, flies to Dominica at least four times a week from Puerto Rico via Saint Martin/Sint Maarten and Guadeloupe and has ticketing agreements with **United**. Alternatively, routes are via Barbados or Antigua, both of which are well served by US and Canadian airlines.

Sea

While St Lucia, Dominica and Martinique are on the itineraries of many cruise lines, and lots of private or chartered yachts also call in on a tour of the Lesser Antilles, the main transport link between the three islands is by international ferry.

L'Express des Iles

L'Express des Iles ① *www.express-des-iles.com*, has at least one daily service in each direction connecting Guadeloupe, Les Saintes, Marie Galante, Dominica, Martinique and St Lucia. Timetables are on the website, but the schedule is subject to change, so

TRAVEL TIP

Ferry times

Castries–Fort-de-France, 1½ hours; Fort-de-France–Roseau, two hours; total time Castries–Roseau with stops, 4¼ hours. Beyond Roseau, the ferry also stops in Portsmouth on its way to/from Guadeloupe.

always check locally. If you are planning to fly home from St Lucia after a trip to Dominica (or the other way around) do not catch the ferry on the same day as your flight; always leave yourself a day in hand in case of delays and cancellations. The fast catamarans carry 300-360 passengers and the larger ones have capacity for 10 cars. They have air conditioning, reclining seats, an open upper deck, and vending machines for drinks/snacks. Immigration and customs formalities and departure taxes have to be complied with at each country and check-in is 1½ hours before departure. Hand luggage and one bag, with a maximum weight of 25 kg, are permitted, although there is the option of paying €20 for a second bag.

Fares are for the full journey – Guadeloupe to St Lucia – regardless of where your final destination is, but you can break the ticket on each island. At the time of writing tickets were EC\$250-380 (€83-126) return, EC\$160-295 (€53-98) one way, depending on the day of the week and the flexibility of the ticket, with about 25% discount for children 2-12 years, and under 2s paying about 10%. You can book online, although the website is not easy to navigate and switches between French and English. Alternatively book through one of the agents and confirm in advance via email, especially if you are travelling at the weekend. All ferry terminals are in walking distance of the town centre and within easy reach of bus routes, although taxis are available.

In St Lucia, the ferry terminal is on La Toc Road, Castries. Departure tax of EC\$33 (US\$13) for all passengers over the age of 12 is paid at the time of the ferry departure (cash only). The ticket agent is **Cox & Company Ltd** ① *office at the ferry terminal, Mon-Fri 0800-1615, also at Castries–Gros Islet Hwy, just north of the roundabout at Vigie, Mon-Fri 0800-1800, T758-456 5022/23/24, www.coxcoltd.com.*

In Dominica, the ferry terminal is on Dame Mary Eugenia Charles Blvd, Roseau. Departure tax of EC\$59 (US\$22) for all passengers over the age of 12 is payable at the time of the ferry departure (cash only). The ticket agent is **HHV Whitchurch & Co Ltd** ① *upstairs in the Whitchurch Centre, Old St, T767-255 1125, www.whitchurch.com, Mon-Fri 0800-1600, Sat 0800-1300.*

In Fort-de-France, Martinique, the ferry operates from the **Terminal Inter-Iles** ① *Bassin de Radoub, T596-(0)596-420405,* just east of La Savane in the centre. There are three L'Express des Iles ticket counters here, but queues build up before a departure so it's best to go early (to check departure times too). There is presently no departure tax from Martinique.

Getting around

Road

Roads are generally in good condition, although in mountainous areas they remain susceptible to landslides after storms, and in urban areas they can be heavily congested. Journey times are often quoted in hours rather than miles, as driving on twisty, hilly roads is time-consuming.

St Lucia has a very busy main road heading north out of Castries to the resort area around Rodney Bay, while the road south down the scenic West Coast Road is less congested, but the terrain requires slow driving as there are many ups and downs and tight curves. The East Coast Road is better and this is the route taken by transport between Hewanorra International Airport and Castries and Rodney Bay further north, as it's quicker. These two roads, together with the transinsular road over the Barre de l'Isle mountains in the middle of the island, make a lovely circular route.

Dominica's roads are mostly tarred, but are generally in poor condition and very narrow, hilly and mountainous (see box, opposite). The exception is the good road north from Roseau to the second city of Portsmouth, which is an attractive drive along the coast. From here you can cross over to the east coast for a spectacular view of the Atlantic side of the island, either turning inland on the Dr Nicholas Liverpool (transinsular) Highway to the Pont Cassé roundabout (a major junction in the interior), or at Canefield or Roseau, or going further south to either Castle Bruce or Rosalie before taking alternative roads to the Pont Cassé roundabout. Roads in the southern third of the island are not all so well maintained and suffered particular damage during Tropical Storm Erika in 2015.

Bus

The cheapest way of getting around St Lucia is by bus. Hotels and tour operators will encourage you to take a taxi, but this is quite unnecessary during the day unless you want to get to somewhere quickly or off the beaten track. Privately owned and operated 14-seater minivans with green M licence plates run individual routes between major communities and, while there is no schedule, they are frequent and well organized with all the bus routes denoted (Castries to Gros Islet is 1A for example). Fares range from US$0.80 for very short distances to US$5 to get from one end of the island to the other. See St Lucia Transport, page 80, for details.

In Dominica the service is similar but more limited. Again they are privately owned and operated 14-seater minivans, here with green H licence plates. Each village, across the island, has its own buses, and each goes to Roseau and back again. This means they are frequent towards Roseau in the morning from 0600-0900 then it goes quiet until about 1330, when the afternoon return trips from Roseau begin. The most frequented route is the main west coast road between Roseau and Portsmouth and points in between. Fares range from US$0.60 for very short distances to US$4 to get from one side of the island to the other. See Dominica Transport, page 119, for details.

> Tip...
> On St Lucia, a few buses run on Sunday in the most popular areas – between Castries and Rodney Bay and Gros Islet, for example; on Dominica no buses run on a Saturday afternoon and all day on Sunday.

TRAVEL TIP
Driving in Dominica

Car hire is generally a good option to explore Dominica given that the public bus system is limited and taxis are expensive. However, driving can be a little challenging to say the least and roads can be simultaneously steep, thin and twisted. While most roads are paved, not many of them are in very good condition and potholes and blind corners are common. Many are lined with deep ditches made from concrete, often hidden by overgrowth, which act as drains to divert water as it comes off the mountains during heavy rains. They also mean that there are very few places to pull over, so you must be prepared to start driving and not stop again until you reach your destination. Pedestrians and livestock on the road create additional hazards; road signs are virtually non-existent; and night-time driving can be dangerous because most areas are unlit. The exception is the good road between Roseau and Portsmouth, which is paved to a good standard, has road signs, even a few traffic lights and a line down the middle. Elsewhere, some visitors have to take anti-nausea medication for the drive between Douglas-Charles Airport at Melville Hall and Portsmouth because there are over 250 twists, turns and curves on this route. Furthermore, the inland Northern Link Road that cuts across the north of the island between Tanetane and Penville has such a sharply winding and precipitous zig-zag ascent/descent, it's first gear all the way with an average of a 10% incline/decline. Be aware that if you arrive at the Douglas-Charles Airport after 1600 and you're picking up a car, it could well be nearly dark by the time you've gone through immigration/customs, claimed your luggage, done the car hire paperwork, etc. Anticipate the following driving times: from the airport to Pagua Bay, 20 minutes; Calibishie, 30 minutes; Rosalie Bay, 1¾-2½ hours; Portsmouth, 1¼ hours; Roseau 1¾-2½ hours if taking the Dr Nicholas Liverpool (transinsular) Highway route – much longer if going via Portsmouth. In short, it takes a long time to drive just about anywhere on Dominica.

Car *Driving is on the left in both St Lucia and Dominica.*

In many ways, **St Lucia** is an easy island to get around by hire car as there really are not many main roads. For example, there is only one navigable road between the tourist area around Rodney Bay in the north and Soufrière in the southwest. Negotiating busy Castries can be a little confusing, there are twists and turns south of Castries towards Soufrière, and some hotels are reached along awful, rutted tracks. But as long as you're a fairly confident driver, a car is highly recommended as it's the best way of getting to see plenty of the island. Be aware, however, that car crime can occur in St Lucia, and obvious tourists in hire cars have been targeted – always drive with doors locked, be conscious that nobody is following you, park in well-lit areas, and do not have valuables on show, especially on the seats in plain view. The use of seat belts is compulsory, and using a cell phone and under the influence of alcohol while driving is illegal. Speed limits are posted in miles: city areas, 10-15 mph, rural areas 30 mph, major highways 40 mph.

There are dozens of car hire companies. If you want a car immediately on arrival at the airport than pre-book; otherwise unless it's in the middle of high season, you can usually organize a car for the next day. All companies will arrange pick-up/drop-off at hotels and can arrange a drop-off at a different location for no extra fee. The minimum age for hiring a car is 25, and a local driver's permit is required (US$22 valid for three months); the car hire companies will arrange this. Choose the type of car for your needs; a normal car is sufficient to get around the island on the main roads but a high-clearance vehicle (a 4WD in the wet) is necessary for access roads to certain hiking trails and minor roads in the interior. See St Lucia Transport, page 80.

Driving in **Dominica** is far more hazardous for the uninitiated (see box, page 135), but is still a good option to explore the island at your own speed if you are a confident, experienced driver. At the very least, a high-clearance vehicle is required, but to get to the access roads for the hiking trails a 4WD is usually essential – most hire companies have more of these than saloon cars. Speed limits are posted in kilometres, and officially are 50 km per hour in towns and 80 km per hour on open roads, but they are rarely adhered to and there are virtually no signs. Many people on the island drive recklessly fast and show no fear of passing on curves or on the crest of hills and, when overtaking, they often pull right up behind your car, honking their horn as they pass.

There are only a few hire companies so it's advisable to pre-book and they can arrange to meet you on arrival at the airport, L'Express des Iles ferry terminal or hotels. Drivers must be between 25 and 65 and have at least two years' driving experience. A local driving permit is required – US$12 valid for one month; the car hire companies will arrange this. See Dominica Transport, page 120.

Taxi

Registered taxis in **St Lucia** have red number plates with the TX prefix. Minibuses have the T prefix. Fares are set by the government and taxi associations, but always verify the rate before embarking on a journey and make sure you are being quoted in EC$, not US$. If in doubt about the amount charged, check with your hotel reception. You can see a copy of the fixed fares at the airport – you could take a photo. Sometimes drivers will cut you a deal if you use them more than once (get their card and/or phone number), and many are generally very knowledgeable about the island and make good tour guides; the rate for six or seven hours is from about US$200 split by four passengers. There are plenty of taxis at both airports, and any hotel and restaurant can phone for one. See St Lucia Transport, page 81.

In **Dominica**, taxis have H, HA or HB on the licence plate. Again fares are fixed by the government and taxi associations so the above rules apply. Almost all taxis are minivans so on arrival at Douglas-Charles Airport or L'Express des Iles ferry it is quite usual to share a vehicle with other people. Any hotel and restaurant can phone for one. However, they can be difficult to find after around 1800 and on Sunday, so book well in advance, especially for your return trip to the airport/ferry. See Dominica Transport, page 120.

Essentials A-Z

Accident and emergency

T911 in St Lucia, T911 or T999 in Dominica.

Customs and duty free

Duty-free imports to St Lucia and Dominica are 1 litre of spirits or wine, 200 cigarettes or 50 cigars, and 60 ml of perfume.

Disabled travellers

Wheelchairs are not accommodated on public road transport and the towns have very uneven pavements. However, in **St Lucia** modern resorts and hotels have rooms with disabled facilities and it's easy enough to get around on an organized tour, in a rented vehicle or by boat. This is not the case in **Dominica**, which is not wheelchair-friendly at all. Accommodation generally does not have facilities and most rooms are difficult to access because of steps, hills and the lack of lifts. Nevertheless, local people will do their very best to help and hiring a taxi (minivan) is an option for getting around.

Drugs

Do not be tempted to dabble in narcotics, all are illegal and the law does not allow for 'personal possession''; there are severe penalties for all drug offences. On both islands, you may be approached to buy drugs on the beach, in a rum shop or at a party – just keep walking and ignore the person.

Electricity

220 volts, 50 cycles. A few hotels are 110 v, 60 cycles. Most sockets take 3-pin square plugs (UK standard), but some take 2-pin round plugs or flat US plugs. Adaptors are generally available in hotels.

Embassies and consulates

For a full list of embassies and consulates in St Lucia and Dominica and St Lucian and Dominican offices abroad, see https://embassy.goabroad.com.

Health

Before you travel
Travel in St Lucia and Dominica poses no health risk to the average visitor provided sensible precautions are taken. See your GP or travel clinic at least 6 weeks before departure for general advice on travel risks and vaccinations. Make sure you have sufficient medical travel insurance, get a dental check, know your own blood group and, if you suffer a long-term condition such as diabetes or epilepsy, obtain a Medic Alert bracelet (www.medicalert.org.uk).

Vaccinations
It is important to confirm your primary courses and boosters are up to date. No special vaccinations are required, but a yellow fever inoculation certificate must be produced on arrival if you have arrived within 5 days of leaving an area in Africa or South America affected with yellow fever. If you bring prescription medication along with you, make sure to pack them in their original containers and that they are clearly labelled.

Health risks
Insect-borne risks The major risks posed in the Caribbean region are those caused by insect disease carriers such as mosquitoes and sandflies. The key parasitic and viral diseases are **dengue fever** and **chikungunya** (also known as chik V). Cases of the **Zika virus**, also spread by mosquitos, have been reported in the Caribbean since early 2016. If pregnant or planning

to become pregnant, it is recommended you check with the **Foreign Office** (www.fco.gov.uk) before travel. Although the risk of contracting any of the above is very low, it is always a good idea to protect yourself against mosquitoes: try to wear clothes that cover arms and legs at dusk and dawn (when mosquitoes are most active) and use effective mosquito repellent. Rooms with a/c or fans also help ward off mosquitoes at night. **Malaria** is not a danger in St Lucia or Dominica.

Snakes There are 4 species of snake on **St Lucia**. The only one that is dangerous is the fer-de-lance ('spearhead' in French), so called due to the shape of its head. It can grow up to 1.8 m in length, although most found are considerably shorter. This very poisonous snake is considered the most dangerous in the Caribbean and if bitten, its venom can cause victims hypertension, gastrointestinal bleeding, loss of consciousness, and eventually death (if not treated). Fortunately, it is only found within a few dry scrub woodland areas along the central east and west coasts and attacks are rare. Nevertheless, give a wide berth to all snakes, take care when walking through the bush, especially at night, and wear shoes or boots and long trousers. On **Dominica**, there are boa constrictors (also on St Lucia) that grow to nearly 3 m in length as well as 4 other types of snakes, but none are poisonous.

Stomach issues

The most common affliction of travellers to any country is probably diarrhoea, and this holds true for St Lucia and Dominica. The standard advice is always to wash your hands before eating and to be careful with drinking water and ice. Also be wary of washed salads and peel all local fruits and vegetables before eating. Tap water is good in most areas in **St Lucia** and many hotels treat it, but bottled water is widely available and recommended. Tap water in **Dominica** should be avoided since it is sometimes drawn straight from the island's many rivers and may be contaminated with bacteria and parasites (that can cause E-coli or giardia, for example); drink bottled water or use a sterilization method. Swimming in sea or river water that has been contaminated by sewage can be a cause of diarrhoea; ask locally if it is safe. Any kind of diarrhoea responds well to the replacement of water and salts. Sachets of rehydration salts can be bought in most pharmacies and can be dissolved in boiled water. If the symptoms persist, consult a doctor.

Sun

The climate is hot, and do not be deceived by cooling sea breezes. Protect yourself adequately against the sun. Apply a high-factor sunscreen (greater than SPF15) and also make sure it screens against UVB. Prevent heat exhaustion and heatstroke by drinking enough fluids throughout the day (your urine will be pale if you are drinking enough). Symptoms of heat exhaustion and heatstroke include dizziness, tiredness and headache. Use rehydration salts mixed with water to replenish fluids and salts and find somewhere cool and shady to recover. If you suspect heatstroke rather than heat exhaustion, you need to cool the body down quickly (cold showers are particularly effective).

If you get sick

St Lucia There are several public hospitals in St Lucia but some are old and not well equipped. If you have adequate insurance, the private hospital and medical centres are the better bet, and the larger hotels and resorts have doctors on call (expect to pay around US$15-20 for a consultation). In the event of a diving emergency, there is a **hyperbaric chamber** at Tapion Hospital in Castries.

Rodney Bay Medical Centre, Providence Commercial Centre, next to Bay Gardens Hotel, Rodney Bay village, T758-452 8621, www.rodneybaymedicalcentre.com. A practice of private doctors and dentists.

Soufrière Hospital, W Quinlan St, Soufrière, T758-459 7257. The public hospital for Soufrière.

St Jude Hospital, St Jude Hwy, Vieux Fort, T758-454 6041, www.stjudehospitalslu.org. The public hospital for Vieux Fort.

Tapion Hospital, Tapion Rd, Castries, T758-459 2000, www.tapion-hospital.com. Private hospital with 24-hr emergency service and A&E, pharmacy, X-ray, CAT scan, laboratory services, specialist doctors.

Victoria Hospital, Hospital Rd, Castries, T758-452 2421/453 7059. The largest public hospital on the island.

Dominica Medical care on Dominica is limited; there are 2 public hospitals on the island but for any serious ailment or surgery, only Princess Margaret Hospital in Roseau is adequately equipped, so ensure you have insurance (see below) that provides for medical evacuation (usually to Barbados or, for serious medical conditions, to your home country). In the event of a diving emergency, there is a hyperbaric chamber at the Princess Margaret Hospital in Roseau.

Portsmouth Hospital, Pembroke St, Portsmouth, T767-445 5237.

Princess Margaret Hospital, Charles Av, Goodwill, Roseau, T767-448 2231. 24-hr A&E.

Useful websites

www.bgtha.org British Global and Travel Health Association.

www.cdc.gov US government site that gives excellent advice on travel health and details of disease outbreaks.

www.fco.gov.uk British Foreign and Commonwealth Office travel site that has useful information on each country, people, climate and a list of UK embassies/consulates.

www.fitfortravel.nhs.uk A-Z of vaccine/health advice for each country.

www.travelhealth.co.uk Independent travel health site with advice on vaccination, travel insurance and health risks.

www.who.int World Health Organization, updates of disease outbreaks.

Insurance

Before departure, it is vital to take out comprehensive travel insurance. There is a wide variety of policies to choose from, so shop around. At the very least, the policy should cover medical expenses, including repatriation to your home country in the event of a medical emergency. Hospital bills need to be paid at the time of admittance, so keep all paperwork to make a claim. There is no substitute for suitable precautions against petty crime, but if you do have something stolen, report the incident to the nearest police station and ensure you get a police report and case number which you will need to make a claim.

Language

English is the official language but Kwéyòl, a French-based patois, is spoken widely on both St Lucia and Dominica. It is very similar to the Creole of Martinique and Haiti.

Money

US$1 = EC$2.70; UK£1 = EC$3.51; €1 = EC$3.12 (Jul 2017).

The currency on St Lucia and Dominica is the EC$ or XCD. Notes are for EC$5, 10, 20, 50 and 100. Coins 5, 10, 25 cents, EC$1 and 2. Some things, such as hotel rates, air fares and sometimes activities such as diving and tours are quoted in US dollars, and you can usually pay in either currency.

Changing money

Banks will exchange major currencies, such as the US$, Can$, € and £. Credit, debit and currency cards are widely accepted, especially at larger establishments such as resorts and restaurants, but smaller local businesses and street vendors will require payment in cash. In **St Lucia** there is an ATM and foreign exchange bureau at the airport and banks and ATMs are available in Castries, Soufrière, Rodney Bay village and Vieux Fort. In **Dominica**, there are banks and ATMs in

Roseau, Marigot and Portsmouth. Inform your bank before you travel so they don't put a stop on your card. Make sure you bring contact details from home of who to call if your card is lost or stolen.

Opening hours

St Lucia

Banks Mon-Thu 0800-1500, Fri 0800-1700, in Rodney Bay village banks open on Sat 0900-1200.

Government offices Mon-Fri 0830-1230, 1330-1600.

Shops Mon-Fri 0800-1700, although a few shut for lunch, Sat 0800-1230. Shopping malls and larger supermarkets have extended hours, usually Mon-Thu 0800-2000, Fri-Sat 0800-2100, Sun 0900-1400.

Dominica

Banks Mon-Thu 0800-1400, Fri 0800-1400.

Government offices Mon-Fri 0800-1300, 1400-1600.

Shops Mon-Fri 0800-1300, 1400-1600, Sat 0800-1300. Many supermarkets in Roseau and Portsmouth stay open at lunch and some until 2000.

Post and courier services

St Lucia The **General Post Office** is on Bridge St, Castries, T758-452 2671, www.stluciapostal.com, Mon-Fri 0830-1630. There are a number of district post offices across the island, open Mon-Fri 1300-1700.

Dominica The **General Post Office** is on Dame Mary Eugenia Charles Blvd, Roseau, T767-266 5209, Mon-Fri 0800-1600. There are a few small district post offices around the island that usually open Mon-Fri for a couple of hours in the afternoon.

For **courier services**, DHL, www.dhl.com, and **Fedex**, www.fedex.com, are both represented on the islands.

Public holidays

St Lucia

1 and 2 Jan New Year
22 Feb Independence Day
Easter Good Fri, Easter Mon
1 May Labour Day
May/June Whit Mon; Corpus Christi
July Carnival
1 Aug Emancipation Day
1st Mon in Oct Thanksgiving Day
13 Dec National Day
25 and 26 Dec Christmas Day and Boxing Day.

Dominica

1 and 2 Jan New Year
Feb/Mar Carnival
Easter Good Fri and Easter Mon
May/Jun 1st Mon; Whit Mon
Aug 1st Mon
3-4 Nov Independence
25 and 26 Dec Christmas Day and Boxing Day

Safety

Most visitors to the islands will have a safe, trouble-free and enjoyable stay. But on both St Lucia and Dominica there are isolated incidents of crime against tourists, including armed robbery, theft from vehicles and sexual harassment. It is always best to travel in a group and keep an eye out for suspicious characters and places. If you are travelling alone, explore more remote areas with a guide or stay where there are others nearby. The general common sense rules apply to prevent petty theft: don't exhibit anything valuable and keep wallets and purses out of sight; do not leave your possessions unattended on the beach; use a hotel safe to store valuables, money and passports; lock hotel room doors as noisy fans and a/c can provide cover for sneak thieves; don't leave items on hotel or villa balconies when you go out; at night, avoid deserted areas, including the beaches, and always take taxis. If hiring a car, don't stop if you're flagged down, keep valuables out of sight and lock car doors when driving.

Tax

St Lucia: VAT of 10% and service charge of 10% is charged by all accommodation options, usually as a single charge of 20%; check if this has been included in quoted rates. In restaurants, menu prices include the 10% VAT and the bill may or may not include the 10% service charge; check before tipping. Activities and tours do not include the 10% VAT on their published prices so don't forget to factor that in.

Dominica: VAT in Dominica is 15% except for accommodation when it is 10%; again VAT of 10% and service charge of 10% is charged by all accommodation options. In restaurants the 15% VAT is included in menu prices, but the service charge of 10% is not usually added to the bill (unless it's a large group) and tipping is discretionary.

Telephone

The international code for **St Lucia** is 758 and for **Dominica** 767. **Digicel**, www.digicel group.com, and **Flow**, www.discoverflow.co, are Caribbean-wide cellular and internet providers. Local SIM cards and start-up packs are available to purchase at phone shops. You'll find these in the major towns, and you can top-up via phone, the websites or buy credit at small shops. Almost all hotels have free Wi-Fi, as well as many restaurants, coffee shops and beach bars.

Time

Atlantic Standard Time: GMT -4 hrs, EST + 1 hr.

Tipping

Tipping is not mandatary as a service charge is added to all hotel bills and most restaurant bills in St Lucia (less so in Dominica). However, given that the islands receive so many cruise ship passengers (the majority from the US) a tipping culture is prevalent, so by all means tip if you want to show your appreciation to extra helpful waiting staff in restaurants, a particularly informative tour guide, a helpful taxi driver or cleaning staff in hotels. A 10% tip is about right for good service, and it will be most appreciated by all hospitality staff.

Tourist information

Local tourist offices can be found at the start of the listings sections on pages 62 (St Lucia) and 107 (Dominica).
St Lucia Tourist Board, www.stlucia.org, has representation in the UK, Europe, USA and Canada.
Discover Dominica Authority, www. dominica.dm, has representation in the UK, USA, Canada, Europe and Scandinavia.

Visas and immigration

Visitors arriving in St Lucia and Dominica must have a passport valid for 6 months after the date of entry and adequate unused pages for stamps. Even though you may not always get asked for it, all travellers need to be able to produce a return or onward ticket, proof that they can support themselves during their stay (a credit card will suffice), and an address at which they will be staying (the hotel on your 1st night should be enough). Most visitors – including citizens of the USA, UK, EU, most Commonwealth countries, South Africa and the Caribbean – do not need a visa. The length of stay usually granted is 28 days but up to 90 days can be requested.

Weights and measures

St Lucia: imperial. **Dominica**: metric.

Index

Entries in bold refer to maps

Credits

Footprint credits

Editor: Felicity Laughton
Production and layout: Emma Bryers
Maps: Kevin Feeney
Colour section: Angus Dawson

Publisher: John Sadler
Head of Publishing: Felicity Laughton
Marketing: Kirsty Holmes
Advertising and Partnerships:
Debbie Wylde

Photography credits
Front cover: shutterstock.com/Judith Lienert
Back cover top: shutterstock.com/
Judith Lienert
Back cover bottom: shutterstock.com/
Richard Goldberg
Inside front cover: Andrew Jalbert/
Shutterstock.com, CKP1001/Shutterstock.
com, Rafal Gadomski/Shutterstock.com.

Colour section
Page 1: agf photo/Superstock.com.
Page 2: PITAMITZ Sergio/Superstock.com.
Page 4: Martin Moxter/Superstock.com,
Styve Reineck/Shutterstock.com,
dpvuestudio/Shutterstock.com.
Page 5: robertharding/Superstock.com,
Jon Arnold Images/Superstock.com,
Jad Davenport/Superstock.com,
Michael Runkel/Superstock.com.
Page 7: age fotostock/Superstock.com,
GIUGLIO Gil/Superstock.com,
Michael Runkel/Superstock.com.
Page 8: Claudio306/Shutterstock.com.

Duotone
Page 28: Travel Bug/Shutterstock.com.

Printed in India

Publishing information
Footprint St Lucia & Dominica
3rd edition
© Compass Maps Ltd
October 2017

ISBN: 978 1 911082 26 2
CIP DATA: A catalogue record for this book
is available from the British Library

® Footprint Handbooks and the
Footprint mark are a registered
trademark of Compass Maps Ltd

Published by Footprint
5 Riverside Court
Lower Bristol Road
Bath BA2 3DZ, UK
T +44 (0)1225 469141
footprinttravelguides.com

Every effort has been made to ensure that
the facts in this guidebook are accurate.
However, travellers should still obtain advice
from consulates, airlines, etc about travel
and visa requirements before travelling.
The authors and publishers cannot
accept responsibility for any loss, injury
or inconvenience however caused.